☞ W9-CMV-070

CAMBRIDGE
EDUCATIONAL SERVICES

AMERICA'S PREMIERE TESTING READINESS PROGRAM

AccelePrep™

for the

ACT® Test

S T U D E N T   T E X T

ACT® • PreACT™ • PLAN® • EXPLORE® • ACT Aspire™ • SAT® • PSAT/NMSQT® • PSAT™ 10 • PSAT™ 8/9 • TSI
GRE® • GMAT® • LSAT® • WorkKeys® • GED® • TASC™ • HiSET® • ITBS®
Victory • AccelePrep™ • Essential Skills • Non-Negotiable Skills™ • CollegePrep™ • College Credit Ready™ • Career Interest Inventory • Learning Styles
PrepCast Videos • Studio Web Courses • Score Booster Practice Tests • iVictory and IlumaPrep eBooks • EduCopy Duplication
Go-Guru Full Service • Print, Digital, and Online Assessment Services • Essay Grading • Analytics • Formative Assessment
Classroom Texts • Teacher Curriculum • Question Writing • Motivation/Admissions Workshops • Professional Development

The above-cited marks are the property of their respective owners.

The ACT, Inc. tests offered by Cambridge Educational Services, Inc. are retired tests, intended by ACT for practice purposes only and not for official administration, and are based on high school curriculum as of
the copyright dates of the tests. Cambridge's products and services, including its score reports, are not approved or endorsed by ACT, with which Cambridge has no affiliation.

Our Mission:

Progress Through Partnership

Cambridge Educational Services partners with educators who share

the significant mission of educational advancement for all students. By

partnering together, we can best achieve our common goals:

to build skills, raise test scores, enhance curriculum, and support

instruction. A leading innovator in education for over twenty-nine years,

Cambridge is the nation's premiere provider of school-based

test preparation and supplemental curriculum services.

Cambridge Publishing, Inc.
www.CambridgeEd.com

© 2019 by Cambridge Publishing, Inc.
All rights reserved. First edition 2016
Second edition 2019

Printed in the United States of America
22 21 20 19   1 2 3 4 5

ISBN-13: 978-1-58894-320-0

© 2019 by Cambridge Educational Services
All rights reserved.

© 2019 by Thomas H. Martinson
All rights reserved.

TABLE OF CONTENTS

POWER UP! THE EXCLUSIVE CAMBRIDGE SAMPLE EXAM — 245

TAKE A TEST DRIVE! POST-TEST — 301

APPENDIX | ANSWER KEY — 307

Course Overview

ACCELEPREP EXCLUSIVES

These powerful tools will help you score higher on test day!

AccelePrep Approach
Master the AccelePrep method for test prep.

Test Specs
Understand the test's format and features.

Pacing Tip
Integrate valuable time-saving tips.

Strategy Alert
Learn vital test-day strategies.

Power Tip
Learn how to test like a pro.

Closer Look
Dissect parts of the test and example questions.

Review
Revisit the core test concepts.

Sum It Up
Recap what you just learned.

Power Practice
Pick up your pencil and see what you learned.

The fact that you're reading this book means just one thing—you've got a big, important test ahead of you. You want to do well—and we want to help you.

We wrote this book to help you do your best on the ACT test. We don't promise to raise your GPA or to get you on the dean's list. And we won't ask you to spend every night for the next six months chained to your desk studying. What we do pledge is that absolutely everything in this book has just one aim: to help you earn the highest ACT score you can.

Cambridge teachers have examined the ACT test question by question and answer choice by answer choice. We've literally taken each test apart, analyzed every component, and then put the pieces back together again. The result of all our efforts is a four-step plan. It's a surefire method that we've made available to you in the pages of this exciting new book. So let's introduce the four steps and then get started!

- **Take a Test Drive! Pre-Test.** A pre-test and score reports help you identify your starting point and prepare for the course.
- **Surge to Success! TestPrep.** Conquer the English, Math, Reading, Science, and optional Writing portions of the test, with a quick review of tested topics and tips on how to answer each question type the test writers will throw at you.
- **Power Up! The Exclusive Cambridge Sample Exam.** Practice with a full-length test to make sure you're ready for test day.
- **Take a Test-Drive! Post-Test.** A post-test helps you to see how far you've come and plan how to continue studying until test day.

Course Overview

Take a Test Drive!
Pre-Test

TAKE THE PRE-TEST

At the beginning of the course, you will take a pre-test. This pre-test is an ACT, Inc. ACT practice exam. When you take the pre-test, you should bring the following items to the classroom, in addition to anything else your teacher instructs you to bring:

1. Sharpened, soft-lead No. 2 pencils.
2. A calculator that is approved for use on the test. This includes any four-function, scientific, or graphing calculator, except for the following:

   - Devices with built-in computer algebra systems.
   - Pocket organizers or PDAs.
   - Handheld, laptop, or tablet computers.
   - Electronic writing pad or pen-input devices.
   - Calculators built into any electronic communication device, such as a cell phone.
   - Models with a QWERTY (typewriter) keypad. (Calculators with letters on the keys are permitted as long as the keys are not arranged in a QWERTY keypad.)

You may use the following types of calculators if you make appropriate modifications:

   - Calculators that can hold programs or documents: remove all documents and remove all programs that have computer algebra system functionality.
   - Models with paper tape: the paper must be removed.
   - Models that make noise: the sound feature must be turned off.
   - Models that have an infrared data port: the port must be covered with duct tape, electrician's tape, or another heavy, opaque material.
   - Models that have a power cord: the power cord must be removed.

(For more detailed information on calculator usage, go to www.actstudent.org/faq/calculator.html.)

3. A watch (to pace yourself as you work through each test section).

If your program has ordered pre-test Student Summary reports, you will receive one of these reports with your pre-test results. You will learn more about how to read and use your Student Summary report in the "Use the Pre-Test Reports" section.

USE THE PRE-TEST REPORTS

Before you dive into the heart of your course, you and your teacher will use the results of your pre-test to recognize your individual strengths and weaknesses. Having this valuable information will allow you to create a study plan so that you can effectively manage your time.

You will receive the results of your pre-test in the form of a Student Summary and a Student Item Analysis. Review the details of the sample Student Summary and Student Item Analysis on the next two pages so that you are familiar with their contents.

STUDENT SUMMARY

The Student Summary reports all your scaled scores based on your test performance. In addition, you are able to see how you performed within specific categories for each of the four subject tests (English, Mathematics, Reading, and Science). For example, English includes the categories Conventions of Standard English (SE), Production of Writing (PW), and Knowledge of Language (KL).

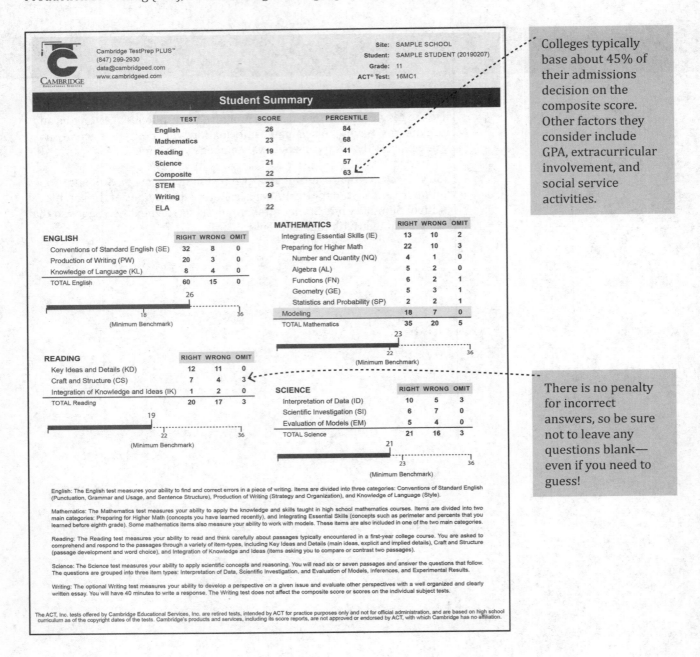

Cambridge TestPrep PLUS™
(847) 299-2930
data@cambridgeed.com
www.cambridgeed.com

Site: SAMPLE SCHOOL
Student: SAMPLE STUDENT (20190207)
Grade: 11
ACT® Test: 16MC1

Student Summary

TEST	SCORE	PERCENTILE
English	26	84
Mathematics	23	68
Reading	19	41
Science	21	57
Composite	22	63
STEM	23	
Writing	9	
ELA	22	

Colleges typically base about 45% of their admissions decision on the composite score. Other factors they consider include GPA, extracurricular involvement, and social service activities.

ENGLISH

	RIGHT	WRONG	OMIT
Conventions of Standard English (SE)	32	8	0
Production of Writing (PW)	20	3	0
Knowledge of Language (KL)	8	4	0
TOTAL English	60	15	0

26
18   36
(Minimum Benchmark)

MATHEMATICS

	RIGHT	WRONG	OMIT
Integrating Essential Skills (IE)	13	10	2
Preparing for Higher Math	22	10	3
Number and Quantity (NQ)	4	1	0
Algebra (AL)	5	2	0
Functions (FN)	6	2	1
Geometry (GE)	5	3	1
Statistics and Probability (SP)	2	2	1
Modeling	18	7	0
TOTAL Mathematics	35	20	5

23
22   36
(Minimum Benchmark)

READING

	RIGHT	WRONG	OMIT
Key Ideas and Details (KD)	12	11	0
Craft and Structure (CS)	7	4	3
Integration of Knowledge and Ideas (IK)	1	2	0
TOTAL Reading	20	17	3

19
22   36
(Minimum Benchmark)

SCIENCE

	RIGHT	WRONG	OMIT
Interpretation of Data (ID)	10	5	3
Scientific Investigation (SI)	6	7	0
Evaluation of Models (EM)	5	4	0
TOTAL Science	21	16	3

21
23   36
(Minimum Benchmark)

There is no penalty for incorrect answers, so be sure not to leave any questions blank—even if you need to guess!

English: The English test measures your ability to find and correct errors in a piece of writing. Items are divided into three categories: Conventions of Standard English (Punctuation, Grammar and Usage, and Sentence Structure), Production of Writing (Strategy and Organization), and Knowledge of Language (Style).

Mathematics: The Mathematics test measures your ability to apply the knowledge and skills taught in high school mathematics courses. Items are divided into two main categories: Preparing for Higher Math (concepts you have learned recently), and Integrating Essential Skills (concepts such as perimeter and percents that you learned before eighth grade). Some mathematics items also measure your ability to work with models. These items are also included in one of the two main categories.

Reading: The Reading test measures your ability to read and think carefully about passages typically encountered in a first-year college course. You are asked to comprehend and respond to the passages through a variety of item-types, including Key Ideas and Details (main ideas, explicit and implied details), Craft and Structure (passage development and word choice), and Integration of Knowledge and Ideas (items asking you to compare or contrast two passages).

Science: The Science test measures your ability to apply scientific concepts and reasoning. You will read six or seven passages and answer the questions that follow. The questions are grouped into three item types: Interpretation of Data, Scientific Investigation, and Evaluation of Models, Inferences, and Experimental Results.

Writing: The optional Writing test measures your ability to develop a perspective on a given issue and evaluate other perspectives with a well organized and clearly written essay. You will have 40 minutes to write a response. The Writing test does not affect the composite score or scores on the individual subject tests.

The ACT, Inc. tests offered by Cambridge Educational Services, Inc. are retired tests, intended by ACT for practice purposes only and not for official administration, and are based on high school curriculum as of the copyright dates of the tests. Cambridge's products and services, including its score reports, are not approved or endorsed by ACT, with which Cambridge has no affiliation.

STUDENT ITEM ANALYSIS

The Student Item Analysis provides a comprehensive breakdown of each item: its category (corresponding to the categories listed on the Student Summary), the correct answer, and how you answered each item.

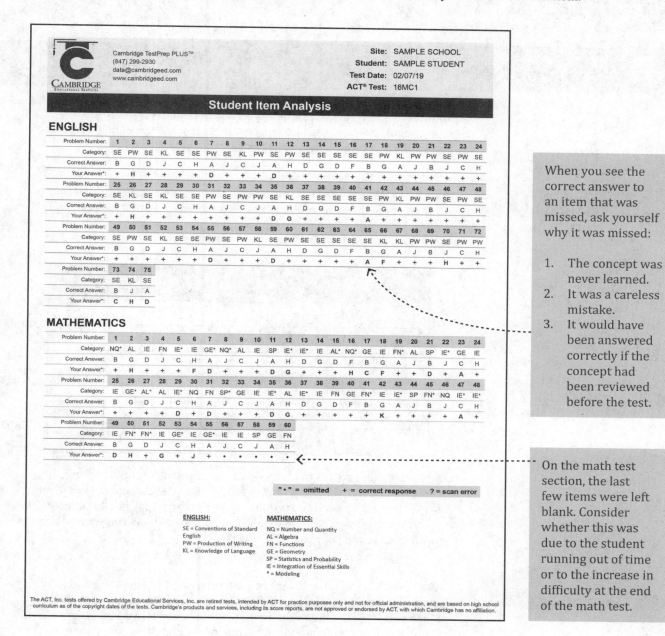

Cambridge TestPrep PLUS™
(847) 299-2930
data@cambridgeed.com
www.cambridgeed.com

CAMBRIDGE
EDUCATIONAL SERVICES

Site: SAMPLE SCHOOL
Student: SAMPLE STUDENT
Test Date: 02/07/19
ACT® Test: 16MC1

Student Item Analysis

ENGLISH

Problem Number:	1	2	3	4	5	6	7	8	9	10	11	12	13	14	15	16	17	18	19	20	21	22	23	24
Category:	SE	PW	SE	KL	SE	SE	PW	SE	KL	PW	SE	PW	SE	SE	SE	SE	SE	PW	KL	PW	PW	SE	PW	SE
Correct Answer:	B	G	D	J	C	H	A	J	C	J	A	H	D	G	D	F	B	G	A	J	B	J	C	H
Your Answer*:	+	H	+	+	+	D	+	+	+	D	+	+	+	+	+	+	+	+	+	+	+	+	+	+
Problem Number:	25	26	27	28	29	30	31	32	33	34	35	36	37	38	39	40	41	42	43	44	45	46	47	48
Category:	SE	KL	SE	KL	SE	SE	PW	SE	PW	PW	SE	KL	SE	SE	SE	SE	SE	PW	KL	PW	SE	PW	SE	SE
Correct Answer:	B	G	D	J	C	H	A	J	C	J	A	H	D	G	D	F	B	G	A	J	B	J	C	H
Your Answer*:	+	H	+	+	+	+	+	+	+	+	D	G	+	+	+	+	A	+	+	+	+	+	+	+
Problem Number:	49	50	51	52	53	54	55	56	57	58	59	60	61	62	63	64	65	66	67	68	69	70	71	72
Category:	SE	PW	SE	KL	SE	PW	SE	PW	KL	SE	PW	SE	SE	SE	SE	SE	SE	KL	PW	SE	SE	SE	PW	PW
Correct Answer:	B	G	D	J	C	H	A	J	C	J	A	H	D	G	D	F	B	G	A	J	B	J	C	H
Your Answer*:	+	+	+	+	+	D	+	+	+	D	+	+	+	+	+	A	F	+	+	+	H	+	+
Problem Number:	73	74	75
Category:	SE	KL	SE
Correct Answer:	B	J	A
Your Answer*:	C	H	D

MATHEMATICS

Problem Number:	1	2	3	4	5	6	7	8	9	10	11	12	13	14	15	16	17	18	19	20	21	22	23	24
Category:	NQ*	AL	IE	FN	IE*	IE	GE*	NQ*	AL	IE	SP	IE*	IE*	IE	AL*	NQ*	GE	IE	FN*	AL	SP	IE*	GE	IE
Correct Answer:	B	G	D	J	C	H	A	J	C	J	A	H	D	G	D	F	B	G	A	J	B	J	C	H
Your Answer*:	+	H	+	+	+	F	D	+	+	+	+	D	G	+	+	+	H	C	F	+	+	D	+	A	+
Problem Number:	25	26	27	28	29	30	31	32	33	34	35	36	37	38	39	40	41	42	43	44	45	46	47	48
Category:	IE	GE*	AL*	AL	IE*	NQ	FN	SP*	GE	IE	IE*	AL	IE*	IE	FN	GE	FN*	IE	IE*	SP	FN*	NQ	IE*	IE*
Correct Answer:	B	G	D	J	C	H	A	J	C	J	A	H	D	G	D	F	B	G	A	J	B	J	C	H
Your Answer*:	+	+	+	+	D	+	D	+	+	+	+	D	G	+	+	+	+	K	+	+	+	+	A	+
Problem Number:	49	50	51	52	53	54	55	56	57	58	59	60
Category:	IE	FN*	FN*	IE	GE*	IE	GE*	IE	IE	SP	GE	FN
Correct Answer:	B	G	D	J	C	H	A	J	C	J	A	H
Your Answer*:	D	H	+	G	+	J	+	•	•	•	•	•

"•" = omitted   + = correct response   ? = scan error

ENGLISH:
SE = Conventions of Standard English
PW = Production of Writing
KL = Knowledge of Language

MATHEMATICS:
NQ = Number and Quantity
AL = Algebra
FN = Functions
GE = Geometry
SP = Statistics and Probability
IE = Integration of Essential Skills
* = Modeling

The ACT, Inc. tests offered by Cambridge Educational Services, Inc. are retired tests, intended by ACT for practice purposes only and not for official administration, and are based on high school curriculum as of the copyright dates of the tests. Cambridge's products and services, including its score reports, are not approved or endorsed by ACT, with which Cambridge has no affiliation.

When you see the correct answer to an item that was missed, ask yourself why it was missed:

1. The concept was never learned.
2. It was a careless mistake.
3. It would have been answered correctly if the concept had been reviewed before the test.

On the math test section, the last few items were left blank. Consider whether this was due to the student running out of time or to the increase in difficulty at the end of the math test.

SET A TEST SCORE TARGET

Your test score target is unique to you and depends on your future educational and career goals. Setting your test score target also involves several steps, outlined below: test, research, and action.

TEST

Your first step is to take the pre-test that is part of your Cambridge course. After you take this test, you will receive a score report that gives you an accurate measure of where you stand. To begin the process of setting a test score goal, fill in your pre-test scores below:

TEST SECTION	SCORE
English	
Mathematics	
Reading	
Science	
Composite	
Writing	

As you use these scores to make a plan for improvement throughout this course, remember that if you had a bad test day (for example, if you were ill or distracted by personal problems), your scores may not be reflective of your true abilities. Be sure to take this into account as you set a goal for your post-test and your real ACT test.

RESEARCH

Now, make a list of schools that you are interested in attending and research the average scores and GPAs of admitted students to get an idea of how you stack up. Fill in the score that you estimate you need for each school. If you are interested in applying for scholarships, make sure you also research the scores each school requires for scholarship eligibility.

School:	Average ACT Test Score of Admitted Students:	
	Average GPA of Admitted Students:	
	Scholarship Score Requirement:	
	Estimated ACT Test Score Needed:	
	Additional Points Needed:	
School:	Average ACT Test Score of Admitted Students:	
	Average GPA of Admitted Students:	
	Scholarship Score Requirement:	
	Estimated ACT Test Score Needed:	
	Additional Points Needed:	
School:	Average ACT Test Score of Admitted Students:	
	Average GPA of Admitted Students:	
	Scholarship Score Requirement:	
	Estimated ACT Test Score Needed:	
	Additional Points Needed:	
School:	Average ACT Test Score of Admitted Students:	
	Average GPA of Admitted Students:	
	Scholarship Score Requirement:	
	Estimated ACT Test Score Needed:	
	Additional Points Needed:	

Once you have this chart filled in for several schools, you should have a good idea of the difference between your pre-test score and the score you will need to get into your schools of interest. Fill in this information below:

Pre-Test Score		Score	

ACTION

How do you translate these numbers into an action plan? See your Student Item Analysis report. This report gives you valuable information for every question on the pre-test. You'll see your answer, the correct answer, and the type of question that was asked. With a little analysis, you can see exactly where your weaknesses are and make a plan to address them.

CREATE A STUDY SCHEDULE

The most significant aspect of an effective study plan is that it is a written plan. A written study plan is more concrete than one that you simply draw on from memory. So, when creating your plan, write out a day-by-day schedule for reviewing all of the materials that are necessary for success in the course. This written format will provide a clear and dependable guide for study. Your schedule should be prioritized according to the time that you need to devote to each of the different subjects, based on the amount of time that you have.

Consider how you can plan your study time so that it corresponds with the course topics. In addition to assignments given in class, you may wish to devote extra study time to your particular areas of weakness. The "to do" list you created based on your Student Summary report is a good place to start. Use the calendar template that follows to develop a plan of action with your teacher. Determine what topics you will study each day and allot time to study those sections of the book and complete the relevant exercises. Remember, it is not necessary for you to do everything all at once. Instead, pick a few things to focus on each week.

MONTH:						

CHAPTER 1

Fast Track to English Mechanics

ENGLISH TEST DESIGN

Here are the basics of the English test design:

- Five passages
- 15 questions per passage, 75 questions total
- 45 minutes

Each of the five passages includes underlined words and phrases that may contain errors in grammar, sentence structure, punctuation, or style. Some passages also include boxed numbers used to ask about passage development and organization.

Essentially, the test is asking you to play editor, and, fortunately, the potential problem areas in a piece of writing are already pointed out with four potential solutions for you to choose from. Everything you need is right there in front of you.

The test includes three main types of tested topics:

- Nuts and Bolts of English Conventions (approximately 40 items)
- Passage Development (approximately 23 items)
- Style (approximately 12 items)

Let's go through these types one by one.

NUTS AND BOLTS

The nuts and bolts of the English test are items that test the conventions of standard English. These items are just what you would expect to find on an "English test" and cover the mechanical aspects of writing.

Example:

1. The recently created wildlife refuge, which includes nearly 30 small ponds for migrating geese and ducks, <u>were</u> made possible by substantial gifts from an anonymous donor to the Wildlife Protection Fund.

   A. NO CHANGE
   B. was
   C. have been
   D. being

TEST SPECS

Nuts and bolts questions ask about basic grammar principles. For example:

- subject-verb agreement
- pronoun-antecedent agreement
- modifier placement
- choice of verb tense

Although these questions test the rules of English usage, you are not required to know any technical jargon. In the question above, for example, you do not have to justify your choice using terms such as "agreement," "subject," and "verb." You just have to recognize the choice with subject-verb agreement.

PASSAGE DEVELOPMENT

Another 23 questions on the English Test belong to the category *Passage Development*, which includes questions that ask about adding topic sentences and choosing effective transitions. Here is an example:

Example:

2. We know that our solar system is part of a much larger system of hundreds of billions of stars. <u>As such</u>, this system is the Milky Way Galaxy, a huge disk of stars and gas.

    F. NO CHANGE
    G. Actually
    H. As a matter of fact
    J. OMIT the underlined phrase

STYLE

Style questions ask about word choice. These questions focus on using word choice that is concise and clear. There are 12 Style questions on the English test.

Example:

3. School officials who work with dropouts <u>who leave school</u> say a student will usually start thinking about dropping out about two years before he or she ceases to attend school.

    A. NO CHANGE
    B. who have left school
    C. who are leaving school
    D. OMIT the underlined phrase

Answers:

1. The correct answer is (B) because the singular subject "refuge" needs a singular verb "was." "Were" is a plural verb. *A verb must agree in both number and person with its subject.*

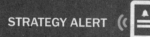

STRATEGY ALERT

Trust your ear. Try reading the sentence and plugging in each answer option. What sounds right probably is right.

2. The problem with the original sentence is that the phrase "as such" doesn't have a meaning that is appropriate here. And neither "actually" nor "as a matter of fact" is any better. The best choice is (J)—simply delete the phrase. The word "this," which modifies "system," refers to the "system" that is discussed in the preceding sentence. The two sentences flow well without any additional phrases.

3. The underlined phrase is a repetition of "dropouts." It should be deleted, (D).

ANATOMY OF ENGLISH

INSIDE THE DIRECTIONS

PACING TIP

On test day, skip the directions. By the time you get to the test you should know what to do.

Let's begin our look inside the English test by reading the directions to see what we can learn about the test.

> **DIRECTIONS:** In the passages below, certain parts of the sentences have been underlined and numbered. In the right-hand column, you will find different ways of writing each underlined part; the original version is indicated by the "NO CHANGE" option. For each item, select the choice that best expresses the intended idea, is most acceptable in standard written English, or is most consistent with the overall tone and style of the passage.
>
> There are also items that ask about a section of the passage or the passage as a whole. These items do not refer to an underlined portion of the passage; these items are preceded by statements that are enclosed in boxes.
>
> Read the passage through once before you begin to answer the accompanying items. Finding the answers to certain items may depend on looking at material that appears several sentences beyond the item. So, be sure that you have read far enough ahead before you select your answer choice.

STRATEGY ALERT

Read the passage and answer questions as you go. This will save you time, as long as you pay attention to the main idea and development of the passage as you read.

The directions tell you to choose answers corresponding to each underlined word or phrase based on correct expression, use of standard English, and consistency of style and tone. But you already knew that. So there's no reason to read the directions on test day.

The directions also tell you to read the whole passage, then answer the items. The test writers tell you to do this because some questions ask about the main idea of the passage, so you need to understand the whole passage. But these questions appear at the end of a paragraph or at the end of the whole passage; so as long as you're paying attention you will save yourself time by reading the passage and answering questions as you go.

INSIDE THE PASSAGES

English passages are approximately 300 words long. The text is interrupted by underlined words and phrases that could contain errors. Think of these passages as minefields, except with the advantage that someone has placed flags where mines might be. If we extend the analogy, we might say that if you needed to walk through a flagged minefield, you would look at the flags, not at the scenery. In the same way, you need to read the passage as you go (so you can answer questions about the main point of the passage, the passage organization, and so on), but you should focus on the underlined words and phrases. Let's look at a sample passage.

Poverty in America

[1]

The defining characteristic of poverty is a lack

of money. A family is characterized as poor when

its annual income <u>is below a certain dollar amount,</u>
1

calculated by the US federal government to be

1. A. NO CHANGE
    B. being under a certain dollar amount,
    C. is under a certain specific dollar amount,
    D. is a certain dollar amount

TEST SPECS

Underlined words or phrases indicate a part of the passage to be considered for revision.

The corresponding item number is located under the underline in superscript.

the minimum a family of their size would need to

maintain a minimally decent standard of living. [2]

2. The first paragraph provides which of the following?

    F   An argument
    G. A comparison
    H. A definition
    J. A narrative

TEST SPECS

Items that ask about a paragraph or particular point within a paragraph refer to the relevant part of the passage with a boxed number.

The corresponding item number is located inside the box.

[2]

In certain areas of rural America, poverty

is the rule rather than the exception. As much as
3

50 percent of the families may earn less than the

poverty level, and some may manage to survive by
4

subsisting somehow or other on amounts even less
4

than half the official poverty level income.

[3]

Although lack of money is the defining

characteristic of poverty, poverty is more than

simply lack of money. Poverty is an entire complex

of symptoms. Low levels of formal schooling among

adults parallel low-income levels. Additionally, in

families below the poverty level, the number of

children and elderly who depend on those who

work is, in general, higher than the national average

for all families. However, fewer workers support a
5

greater number of non-workers than in other, more

prosperous families.

3.   A.   NO CHANGE
      B.   As many as
      C.   So many as
      D.   So much

4.   F.   NO CHANGE
      G.   some folks may manage to survive by subsisting somehow
      H.   some may manage to subsist somehow or other
      J.   some may subsist

TEST SPECS

Bracketed numbers serve to numerate paragraphs and sentences, especially when a question asks about the best order for a series of paragraphs or sentences. In this case, the paragraph numbers are located inside the brackets for illustration.

5.   A.   NO CHANGE
      B.   As a consequence
      C.   Surprisingly
      D.   Fortunately

Item #6 asks about the preceding passage as a whole.

TEST SPECS

Items that ask about the passage as a whole are preceded by a box with the item number.

6.   The author does NOT use which of the following in the development of the essay?

      F   Definitions
      G.   Personal experience
      H.   Statistics
      J.   Explanation

INSIDE THE QUESTIONS

CLOSER LOOK

Items #1 and 3 are nuts and bolts questions about standard written English.

1. **(A)** Some questions can be answered just by reading a single sentence. In this case, you need to find the most grammatically correct way to write the underlined phrase. The original sentence is correct. (B) and (C) are awkward and wordy by comparison. (D) destroys the structure of the sentence. This question demonstrates that the original can be correct. Don't be afraid to choose "No Change."

2. **(H)** In the first paragraph the author provides the definition of "poor," so (H) is correct.

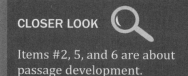

CLOSER LOOK

Items #2, 5, and 6 are about passage development.

3. **(B)** This question is like question 1. You can answer it by reading this one sentence and finding the idiomatic phrase. Since families come in discrete units, the correct idiom is "many," not "much."

4. **(J)** This is a style question, and it illustrates a couple of features of style items. First, the answer choices get shorter, showing that there is excess verbiage in the original sentence, so eliminate (F). There is also informal usage, "folks" in (G) and "somehow or other" in (H), so they can be eliminated. (J) is the most concise and idiomatic answer choice.

CLOSER LOOK

Item #4 asks about style.

5. **(B)** The last sentence of the paragraph expresses an idea that follows from, or is the result of, the idea that precedes it. The phrase "as a consequence" signals the reader that the second idea is the result of the first.

6. **(G)** The author supplies a definition in the first paragraph and statistics in the second paragraph. Throughout the selection the author offers explanations. The only answer choice the author doesn't provide is a personal example, (G).

PACING

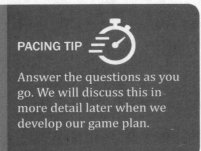

PACING TIP

Answer the questions as you go. We will discuss this in more detail later when we develop our game plan.

The ACT English test consists of five passages, each approximately 300 words in length and each with 15 corresponding items, for a total of 75 items. The time limit is 45 minutes. So, a fairly simple and easy-to-follow plan is to spend nine minutes on each of the five passages.

TASK	ALLOTTED TIME	REMAINING TIME
Answer questions accompanying first passage	9 minutes*	36 minutes
Answer questions accompanying second passage	9 minutes*	27 minutes
Answer questions accompanying third passage	9 minutes*	18 minutes
Answer questions accompanying fourth passage	9 minutes*	9 minutes
Answer questions accompanying fifth passage	9 minutes*	0 minutes

*Approximately 36 seconds per question

In a perfect world, you would spend exactly 36 seconds per question; but of course, the ACT test does not take place in a perfect world. Some items are going to take longer than others, particularly those that ask about the overall development of the passage.

To do well on the test you'll need to spend less time on the simple grammar items, building up a time reserve for those more difficult items that are coming. And the more difficult items are usually placed at the end of a passage because that's where it makes sense to ask, "What is the main idea?" and "How could the passage be improved?"

The schedule actually gives you a feedback loop that lets you know whether you need to skip some items. For example, if you are nearing the nine-minute mark and still have two or three items to do on the first passage, then skip any Passage Development items and go straight to the next passage. The Passage Development items take longer, and there will be some simple grammar items waiting to be easily completed in the next passage. Each problem should be answered even if you must turn to guessing. There is no penalty for wrong answers.

THE CAMBRIDGE GAME PLAN

Cambridge has a game plan for answering English questions. The plan includes five important strategies. Let's look at them one at a time.

READY. SET. GO.

PACING TIP

Each question is worth one point, so improve your score by completing the easy questions and skipping the more time-consuming questions.

But even if you aren't able to answer all the questions, don't forget to guess.

When you open your test booklet, start reading.

The questions are presented in order of the text (asking about particular points in the text). That means you don't need to read the entire passage before you can answer questions. Look ahead one or two sentences if necessary, but answer the questions as you go.

At the end of the passage, you may be asked some questions about the overall development of the passage. These questions usually take a little more time. Check the clock. If you've used up your nine minutes to answer the questions for that passage, circle those questions in your test booklet and move on to the next passage. You can come back to them at the end if there's time, or guess if necessary.

CIRCLE THE ERRORS IN THE UNDERLINED PARTS

Most items with the following format contain an error that must be corrected:

Example: A moral philosopher and pioneer of political economy, <u>Adam Smith's classic work, *The Wealth of Nations*, is widely acknowledged to be the "father of modern economics," yet the book</u> is rarely studied in university courses.

For these questions you must pick the one choice that is entirely correct. First, ignore the answer choices and look for an error in the underlined part. If you find an error, circle it.

The primary weakness of the sentence above is a misplaced modifier. The introductory phrase "A philosopher and pioneer" connects to the first important noun following it—in this case, "work." But a "philosopher and pioneer" is not a written work. The phrase really means to modify "Adam Smith," the thinker. So circle "Adam Smith's classic work."

WORK BACKWARD FROM THE ANSWERS

After identifying the error in the item stem, look at the answer choices to see which ones correct the error. What if more than one choice corrects the error? Then compare them to figure out the differences and determine which choice is entirely correct and doesn't introduce any other errors.

Example:

Q A moral philosopher and pioneer of political economy, <u>Adam Smith's classic work, *The Wealth of Nations*, is widely acknowledged to be the "father of modern economics," yet the book</u> is rarely studied in university courses.

A. NO CHANGE
B. Adam Smith's classic *The Wealth of Nations* is widely acknowledged to have been written by the "father of modern economics," Adam Smith;
C. Adam Smith is widely acknowledged to be the "father of modern economics," yet his classic work, *The Wealth of Nations*,
D. Adam Smith wrote the classic work, *The Wealth of Nations* and is widely acknowledged to be the "father of modern economics," yet the book

A Both (C) and (D) correct the original error, so compare them to see how they are different. (D) destroys the connection between the author and the work, obscuring the fact that it was Smith's authorship of the book that gave Smith his status, so (C) must be correct.

STRATEGY ALERT

Use the Process of Elimination.

- Eliminating one choice gives you a 33% chance of guessing correctly.
- Eliminating two choices gives you a 50% chance of guessing correctly.

POWER PRACTICE 1

> **DIRECTIONS:** Read the sentences below and circle any error in the underlined part. Then select the correct answer.

1. The supporters of the volunteer ambulance corps were assured <u>as to the deductibility of their donations on their tax returns</u>.

   A. NO CHANGE
   B. as to their donations being deductible on their tax returns
   C. that their, the supporters', donations are deductible on their tax returns
   D. that their donations are deductible on their tax returns

2. Most often, the reasons given for increasing physicians' fees <u>is they pay increasing malpractice insurance premiums and invest</u> in costly equipment.

   F. NO CHANGE
   G. are they pay increasing malpractice insurance premiums and invest
   H. are that physicians pay increasing malpractice insurance premiums and that they invest
   J. is increasing malpractice insurance premiums and investing

3. Visiting Europe as a tourist ten years after the end of the war, <u>the rapid pace of the postwar reconstruction amazed the former soldier</u>.

   A. NO CHANGE
   B. the postwar reconstruction that had taken place at a rapid pace amazed the former soldier
   C. the former soldier was amazed at the rapid pace of the postwar reconstruction
   D. the former soldier who was amazed at the rapid pace of the postwar reconstruction

4. Because Ian had been wounded in the European <u>Campaign, so he was asked</u> to serve as Grand Marshal of the Memorial Day Parade.

   F. NO CHANGE
   G. Campaign, he was asked
   H. Campaign, they asked him
   J. Campaign, so they asked him

5. The present administration <u>has always and will continue to be</u> committed to a policy of guaranteeing a good education to every child in the district.

   A. NO CHANGE
   B. has always and continues to be
   C. has always been and will continue
   D. has always been and will continue to be

ANSWERS

1. **(D)** *English/Conventions of Standard English/ Grammar and Usage/Diction*

   The phrase "as to" is generally not acceptable in standard written English, so (A) is incorrect. A noun clause is required: the supporters were assured that is the case. (B) fails to make this correction. (C) is wrong because the parenthetical expression is unnecessary and disrupts the logical flow of the sentence.

2. **(H)** *English/Conventions of Standard English/ Grammar and Usage/Subject-Verb Agreement and Nouns and Noun Clauses and Pronoun Usage*

   The original sentence suffers from three weaknesses. First, the subject of the sentence is the plural noun "reasons," so the verb should be the plural "are." Second, the pronoun "they" has no referent. It could refer to "physicians" if that word appeared in the sentence, but "physicians" does not appear—only "physicians' fees." Third, the material that follows "is" must be a noun or a noun substitute such as a noun clause. However, in the original, an independent clause follows "is." (H) corrects these errors. It uses the plural "are"; it creates a noun clause by using "that"; and it uses the noun "physicians" in place of the incorrect pronoun. (G) and (J) fail to correct the errors.

3. **(C)** *English/Conventions of Standard English/ Sentence Structure/Misplaced Modifiers*

   The original sentence has the notorious misplaced modifier. In general, a modifier should be placed as close as possible to what it modifies. Here, "visiting" is intended to modify "soldier," but those two words could not be farther apart. Consequently, the natural tendency, when reading this sentence, is to hook "visiting" to

the first noun in the main clause: "pace." Thus, the sentence seems to assert "the rapid pace of reconstruction is visiting Europe." (C) corrects this by placing the modified word in its proper position. (B) fails to make the needed correction and seems to assert that the reconstruction is visiting Europe. (D) does make the needed correction, but the use of "who" in (D) places the verb "was amazed" in a relative clause and turns the entire sentence into a fragment.

4. **(G)** *English/Knowledge of Language/Style/ Idiomatic Expression*

   The construction "because. . .so" is not idiomatic English. The subordinating conjunction "because" connects the two clauses and makes the "so" redundant. (G) solves this problem by eliminating the word. (H) and (J) do make the needed correction but use the pronoun "they," which has no referent.

5. **(D)** *English/Conventions of Standard English/ Sentence Structure/Incomplete Split Constructions*

   The original is an incomplete split construction. The sentence has a two-part verb: the administration "has always. . .committed" and "will continue to be committed." Removing the second part makes the error easier to identify. The verb "has" should be "has. . .been." (D) corrects this problem by supplying the missing word. (B) fails to supply the needed word. (C) does include "been," but it creates a new error in the second half of the construction. It reads "will continue committed," which doesn't make sense.

DON'T BE AFRAID TO PICK "NO CHANGE"

ACCELEPREP APPROACH

Don't believe NO CHANGE is statistically as likely to be correct? We checked over 200 questions, and NO CHANGE was right about 22% of the time. And on three recent tests, NO CHANGE was actually more likely to be correct than the other answer choices.

Choose "NO CHANGE" if you think that the original is correct as written. Many students automatically refuse to pick "NO CHANGE" because they figure that there must be something wrong with the original—even if they are unable to say what. But this reasoning is faulty. "NO CHANGE," when it is an option, is statistically as likely to be correct as is one of the other three choices.

POWER PRACTICE 2

DIRECTIONS: Read the following statements and circle any error in the underlined part. Then select the correct answer.

1. The gift certificate for a hot-air balloon ride gives the recipient the option that you may exchange the certificate for cash.

   A. NO CHANGE
   B. that the certificate may be exchanged
   C. of exchanging the certificate
   D. of your exchanging the certificate

2. Ignoring a projected decline in births over the next decade, the school board allocated funds for a new elementary school based upon an increase in the infant population last year.

   F. NO CHANGE
   G. By ignoring a projected decline in births over the next decade
   H. To ignore a projected decline in births over the next decade
   J. The next decade's projected decline in births having been ignored

3. Greek fire, a gelatinous, incendiary mixture, was used in warfare before gunpowder was invented.

   A. NO CHANGE
   B. Greek fire, a gelatinous, incendiary mixture, was used during warfare before the invention of gunpowder.
   C. Greek fire, a gelatinous, incendiary mixture before the invention of gunpowder, was used in warfare.
   D. A gelatinous, incendiary mixture, warfare involved the use of Greek fire before the invention of gunpowder.

4. The possibility of massive earthquakes are regarded by most area residents with a mixture of skepticism and caution.

   F. NO CHANGE
   G. is regarded by most area residents with
   H. is regarded by most area residents as
   J. is mostly regarded by area residents with

5. According to tradition, Vishnu appeared as Krishna to rid the world of a tyrannical king named Kamsa, the son of a demon.

   A. NO CHANGE
   B. Due to tradition,
   C. Because of tradition,
   D. Tradition has it that

ANSWERS

1. **(C)** *English/Knowledge of Language/Style/Idiomatic Expression*

   The original sentence suffers from two defects. First, "you" seems to refer to "recipient," but it is a second-person pronoun and cannot be substituted for "recipient," a third-person antecedent. Second, modifying "the option," as (C) does, produces a more concise sentence than adding a descriptive clause, as the original, (A), and (B) do. (C) avoids both errors. (D) corrects the second error but not the first, whereas (B) corrects the first error but not the second.

2. **(F)** *English/Knowledge of Language/No Change*

   The original sentence is correct as written. The changes suggested by the other choices distort the meaning of the original sentence or result in sentences that are very awkward.

3. **(A)** *English/Knowledge of Language/No Change*

   The sentence is correct as originally written. The use of "during" in (B) is not idiomatic. (C) changes the meaning of the original by illogically implying that Greek fire was only a gelatinous, incendiary mixture before the invention of gunpowder and that it then became something else. (D) is not only awkward when compared with the original, but the proximity of "warfare" to the introductory modifier implies that warfare is a gelatinous, incendiary mixture.

4. **(G)** *English/Conventions of Standard English/ Grammar and Usage/Subject-Verb Agreement*

   The original sentence contains an error of grammar. The verb "are" fails to agree with its subject, "possibility." The correct verb is "is." Each of the other choices makes the needed correction, but three of them introduce new problems. (H) changes the meaning of the original. The use of "as" implies that the residents think earthquakes are like a mixture of skepticism and caution. (J) changes the meaning of the original by qualifying the belief with "mostly" (informal usage in itself) and failing to quantify the number of residents who hold the belief.

5. **(A)** *English/Knowledge of Language/No Change*

   The original sentence is correct. (B) and (C) both imply that it was tradition that caused Vishnu to appear as Krishna. (In any event, "due to" is not acceptable in standard written English as a substitute for "according to.") (D) is informal usage. Remember that you should not make a change from the original unless you know that the change is an improvement over the original.

ZOOM OUT FOR THE BIG PICTURE

Some questions on the test will require you to know the context of the passage. These questions ask how to improve the organization of the passage or whether and where to include new information. When you answer these questions, remember your summary of the passage. Zoom out and think about the passage as a whole.

SUM IT UP - GAME PLAN

1. **Ready. Set. Go.**
   You can't afford to waste time, so don't read the directions. Start reading the passage and answer questions as you go.

2. **Circle the Errors in the Underlined Parts**
   Narrow your focus to any errors in the original to easily spot the answer.

3. **Work Backward from the Answers**
   Test the answer choices to figure out which one is correct.

4. **Don't Be Afraid to Pick "NO CHANGE"**
   It's just as likely to be correct.

5. **Zoom Out for the Big Picture**
   Mentally summarize a passage to answer questions about main idea or organization.

POWER PRACTICE 3

DIRECTIONS: In the passages below, certain parts of the sentences have been underlined and numbered. In the right-hand column, you will find different ways of writing each underlined part; the original version is indicated by the "NO CHANGE" option. For each item, select the choice that best expresses the intended idea, is most acceptable in standard written English, or is most consistent with the overall tone and style of the passage.

There are also items that ask about a section of the passage or the passage as a whole. These items do not refer to an underlined portion of the passage; these items are preceded by statements that are enclosed in boxes.

Read the passage through once before you begin to answer the accompanying items. Finding the answers to certain items may depend on looking at material that appears several sentences beyond the item. So, be sure that you have read far enough ahead before you select your answer choice.

[1]

Republican candidate George W. Bush won the presidential election held on November 7, 2000. While votes were cast for other <u>candidates,</u> <u>with Ralph Nader receiving over two million votes</u>,
¹ no candidate other than Bush or Gore received a significant number of electoral votes. The election was not finally decided until December 12 after various recounts, court appeals, and a Supreme Court decision. News coverage of the election results was faulty and contributed to the confusion.

1. A. NO CHANGE
   B. candidates with Ralph Nader receiving over two million votes
   C. candidates with Ralph Nader, receiving over two million votes
   D. candidates, with Ralph Nader receiving over two million votes

[2]

By 8 p.m. EST on election day, all major television news networks declared that Gore had won Florida's 25 electoral votes. The prediction was based on exit polls asking <u>voters which candidates</u> <u>they had selected, in the actual vote tally, Bush</u> took
² an early lead in Florida. By 10 p.m. EST the networks

2. F. NO CHANGE
   G. voters which candidates they had selected, in the actual vote tally Bush
   H. voters which candidates they had selected in the actual vote tally, Bush
   J. voters which candidates they had selected. In the actual vote tally, Bush

put Florida back into the "undecided" column. At

approximately 2:30 a.m., with some 85% of the votes

counted in Florida and Bush leading Gore by more

than 100,000 votes, the networks declared that

Bush had carried Florida and, therefore, based on

voting results from other states, had been elected

president.

[3]

Similarly, most of the remaining votes to
    3
be counted in Florida were located in just three

counties Broward, Miami-Dade, and Palm Beach.
    4
These counties are heavily Democratic. As these

additional votes were reported, Gore began to gain

on Bush. By 4:30 a.m., after all votes were counted,

Gore had narrowed Bush's margin to just over 2,000

votes, and the networks retracted their predictions
    5
that Bush had won Florida and the presidency. By

the time a mandatory recount was completed later

in the week, Bush's lead had dwindled to about

300 votes. A count of overseas military ballots later

boosted his margin to about 900 votes. Eventually,

after a US Supreme Court decision, Bush was

declared the winner and became the president of the

United States.

3. Which of the following would be the most effective transition between the two paragraphs?

    A. NO CHANGE
    B. Therefore
    C. Instead of
    D. However

4. F. NO CHANGE
   G. counties Broward Miami-Dade and Palm Beach
   H. counties: Broward, Miami-Dade, and Palm Beach
   J. counties, Broward Miami-Dade and Palm Beach

5. Select the choice that best fits the meaning of the sentence.

    A. NO CHANGE
    B. denied
    C. falsified
    D. invalidated

[4]

The faulty journalism resulted from excessive speed and competition, combined with overconfidence in experts and polls. The desire to be first, combined with the goal of offering viewers unique insights, led the networks to make unwise calls based on sketchy and sometimes <u>mistaken and</u>
<u>erroneous</u> information.
6

[5]

[1] Ultimately, the business imperative to win high ratings took priority. ☐7 [2] Ratings (that is, the size of the audience) determine the price of commercials. [3] Better ratings mean that networks can charge advertisers higher prices for commercial time. ☐8 [4] The revenue from commercials determines the bottom-line profits of the corporations that own the network.

[5] <u>What results being</u> a speed trap in which
9
all of the networks are doing their complicated calculations under maximum competitive pressure in minimum time, usually making their projections minutes apart. [6] The desire for high ratings, combined with the competitive pressure of the business, overrode journalistic standards. ☐10

6. F. NO CHANGE
   G. mistaken
   H. mistaken and erroneously wrong
   J. erroneously wrong

7. Sentence 2 would be most effectively placed

   A. where it is now.
   B. before sentence 1.
   C. after sentence 3.
   D. after sentence 4.

8. Which of the following is the best way of joining sentences 3 and 4?

   F. time, and the
   G. time and the
   H. time, the
   J. time and, the

9. A. NO CHANGE
   B. What results were
   C. Results are
   D. What results is

10. Paragraph 5 would be most effectively placed

    F. where it is now.
    G. after the first paragraph.
    H. after the second paragraph.
    J. after the third paragraph.

ANSWERS

1. **(A) *English/Conventions of Standard English/No Change***

    Notice that all four choices here use exactly the same words in the same order, so the issue has to be one of punctuation. The correct answer is (A). The information about the number of votes cast for Ralph Nader is parenthetical, so two commas are needed, one at the opening and one at the closing of the phrase.

2. **(J) *English/Conventions of Standard English/Sentence Structure/Run-On Sentences***

    Here we have another punctuation item. The problem with the original is that it is a run-on sentence. The "in the actual vote tally" is intended to modify "Bush," not "selected." So the break needs to be made just before "in."

3. **(D) *English/Production of Writing/Strategy/Effective Transitional Sentence***

    The author intends a contrast here, so you need a conjunctive adverb to show the reversal of ideas. Only "[h]owever" does the job.

4. **(H) *English/Conventions of Standard English/Punctuation/Dashes and Colons***

    This sentence, which lists specific counties, is an appropriate occasion for a colon. Here it is used to signal a list of specific counties that fit the general description given earlier in the sentence.

5. **(A) *English/Knowledge of Language/No Change***

    Once the networks realized that they were wrong, they retracted or withdrew their statement. The other choices have meanings that are suggested by the text, but they just don't fit well here.

6. **(G) *English/Knowledge of Language/Style/Conciseness***

    The original "mistaken and erroneous" is redundant, and only (G) solves this problem. (H) and (J) are also redundant.

7. **(A) *English/Production of Writing/Organization/Paragraph-Level Structure***

    Sentence 2 describes how ratings, which are determined by the size of the audience, determine the price of commercials. Sentence 2 is best placed where it is now, so it can introduce sentence 3, which discusses why ratings are so important.

8. **(F) *English/Production of Writing/Organization/Sentence-Level Structure***

    You can join two independent clauses or sentences by using a comma and a coordinating conjunction. (G) is wrong because some sort of punctuation is needed. (H) is wrong because a comma by itself is not strong enough to do the job (though you might use a semicolon without a conjunction). (J) is wrong because the comma is placed in the wrong spot.

9. **(D) *English/Conventions of Standard English/Grammar and Usage/Verb Tense***

    The problem with the original is that "being" is not a conjugated verb and so the word grouping is only a fragment. You need a conjugated verb, but both (B) and (C) introduce errors of agreement. The subject of the sentence, "what results," is singular.

10. **(F) *English/Production of Writing/Organization/Passage-Level Structure***

    The paragraph does not really belong to the main development of the essay. Instead, it is a different issue and is correctly placed at the end of the essay.

CHAPTER 2

HyperPrep English

GRAMMAR AND USAGE

TEST SPECS

Of all the Grammar and Usage questions on the test, questions involving pronouns, nouns and noun clauses, verb tense, and diction appear most frequently.

Grammar and Usage problems test your ability to edit texts to conform to the conventions of standard written English. You need to know five key Grammar and Usage topics:

1. Subject-Verb Agreement
2. Pronoun Usage
3. Nouns and Noun Clauses
4. Verb Tense
5. Diction

SUBJECT-VERB AGREEMENT

One common grammatical error is lack of agreement between subject and verb. The simplest subject-verb disagreements are usually obvious, as in the following example:

Example:

The books is on the shelf. ✘
The books are on the shelf. ✔

This example is very simple. The error is easy to spot because the subject and verb are next to each other. Often, however, errors occur when the subject and the verb are separated, when the sentence structure is inverted, or when it is not clear whether the subject is singular or plural.

MATERIAL INSERTED BETWEEN SUBJECT AND VERB

The test-writers insert material between the subject and verb to obscure their connection. If you are not careful, by the time you reach the verb, you will have forgotten the subject, and it will not be easy to determine whether the verb agrees with it. Consider the following examples:

Examples:

Star performers in the movies or on television usually earns substantial income from royalties. ✘

One school of thought maintains that the federal deficit, not exorbitant corporate profits and excessively high wages, cause most of the inflation we are now experiencing. ✘

A recent survey shows that a household in which both the wife and the husband are pursuing careers stand a better chance of surviving intact than one in which only the husband works. ✘

POWER TIP

Whack down the word weeds. When you are trying to check for subject-verb agreement, isolate the subject and verb. Ignore the extra words and phrases between the subject and verb.

In each of these three sentences, the subject and verb do not agree: "performers . . . earns," "deficit . . . cause," and "household . . . stand." However, the errors may not be obvious because of the intervening material. In the first sentence, the subject is separated from the verb by prepositional phrases. In the second sentence, the subject and the verb are separated by a parenthetical expression. In the third sentence, a clause intervenes between the subject and the verb.

Watch out for words or phrases near the verb that might be mistaken for the subject, as in the above examples: "television . . . earns," "wages . . . cause," and "careers . . . stand." If the first word of each of these pairs had been the subject, then there would have been no failure of agreement.

INVERTED SENTENCE STRUCTURE

A second common problem of subject-verb agreement is inverted sentence structure. In an inverted sentence, the verb precedes the subject. You should pay careful attention to the connection between subject and verb, no matter how those elements are ordered.

Examples:

Although the first amendment to the Constitution does guarantee freedom of speech, the Supreme Court has long recognized that there has to be some restrictions on the exercise of this right. ✗

Jennifer must have been doubly pleased that day, for seated in the gallery to watch her receive the award was her brother, her parents, and her husband. ✗

In both of these sentences, the subjects and verbs do not agree. The relationships are obscured by the order in which the elements appear in the sentence—the verbs come before the subjects. These sentences should read:

Examples:

Although the first amendment to the Constitution does guarantee freedom of speech, the Supreme Court has long recognized that there have to be some restrictions on the exercise of this right. ✓

Jennifer must have been doubly pleased that day, for seated in the gallery to watch her receive the award were her brother, her parents, and her husband. ✓

COMPOUND SUBJECTS

Finally, be alert for compound subjects. Usually, when the subject of a sentence consists of two or more elements joined by the conjunction "and," the subject is considered plural and requires a plural verb. Consider the following example:

POWER TIP

When elements of the subject are joined by "or," the verb must agree with the element nearest to it.

Of the seven candidates, John, Bill, or Jim is likely to win.

The elements are joined by "or," so the verb must agree with the closest element, "Jim."

Example:

Of the seven candidates, only John, Bill, and Jim was past office holders. ✗

The subject, "John, Bill, and Jim," is compound (joined by "and") and requires the plural verb "were"—even though the individual nouns are singular.

PRONOUN USAGE

PRONOUNS MUST HAVE ANTECEDENTS

STRATEGY ALERT

Trace it to the source. When an underlined phrase includes a pronoun, back up in the sentence until you find the antecedent. No antecedent? Unclear antecedent? Then you know the problem the correct answer needs to fix.

Except for a few idiomatic expressions ("It" is getting late; "It" will be sunny today), every pronoun must have an antecedent (a word the pronoun is replacing). An antecedent must be a noun, not a thought or phrase. Identify a pronoun's antecedent and then check that it is correct by substituting the antecedent for the pronoun in the sentence.

Example: **1.** During her rise to fame, she betrayed many of her friends, <u>and because of it</u>, very few people trust her.

    A. NO CHANGE
    B. and in spite of it
    C. and even though
    D. and because of her behavior

ANTECEDENTS MUST BE CLEAR

Explanations for the example questions are included later in the chapter. Circle your answers now. Later when you reach the explanations at the end of the section, come back and check to make sure you answered the questions correctly.

The antecedent of a pronoun must be made clear from the structure of the sentence.

Example: **2.** Ten years ago, the United States imported ten times as much French cheese as Italian cheese, but today Americans are eating more <u>of it</u>.

    F. NO CHANGE
    G. of them
    H. French cheese
    J. Italian cheese

PRONOUN-ANTECEDENT AGREEMENT

The pronoun must agree with its antecedent in number.

Example: **3.** Although a college dean used to be a symbol of authority, today <u>they receive</u> little respect from most students.

    A. NO CHANGE
    B. they received
    C. he or she receives
    D. college deans can receive

Remember also to watch for shifting subject errors. These errors occur if different forms of the same pronoun are used to refer to the antecedent.

Example: **4.** After three years of college education, one should be allowed to apply to graduate school, because by that time <u>you are ready to choose a profession</u>.

    F. NO CHANGE
    G. a profession can be chosen
    H. your profession is ready to be chosen
    J. one is ready to choose a profession

A PRONOUN MUST HAVE PROPER CASE

A pronoun must agree with its antecedent in case, number, and person. The pronoun's function in a sentence determines which case should be used. A noun's or a pronoun's case shows its relationship with the other words in a sentence.

Some pronouns are either singular or plural, while others can be both. The structure and intended meaning of the sentence indicate whether these pronouns are singular or plural.

Example:

5. The judges were unable to make a final decision on a single winner, so they divided the first prize between <u>John and he</u>.

 A. NO CHANGE
 B. he and John
 C. John and himself
 D. John and him

POWER TIP

An easy way to remember when to use "who" versus "whom" is that in those situations that "him" or "her" would be appropriate, "whom" should be used; in those situations that "he" or "she" would be appropriate, "who" should be used.

SUM IT UP - PRONOUN USAGE

1. A pronoun must have an antecedent to which it refers.

2. The pronoun must refer clearly to the antecedent.

3. The pronoun and antecedent must agree in number.

4. The pronoun must have the proper case.

NOUNS AND NOUN CLAUSES

Nouns are names of people, places, things, or ideas; they are used to indicate the subject of a sentence. A *noun clause* is a group of words that functions as the subject (or another noun usage) of a sentence. "That" is often the best word to use to introduce noun clauses.

Example: <u>That Judy was chosen for the promotion</u> is not surprising. ✓

"That" by itself is not the noun, nor is "Judy was chosen for the promotion" a noun. However, the two combined create a noun clause and function as the noun.

Do NOT use "where" for "that" in object clauses. However, if the subject of the sentence actually is about where something is, then use "where."

Examples: I saw in the bulletin <u>where</u> Mrs. Wagner's retirement was announced. ✗
I saw in the bulletin <u>that</u> Mrs. Wagner's retirement was announced. ✓

<u>Where</u> he went is not known now. ✓

Example **6.** <u>The reason the manager changed pitchers was because</u> he knew that the opposing side had a left-handed batter.

    F.   NO CHANGE

    G.   The reason that pitchers were changed by the manager was because

    H.   The reason the manager changed pitchers which

    J.   The manager changed pitchers because

SUM IT UP - NOUNS AND NOUN CLAUSES

1. "That" is often the best word to introduce a noun clause.

2. Do not use "because" or "why" to introduce a noun clause.

3. Do not use "where" to introduce a noun clause unless the sentence talks about something or someone's location.

VERB TENSE

The same verb tense should be used whenever possible within a sentence or paragraph. Avoid shifts in verb tense unless there is a valid reason.

Verb tense expresses when the action the verb is describing occurs or occurred. Verb tenses can be separated into three primary divisions of time: past, present, and future. Future tense is formed by adding "will" to the verb stem. Most verbs are called regular verbs because the past tense is formed by adding "-d" or "-ed" to the verb stem:

Present Tense	Past Tense	Future Tense
borrow, dare, guard, miss, staple	borrowed, dared, guarded, missed, stapled	will borrow, will dare, will guard, will miss, will staple

IRREGULAR VERBS

Some verbs, however, do not follow the usual rules. They are called irregular verbs:

Present Tense	Past Tense	Future Tense
see, say, go	saw, said, went	will see, will say, will go

Example: **7.** As soon as Linda finished writing her dissertation, she <u>will take</u> a well-earned vacation in Paris.

    A.   NO CHANGE

    B.   takes

    C.   took

    D.   will be taking

WHEN TO USE
THE PERFECT TENSES

STRATEGY ALERT

Trust your ear to help you eliminate incorrect answers that have to do with tense. Read the sentence in your head. If it sounds wrong, it probably is wrong.

Use the *present perfect* for an action begun in the past and extended to the present.

Example: I am glad you are here at last to keep me company; I have waited an hour already and the plane is not due to land for another 45 minutes. ✓

The action "have waited" (present perfect) began in the past and extended to the present.

Example: **8.** Elaine is the favorite to win the final event because she had always run well at the 100-meter distance.

F.   NO CHANGE
G.   has always run
H.   always ran
J.   will always run

Use the *past perfect* for an action begun and completed in the past before some other past action.

Example: Stacy had biked twelve miles before she realized her tire was going flat. ✓

In this case, both actions are completed in the past, but "biked" is completed before "realized," so "biked" must be expressed as the past perfect "had biked."

Use the *future perfect* for an action begun at any time and completed in the future. When there are two future actions, the action completed first is expressed in the future perfect tense.

Example: By the time I reach Chicago tonight, the Cubs will have played their first game of the season. ✓

The action "will have played" is going to take place before the action "reach," although both actions will occur in the future.

REVIEW

1. **Present Tense:** talk, write
2. **Past Tense:** talked, wrote
3. **Future Tense:** will talk, will write
4. **Present Perfect Tense:** have talked, has written
5. **Future Perfect Tense:** will have talked, will have written
6. **Past Perfect Tense:** had talked, had written

 SUM IT UP - VERB TENSE

1. Avoid unnecessary shifts in verb tense.
2. Use the correct verb tense.

DICTION

Diction is an important component of proper usage; it involves choosing the appropriate word in order to convey the desired meaning. Standard English contains numerous idioms and two-word verbs that are perfectly acceptable to use.

There are several things to check when looking for errors in diction.

WRONG PREPOSITION

In standard written English, only certain prepositions can be used with certain verbs. Daily practice reading and writing helps you learn idiomatic prepositional usage.

POWER TIP

Checklist for diction errors:

1. Wrong preposition
2. Wrong word choice
3. Gerund versus infinitive

Example: **9.** <u>In contrast of</u> the prevailing opinion, the editorial lays the blame for the strike on the workers and their representatives.

A. NO CHANGE
B. In contrast about
C. In contrast to
D. In contrast with

WRONG WORD CHOICE

The second category of diction errors involves word choice. Sometimes, words whose meanings are very similar are used incorrectly and lead to constructions that are non-idiomatic or are not acceptable standard written English. Some sentences are incorrect because they include words that fail to convey the author's intended meaning.

POWER TIP

Make sure you know the difference between these frequently confused words:

- accept/except
- fair/fare
- here/hear
- its/it's
- site/sight/cite
- their/there/they're
- then/than
- your/you're

Example: **10.** The <u>raise</u> in the number of accidents attributable to drunk drivers has prompted a call for stiffer penalties for driving while intoxicated.

F. NO CHANGE
G. raising
H. rise
J. rising

GERUND VERSUS INFINITIVE

The gerund is the "-ing" form of a verb, and it is used as a noun. The infinitive is the "to" form of a verb. It is also used as a noun. In some circumstances, you can use either the gerund or the infinitive.

Examples: <u>Adding</u> an extra room to the house is the next project. ✓
<u>To add</u> an extra room to the house is the next project. ✓

However, in some circumstances, the gerund and the infinitive are NOT interchangeable. The difference is not a matter of grammar because both the infinitive and the gerund are used as nouns. Instead, the difference is a matter of what fluent English speakers would regard as idiomatic.

Examples:

Tania says that <u>to open</u> the window will keep the room cool. ✗
(The infinitive is not idiomatic.)

Tania says that <u>opening</u> the window will keep the room cool. ✓
(The gerund is idiomatic.)

11. The idea of trying <u>completing</u> the term paper by Friday caused Ken to cancel his plans for the weekend.

   A. NO CHANGE
   B. complete
   C. to complete
   D. to completing

SUM IT UP - DICTION

1. Use prepositions idiomatically.

2. Make sure word choice conveys the intended meaning of the sentence.

3. Check for correct use of gerund and infinitive forms.

Answers:

TEST SPECS

We've covered the highest value topics in this Grammar and Usage review. Less frequently tested topics include:

- Adjective and Adverb Use
- Double Negatives
- Faulty or Illogical Comparisons

Return to the pages below to review each item:

1. p. 32
2. p. 32
3. p. 32
4. p. 32
5. p. 33
6. p. 34

1. A pronoun must have an antecedent, but "it" does not refer to anything. "It" wants to refer to the woman's "behavior," but that word does not appear in the original sentence. Corrected, the sentence reads "because of her behavior, (D)."

2. The antecedent of "it" is unclear. Does the sentence mean to state that Americans are eating more French cheese or more Italian cheese? "But" implies that "it" refers to the Italian cheese. However, the sentence would be better written by specifying which cheese the antecedent "it" refers to: " . . . cheese, but today Americans are eating more Italian cheese," (J).

3. The pronoun "they" refers to "college dean," which is singular. The best way to correct it is to say "he or she receives," (C).

4. "You" is a second-person pronoun and doesn't match up with the third-person pronoun used earlier in the sentence: "one." The sentence can be corrected by changing "you are" to "one is," (J).

5. "He" cannot serve as the object of a preposition since "he" is a subject pronoun. The correct pronoun here is the object pronoun "him," (D).

6. The original sentence makes the error of using "because" to introduce a noun clause. (J) corrects the error by eliminating the need for a separate noun clause. (G) not only fails to correct the error, but it introduces additional awkwardness into the sentence. (H) introduces a new error as well, because with (H), the sentence would have no main verb at all.

Return to the pages below to review each item:
7.   p. 34
8.   p. 35
9.   p. 36
10. p. 36
11. p. 37

7. The initial verb phrase ("As soon as Linda finished") describes an action that was entirely completed in the past; however, the subsequent verb phrase ("she will take") makes it sound as if that first action had not been completed and was instead ongoing. (C) corrects this error by stating that both events are completed and the writing preceded the vacation.

8. The present perfect is used to describe an action begun in the past and extended into the present. Since Elaine is currently the favorite to win the final event, her habit of running well at the 100-meter distance occurred in the past but continues into the present. So, the present perfect form "has run" should be used in place of the past perfect form "had run." Therefore, (G) is correct.

9. The expression "in contrast of" is an error in diction. The expression should be "in contrast to," (C).

10. "Raise" is not the correct word to use, here. While "raise" does mean "to lift," this sentence is referring to a specific number or statistic. The correct way to say this is "rise," (H).

11. Although "completing" can be a noun, only the infinitive form makes sense here. The sentence should read "trying to complete," (C).

POWER PRACTICE 1

> **DIRECTIONS:** Read the following statements and circle any errors in the underlined parts. Then select the correct answer. Answers are on p. 308.

1. In New York City, <u>they are</u> brusque and even rude but quick to come to one another's assistance in a time of crisis.

   A. NO CHANGE
   B. the people there are
   C. people are
   D. some are

2. I read in a magazine <u>where</u> scientists believe they have discovered a new subatomic particle.

   F. NO CHANGE
   G. in which
   H. that
   J. about

3. The sheriff called off the search for the escaped convict because he doubted that <u>the convict can successfully cross the river because the current was</u> so swift.

   A. NO CHANGE
   B. the convict successfully crossed the river because the current was
   C. the convict would have been successful in crossing the river, the current being
   D. a successful attempt to cross the river was made by the convict because the current was

4. Diplomats sent to an unstable region or a genuinely hostile territory usually <u>is assigned an aide or chauffeur who function</u> also as a bodyguard.

   F. NO CHANGE
   G. are assigned an aide or chauffeur who function
   H. are assigned an aide or chauffeur who functions
   J. is assigned an aide or chauffeur that function

5. Although ballet and modern dance are both <u>concerned in</u> movement in space to musical accompaniment, the training for ballet is more rigorous than that for modern dance.

   A. NO CHANGE
   B. concerned with
   C. concerning
   D. concerned to

SENTENCE STRUCTURE

TEST SPECS

Of all the Sentence Structure questions on the test, questions involving fragments, faulty parallelism, comma splices, and coordination and subordination appear most frequently.

We've reviewed the key Grammar and Usage topics, which focus on individual words or phrases within sentences. Now it's time to review Sentence Structure. You need to learn to watch for four key Sentence Structure errors:

1. Fragments
2. Faulty Parallelism
3. Comma Splices
4. Problems of Coordination and Subordination

FRAGMENTS

POWER TIP

If you're not sure whether a sentence is a fragment, ask yourself:

1. Does the sentence have a verb?
2. Does the sentence have a subject?

Dependent clauses by themselves are sentence fragments.

A sentence fragment, as the name suggests, is an incomplete piece of a sentence. By itself, a fragment does not constitute a complete thought. A typical fragment might lack a verb, a subject, or both. Sometimes a fragment is a dependent clause or a prepositional phrase that needs an independent clause to be complete. Fragments can be corrected by supplying the missing elements.

Example: **1.**   Most of the delegates, who were from smaller villages and <u>rural areas and so opposed</u> any plans to improve conditions in the large cities.

    A. NO CHANGE
    B. rural areas and so opposed to
    C. rural areas, they opposed
    D. rural areas, opposed

Explanations for the example questions are included later in the chapter. Circle your answers now. Later when you reach the explanations at the end of the section, come back and check to make sure you answered the questions correctly.

FAULTY PARALLELISM

POWER TIP

Check that all elements of a sentence are parallel—including verb forms, noun forms, and word pairs such as "this . . . that," "either . . . or," and "neither . . . nor."

Whenever elements of a sentence perform similar functions, they should have the same form. If they do not, the sentence is considered to have faulty parallelism.

Example: **2.** To abandon their homes, leave behind their families, and <u>traveling across the ocean</u> required great courage on the part of the immigrants who moved to America.

    F.   NO CHANGE
    G.   travel across the ocean
    H.   to travel across the ocean
    J.   while traveling across the ocean

SUM IT UP - FAULTY PARALLELISM

1. Make sure sentences are not fragmented or missing elements.

2. Elements of a sentence that have similar functions must take the same form or be parallel.

COMMA SPLICES

A comma splice results from the incorrect use of a comma to separate two independent clauses. Comma splices can be corrected in one of three ways: replace the comma with end-stop punctuation, with a semicolon, or with an appropriate connector.

Example: **3.** The weather forecast predicted heavy <u>rain, the</u> baseball game was postponed until the following day.

    A.   NO CHANGE
    B.   rain while the
    C.   rain, so the
    D.   rain the

PROBLEMS OF COORDINATION AND SUBORDINATION

TEST SPECS

We've covered the highest value topics in this Sentence Structure review. Less frequently tested topics include:

1. Run-On Sentences
2. Incomplete Split Constructions
3. Misplaced Modifiers
4. Unintended Meanings

On the ACT English Test, items may contain incorrect coordinating or subordinating conjunctions that join together two or more clauses. Always check to see whether the conjunction creates a logical connection.

Example: The car skidded across the <u>street, but</u> the ground was icy. ✗
The car skidded across the <u>street because</u> the ground was icy. ✓

In the example above, the coordinating conjunction "but" creates a nonsensical sentence. The intended meaning of the sentence is properly presented in the second version. The car skidded as a result of the icy ground (not in spite of the icy ground).

Example: Kari was just about to mail in her deposit for her second-choice school <u>and that was when the letter arrived notifying her</u> of her acceptance at her first choice. ✗

Kari was just about to mail in her deposit for her second-choice school <u>when she learned</u> of her acceptance at her first choice. ✓

In this example, the "and" seems to join the first clause of the sentence to an idea of equal importance, but the writer intends the second idea to be dependent on the timing of the first idea. The correction makes this clear by creating a dependent clause introduced by the subordinating conjunction "when."

Answers:

1. The original construction is a sentence fragment. None of the verbs in this construction can function as the main verb because they all belong to a subordinate clause. (D) is the correct answer choice because "opposed" functions as the main verb of the sentence ("most of the delegates . . . opposed any plans").

Return to the pages below to review each item:
1. p. 40
2. p. 41
3. p. 41

2. The three verb forms should be parallel, so change "traveling" to "travel." Therefore, (G) is the correct answer.

3. The original is a comma splice. This problem can be solved by adding a conjunction that correctly expresses the relationship between the two ideas. In this case, the conjunction "so" indicates the cause and effect relationship between the quality of the weather and the postponement of the baseball game. Therefore, (C) is the correct answer.

POWER PRACTICE 2

DIRECTIONS: Read the following statements and circle any errors in the underlined parts. Then select the correct answer. Answers are on p. 308.

1. <u>Although the American relay team did not qualify for the finals, the</u> anchor runner dropped the baton shortly after the hand-off.

   A. NO CHANGE
   B. When the American relay team did not qualify for the finals, the
   C. The American relay team did not qualify for the finals, and
   D. The American relay team did not qualify for the finals because the

2. The first astronauts were true <u>pioneers, they</u> volunteered at a time when the plans for space travel were only on paper and no one knew what the chance of success was.

   F. NO CHANGE
   G. pioneers but
   H. pioneers. They
   J. pioneers yet

3. <u>The audience, dazzled by the sequined costumes and brilliant lights and applauded wildly.</u>

   A. NO CHANGE
   B. The audience, dazzled by the sequined costumes and brilliant lights, applauded wildly.
   C. The audience, applauding wildly and dazzled by the sequined costumes and brilliant lights.
   D. Dazzled by the sequined costumes and brilliant lights, the applauding audience.

4. To acknowledge that one has something to learn is <u>taking the first step</u> to true wisdom.

   F. NO CHANGE
   G. taken the first step
   H. to taking the first step
   J. to take the first step

5. The devastation caused by the flood was so <u>complete, it</u> was impossible to tell that the pile of debris had once been a house.

   A. NO CHANGE
   B. complete, and it
   C. completely, it
   D. complete that it

PUNCTUATION

TEST SPECS

Of all the punctuation questions on the test, comma, colon, and apostrophe usage questions appear most frequently.

The last Standard English Conventions topic to review is Conventions of Punctuation. There are three commonly tested types of punctuation:

1. Commas
2. Colons
3. Apostrophes

COMMAS

Explanations for the example questions are included later in the chapter. Circle your answers now. Later when you reach the explanations at the end of the section, come back and check to make sure you answered the questions correctly.

To be successful with commas, you must know five easy comma rules:

1. Use commas between independent clauses joined by coordinating conjunctions.
2. Use commas for clarity.
3. Use commas to separate words in a series.
4. Use commas after introductory dependent phrases.
5. Use pairs of commas to set off "interruptions" in a sentence.

JOIN INDEPENDENT CLAUSES

STRATEGY ALERT

Use the breath test to check for correct comma usage. Commas are usually associated with a natural pause in our speech. Reading the sentence to yourself can help you find the correct answer.

Coordinating conjunctions ("and," "but," "nor," "or," "for," "yet," "so") join two independent clauses. Use a comma before coordinating conjunctions unless the two clauses are very short (think two or three words per clause).

Example: **1.** Practically all nitrates are <u>crystalline and readily soluble, and</u> they are characterized by marked decrepitation when heated on charcoals by a blowpipe.

    A. NO CHANGE
    B. crystalline and readily soluble and
    C. crystalline, and readily soluble, and
    D. crystalline and readily soluble and,

USE COMMAS FOR CLARITY

Use a comma to clarify the meaning of a sentence. Some sentences can mean two different things if a comma is missing, as the following example illustrates:

Example: The business owners who closed their businesses yesterday are in serious financial trouble.
(Those business owners who closed yesterday are the ones who are in trouble. Those who remained open yesterday are not in trouble.)

The business owners, who closed their businesses yesterday, are in serious financial trouble.
(The whole group of business owners are in trouble, and all of them closed yesterday.)

USE COMMAS TO SEPARATE LISTS

Use commas to separate the words in a series when three or more elements are present.

Example: Coats, umbrellas, and boots should be placed in the closet at the end of the hall. ✓

Is it correct to use a serial comma (a comma before "and" or "or")? It depends on the style guide you use. The ACT test writers prefer the serial comma, but whether you should use it isn't tested because there is no right or wrong choice. It's just a matter of style.

INSIDE LOOK

The test measures application of straightforward punctuation rules. For example, you won't be asked to choose between two answer choices that are different only because one uses a serial comma and the other does not.

Example: **2.** The procedure requires that you open the outer cover <u>plate remove, the thermostat replace the broken switch, and</u> then replace the thermostat.

    F.   NO CHANGE
    G.   plate remove the thermostat, replace the broken switch; and
    H.   plate, remove the thermostat, replace the broken switch, and
    J.   plate remove the thermostat replace the broken switch and

USE COMMAS WITH INTRODUCTORY DEPENDENT CLAUSES

Use a comma after an introductory phrase or word group that precedes the subject of the sentence.

RULE 1: Place a comma after an introductory phrase of five or more words.

Example: Because the prisoner had a history of attempted jailbreaks, he was put under heavy guard. ✓

RULE 2: Use a comma after a short introductory phrase whenever the comma would aid clarity.

Example: To Dan, Phil was a friend as well as a brother. ✓

RULE 3: Use a comma after introductory gerunds, participles, and infinitives.

Examples: To walk, he needed a cane. ✓

3. When Pat explained to his <u>mother that ten was the highest mark given on the entrance test</u> she breathed a sigh of relief.

   A. NO CHANGE
   B. mother, that ten was the highest mark given on the entrance test,
   C. mother that ten was the highest mark given on the entrance test,
   D. mother that ten was the highest mark given on the entrance test;

USE COMMAS TO SET OFF INTERRUPTIONS

STRATEGY ALERT

Watch out for superfluous commas. Commas should NOT separate a subject from its verb or separate the components of a compound verb.

Use commas before and after words and phrases that provide additional, nonessential information or that interrupt the flow of a sentence. These words and phrases can take a few different forms.

FORM 1: An appositive phrase follows a noun or pronoun and has the same meaning as that noun or pronoun. For example, "Mrs. Walker, a teacher, walked up the steps."

Examples: Mr. Dias, <u>our lawyer,</u> gave us some great advice. ✓

Bob, <u>an industrious and hard-working student,</u> will run for class treasurer. ✓

FORM 2: Parenthetical expressions are words that interrupt the flow of the sentence without changing the meaning of the sentence. Examples include "however," "though," "for instance," "by the way," "to tell the truth," "believe me," "it appears to me," "I am sure," and "as a matter of fact."

Examples: This book, <u>I believe,</u> is the best of its kind. ✓

Julie and her three dogs, <u>I am sure,</u> will not easily find an apartment to rent. ✓

FORM 3: A nonrestrictive element introduces material that is not essential to the sentence and, if removed, will not change the meaning of the original sentence. For example, "The blanket, which was red, lay on the grass."

Examples: Sam, <u>who is a very well-behaved dog,</u> never strays from the front yard. ✓

Millie, <u>who is a fine student,</u> has a perfect attendance record. ✓

In general, if material can be omitted without changing the meaning of the main clause, the material is nonrestrictive and should be set off by commas.

Example: 4. <u>Niagara Falls, which forms part of the border between the United States and Canada,</u> was the site of a saw mill built by the French in 1725.

   F. NO CHANGE
   G. Niagara Falls forms part of the border between the United States and Canada
   H. Niagara Falls, which forms part of the border between the United States and Canada—
   J. Niagara Falls, which forms part of the border between the United States and Canada; it

**WHEN COMMAS
SHOULD NOT BE USED**

Many items on the English test include commas used incorrectly. Watch out for three major errors in comma use.

Do NOT use a comma to separate a subject from its verb.

Example:

Students who plan to graduate with joint majors, must declare their intention and identify the two areas of study by the end of their junior year. ✗

Students who plan to graduate with joint majors must declare their intention and identify the two areas of study by the end of their junior year. ✓

There is no good reason to put a comma into this sentence. The comma separates the subject from its verb and disrupts the logical flow of the sentence.

Do NOT use commas to set off a restrictive or necessary clause or phrase.

Example:

That dog was barking, for attention.

Do NOT use a comma in place of a conjunction.

Example:

We went to the store, picked up a gallon of milk.

STRATEGY ALERT

Trust your ear to tell you if commas should be used to set off a parenthetical expression. Read the sentence. If you pause before and after the parenthetical expression, use commas to set it off.

TEST SPECS

We've covered the highest value topics in this Punctuation review. Less frequently tested topics include:

- Semicolons
- Dashes
- Quotation Marks

SUM IT UP - COMMAS

1. Use commas between independent clauses joined by coordinating conjunctions.
2. Use commas for clarity.
3. Use commas to separate words in a series.
4. Use commas after introductory dependent phrases.
5. Use pairs of commas to set off "interruptions" in a sentence.

COLONS

You need to know two key colon usage rules:

1. **A colon may be used to precede a list of three or more items or a long quotation.**
2. **A colon may be used to call attention to an elaboration or explanation.**

POWER TIP

DO NOT use colons after expressions such as "like," "for example," "such as," and "that is."

Examples:

In the United States there are three branches of government: executive, judicial, and legislative. ✓

We all thought Jacob had retired to do more traveling, but he explained that another factor contributed to his retirement: lack of research funding. ✓

DO NOT use colons after expressions such as "like," "for example," "such as," and "that is." Colons are intended to replace these terms, so including both is redundant.

Example:

5. The seemingly tranquil lane has been the scene of many crimes <u>including: two assaults, three robberies, and one murder</u>.

   A. NO CHANGE
   B. including two assaults, three robberies, and one murder.
   C. including two assaults three robberies and one murder.
   D. including: two assaults three robberies and one murder.

APOSTROPHES

WHEN TO USE AN APOSTROPHE

Apostrophes are most commonly used to show possession.

> *Examples:*
> Clyde's bicycle
> anyone's car
> the teachers' lounge
> the soldiers' weapons

POWER TIP

Singular nouns and indefinite pronouns add the apostrophe and "-s." Plural nouns ending in "-s" add only the apostrophe.

An apostrophe is also used to show that a noun is used to modify another noun in two special cases. First, apostrophes are placed after nouns in time relationships.

> *Examples:*
> a day's ride from camp
> three weeks' wages

Apostrophes are also placed after nouns that modify gerunds.

Examples:
the coach's constant urging
a member's making a motion

WHEN NOT TO USE AN APOSTROPHE

DO NOT use an apostrophe with a personal pronoun. The possessive forms of the personal pronouns are "my," "mine," "your," "yours," "his," "her," "hers," "its," "our," "their," and "theirs."

Answers:

1. Use a comma before "and," "but," "so," "yet," "or," "for," and "nor" when any of these are used to join two independent clauses. Therefore, (A) is the correct answer.

Return to the pages below to review each item:
1. p. 44
2. p. 45
3. p. 46
4. p. 46
5. p. 48

2. A comma should separate the elements in the series. Only (H) correctly separates the elements.

3. A comma should follow the introductory clause ("When Pat explained to his mother . . . entrance test"). However, if the subordinate clause follows the main clause in a sentence, you do not need to set it off with a comma. Therefore, (C) is the correct answer.

4. The sentence is correct as written. The commas are used correctly to set off the nonrestrictive material.

5. The colon in this sentence is unnecessary because the elements in the series are signaled by the word "including," so eliminate (A) and (D). The commas are necessary to separate the elements in the series, so eliminate (C). Therefore, (B) is correct.

POWER PRACTICE 3

DIRECTIONS: Read the following statements and circle any errors in the underlined parts. Then select the correct answer. Answers are on p. 308.

1. According to legend, <u>King Arthurs court</u> consisted of twenty-four knights, each of whom was chosen by King Arthur for a special talent or virtue.

   A. NO CHANGE
   B. King Arthurs'
   C. King Arthur's court
   D. Kings' Arthur Court

2. In the turmoil of our <u>modern times</u>, it is important to try to keep in mind the fundamental moral values that structure our society.

   F. NO CHANGE
   G. modern times'
   H. modern time's
   J. modern-like times'

3. A full train crew consists of a <u>motorman, a brakeman, a conductor, and</u> two ticket takers.

   A. NO CHANGE
   B. motorman, a brakeman, a conductor and,
   C. motorman, a brakeman a conductor and
   D. motorman a brakeman a conductor, and

4. After Peter finished painting the bird <u>feeder he and Jack</u> hung it from a limb of the oak tree.

   F. NO CHANGE
   G. feeder, he and Jack
   H. feeder; he and Jack
   J. feeder, he and Jack,

5. In addition to test scores, college admissions officers take into consideration many other <u>factors such as: grades, extracurricular activities,</u> and letters of recommendation.

   A. NO CHANGE
   B. factors such as grades, extracurricular activities,
   C. factors: such as grades, extracurricular activities,
   D. factors such as grades extracurricular activities

STRATEGY AND ORGANIZATION

TEST SPECS

Of all the Strategy questions on the test, questions involving supporting material, transitional sentences, and main idea appear most frequently.

Strategy questions ask you about the author's development of the passage. Three key Strategy questions ask you to think about the structure of the author's argument:

1. Appropriate Supporting Material
2. Effective Transitional Sentences
3. Main Idea

APPROPRIATE SUPPORTING MATERIAL

PACING TIP

The English Test includes five full-length passages. Remember to read for comprehension as you answer the items so that you don't have to go back and re-read the passage when you get to a Strategy question.

Effective development of an essay depends largely on the appropriateness of the materials presented in the essay. Extraneous or irrelevant information distracts the reader from the main purpose of the essay and decreases the readability and effectiveness of a composition.

Each sentence and paragraph functions to develop an essay; therefore, it is important to find an answer choice that is correct in the context of the paragraph or the essay. When confronted with items that ask about the addition or revision of appropriate material, first identify the overall idea of the selected portion, and then determine whether an addition or revision is in order.

You should be familiar with some of the strategies writers use to support their claims:

- providing an interpretation of a statement
- clarifying a general statement with examples
- furthering an argument with information and logical reasoning
- quoting an expert on the issue

Understanding these strategies will help you quickly identify the purpose of supporting material and evaluate the appropriateness of the strategy in the context of the selection.

Example:

[1] An even more important aspect of the healthcare problem in America is the choices that people make for themselves. [2] Take smoking, for example. [3] Scientific evidence proves that smoking causes lung cancer and other diseases. [4] Yet many people continue to smoke, and young people continue to start smoking. [5] There are other health problems, such as being overweight and using drugs, that may also come from private choices.

STRATEGY ALERT

Resist the temptation to select an answer choice simply because it resuses terminology from the passage. A favorite trick of test writers is to include a detail that sounds important but is totally irrelevant to the topic of the paragraph or passage.

1. The author is considering inserting the following factual statement between sentences 4 and 5:

> Nicotine, which is found in tobacco, is one of the most addictive chemicals known to science.

Would this statement add to the development of the paragraph?

A. Yes, because the paragraph identifies smoking as a serious problem.
B. Yes, because the sentence explains why young people start to smoke.
C. No, because scientific evidence is irrelevant to the author's point.
D. No, because the addictive mechanism behind smoking is not relevant.

Example:

Explanations for the example questions are included later in the chapter. Circle your answers now. Later when you reach the explanations at the end of the section, come back and check to make sure you answered the questions correctly.

My favorite opera is *La Bohème* by Puccini. The action of the opera takes place on the Left Bank of Paris in the 1830s. The Left Bank is where the struggling artists and students lived. Four of the main characters in the opera are a painter, a philosopher, a musician, and, most important for me, a poet. The sets include a sidewalk café and a garret room. The opera even has a passionate romance with a tragic ending.

2. The writer wants to add that the Left Bank is also called the Latin Quarter. Which revision to the underlined sentence best accomplishes that goal?

F. The Latin Quarter is another name for the Left Bank. The Left Bank is where the struggling artists and students lived.
G. The Latin Quarter and the Left Bank are the same thing. The Left Bank is where the struggling artists and students lived.
H. The Left Bank, also called the Latin Quarter, is where the struggling artists and students lived.
J. The Left Bank is where the struggling artists and students lived. The Left Bank is also called the Latin Quarter.

EFFECTIVE TRANSITIONAL SENTENCES

INSIDE LOOK

Here are some transitional words that have shown up on ACT tests.

- alternatively
- finally
- nevertheless
- consequently
- previously
- although
- therefore
- notwithstanding
- however
- thus
- also
- moreover
- furthermore
- subsequently
- likewise

The transitional sentences in an essay offer signposts for the reader. Transitional sentences link the different ideas in a composition together, contributing to the development and flow of an essay. Answer choices for transitional statements generally offer the most logical connection between two paragraphs or sentences.

Example:

My first real job was working at the Burger Barn, where there are rules for everything. There must be so many orders of fries under the warming lamp and a certain number of burgers on the grill. <u>However</u>, paper products and condiments must be restocked every half hour, and employees receive five-minute breaks every two hours and 20 minutes for lunch during a six-hour shift. To outsiders, these rules may seem silly, but they are necessary to make sure that the food we serve is safe to eat and that during evening rush we can serve as many as 150 people.

3. Which of the following represents the best revision of the underlined word?

   A. NO CHANGE
   B. In addition
   C. Therefore
   D. Perhaps

MAIN IDEA

From the time that you were first assigned an essay to write, you've been admonished, "Your essay must have a main idea." Sometimes teachers say, "Make sure your writing has a focus"; other times they might say, "Your essay must have a main point"; and maybe they have also said, "The essay has to develop your thesis." All of these different instructions—main idea, main point, focus, theme, thesis—are essentially the same: every piece of writing should have a central or main point.

Example:

Huey Long was governor of Louisiana from 1928 to 1932 and became a United States Senator in 1932. Although he claimed to be a Democrat, Huey Long was actually a radical populist. He wanted the government to confiscate the wealth of the nation's rich and privileged. He called his program "Share Our Wealth." He called upon the federal government to guarantee every family in the nation an annual income of $5,000, so they could have the necessities of life, including a home, a job, a radio, and an automobile. He also proposed limiting private fortunes to $50 million, legacies to $5 million, and annual incomes to $1 million. Everyone over age 60 would receive an old-age pension. His thinking was summarized in his slogan, "Every Man a King."

4. The writer is primarily interested in:

F. discussing Huey Long's political philosophy.
G. describing Huey Long's achievements.
H. supporting the "Share Our Wealth" program.
J. criticizing the idea that every man is a king.

TEST SPECS

We've covered the highest value topics in this Strategy review. Another less frequently tested topic is Audience.

SUM IT UP - MAIN IDEA

1. Every piece of writing should have a central or main point.

2. As a writer, you must make sure that your essays always have a main idea. As a reader, you must be able to identify the writer's main idea.

ORGANIZATION

TEST SPECS

There are three types of organization questions, focusing on three levels of organization: sentence-level structure, paragraph-level structure, and passage-level structure. Questions about sentence-level structure appear most frequently.

Organization questions focus on the logical order of sentences in a paragraph and paragraphs in a passage. You should become familiar with the basic design of a passage.

A basic passage includes an introduction, supporting paragraphs, and a conclusion. The first paragraph of a passage introduces the topic upon which the rest of the passage will elaborate. Several supporting paragraphs will follow, with each successive paragraph presenting information to further the topic that is set forth in the introductory paragraph. The last paragraph of the essay is the conclusion, which sums up the main idea of the passage.

Organization items that deal with sentence-level structure may ask about the best placement for a particular sentence or the best order of sentences within a paragraph. These items may also ask whether a sentence should be deleted or changed in some way.

You should approach items that ask to reorder sentences in a paragraph by looking for structural clues, such as topic sentences and transitions. When deciding the proper order for sentences, note that topic sentences are generally placed at the beginning of a paragraph as an introduction. If the paragraph follows an inductive method of development, where details are presented leading up to a general statement, the topic sentence will come last. Always make sure that the resulting organization makes sense and follows a logical pattern.

Example:

[1] In the past several years, lawyers have increasingly been in the negative public spotlight. [2] A group of students hire a lawyer to sue their school because they don't like the mascot. [3] A driver sues a take-out restaurant because he was scalded by the hot coffee

he spilled while driving. [4] A prison inmate goes all the way to the Supreme Court because the jail uses the wrong kind of peanut butter.

5. Which of the following would be the most suitable sentence to insert immediately after sentence 1?

    A. Lawyers go to school for an additional three years after college.
    B. The news runs daily stories of how people have been injured.
    C. I have often thought about becoming a lawyer after I graduate.
    D. It seems as though every day we hear of another frivolous lawsuit.

POWER TIP

Use the transitional words in a sentence as clues when reorganizing sentences. For examples, reference the list of transitional words in the previous section.

Answers:

Return to the pages below to review each item:

1. p. 51
2. p. 51
3. p. 52
4. p. 53
5. p. 54

1. This paragraph is devoted to describing different lifestyle choices that are harmful to a person's health (e.g., smoking, obesity, and drug use). Therefore, it is the simple fact that tobacco is harmful ("smoking causes lung cancer and other diseases") that makes it relevant in this context. The statement about nicotine is unnecessary because the nature of tobacco and the addictive mechanism of smoking is not relevant in this essay. Therefore, the correct answer is (D).

2. Inserting the information as a parenthetical expression helps to preserve the flow of the first paragraph. In addition, the information must accurately and effectively refer to "Left Bank." So, (H) is the best choice. The other choices suggest complete sentences, and inserting a whole sentence into the paragraph is likely to be distracting to the reader and give too much importance to a fairly minor detail.

3. This paragraph gives several examples of rules that the Burger Barn employees must follow in order to ensure adequate amounts of safe food. The second sentence of the paragraph states that "[t]here must be so many orders of fries under the warming lamp and a certain number of burgers on the grill." The third sentence continues to give additional rules. Therefore, the best answer is choice (B): "In addition, paper products and condiments must be restocked every half hour." None of the remaining choices are logical in the context of the paragraph.

4. The correct answer is (F). The writer is neither defending nor attacking Long, so you can rule out (H) and (J) as possible choices. Then, you can rule out (G) because the writer is more concerned with Long's vision and philosophy than with his actual achievements.

5. The writer has started off by saying generally that lawyers get bad press and then has followed up with three specific examples. Therefore, a sentence that provides a transition would be appropriate, and (D) does this by introducing the three examples that follow.

POWER PRACTICE 4

DIRECTIONS: The following questions refer to sections of the passage below, or to the passage as a whole. Answers are on p. 308.

[1]

[1] On my vacation to Alaska, I took a trip to Porcupine. In 1905, Porcupine was a thriving town of 2,000 people, retail stores, and a post office. [2] Hardly any of the town remains today, but there is still gold there, and our guide showed us how to pan for gold. [3] It's easy to learn how, and anyone can do it.

[2]

[4] The technique of panning depends on the weight of gold. [5] It's about 20 times heavier than water, so the gold stays at the bottom of a stream and gets caught in the sand in slow-flowing water around bends and along the edge of the stream. [6] It can also get stuck in small crevices of rock and even wedged into pieces of wood.

[3]

[7] You need to find where the gold is. There's no sense in panning for gold in a stream where there isn't any, so go to a stream where people have found gold before. [8] Then concentrate on those areas that are most likely to trap the little bits of gold.

[4]

[9] To start panning, put a few handfuls of material into your gold pan. [10] Then submerge the pan in the water of the stream. [11] Hold the pan under the surface and move it in a circular motion so that the lighter material sloshes over the edge. [12]

1. Which of the following sentences inserted after sentence 3 would best introduce the remaining paragraphs of the essay?

    A. Gold is one of the most valuable substances on earth.
    B. Just follow these simple instructions.
    C. I try to do a lot of different things on my vacations.
    D. Did you even know that there was a gold rush in Alaska?

2. The best placement for sentence 6 would be:

    F. where it is now.
    G. before sentence 4.
    H. after sentence 4.
    J. as the first sentence of paragraph 3.

You have to be careful not to be too aggressive or you'll send your gold downstream along with the silt and other debris.

[5]

[13] Keep moving the pan until about half the original material has been carried away. [14] Lift the pan out of the water, tilt it toward the side with the riffles (the small ridges), and swirl until the water is gone. [15] Repeat this process until nearly all the material is gone.

[6]

[16] Use a small stream of water suction pipette (or even a spray bottle with a concentrated setting on the nozzle) to sort the gold from the remaining debris. [17] Pick up the flecks with tweezers or your fingers and place them in a small glass container such as a test tube or a medicine bottle.

[7]

[18] Panning takes practice, patience, and luck, but even a little bit of gold is a big thrill. [19] You're probably not going to find a lot of gold.

3. Is the parenthetical note following the word "riffles" in paragraph 5 appropriate?

    A. Yes, because it clarifies a technical term for the reader.
    B. Yes, because it presents an idea that is essential to the passage.
    C. No, because it distracts the reader from the directions for panning.
    D. No, because the author does not cite a source for the definition.

4. The best placement for sentence 18 would be:

    F. where it is now.
    G. at the end of the passage.
    H. at the beginning of Paragraph 2.
    J. at the end of Paragraph 6.

5. Suppose the author had been assigned to write a brief essay on an interesting travel destination. Assuming that all of the following statements are true, would this essay successfully fulfill the assignment?

    A. Yes, because many gold-seekers came to Porcupine during the nineteenth century.
    B. Yes, because panning for gold would be a fun activity on a trip.
    C. No, because very little remains today of the town of Porcupine.
    D. No, because most people have never before heard of Porcupine.

STYLE

TEST SPECS

Of all the style questions on the test, questions involving conciseness and clarity of meaning appear most frequently.

Style questions ask about word choice in the passage and whether the language is effective and rhetorically appropriate. You need to watch for two style errors:

1. Lack of conciseness
2. Lack of clarity

CONCISENESS

There are numerous types of concision errors. The major types are illustrated below.

WHEN TO REWORD A SENTENCE

First, a sentence may be grammatically and logically correct and yet be in need of correction because it is awkward.

Examples:

The giant condor is able to spread its wings up to 25 feet. ✗
The giant condor has a wingspan of up to 25 feet. ✓

Given that the Incas lacked the wheel, the buildings at Machu Picchu are more astonishing than any Greek temples that are comparable as an achievement. ✗

Given that the Incas lacked the wheel, the buildings at Machu Picchu are more astonishing than any comparable Greek temples. ✓

In both cases, the second sentence is less awkward and clearly renders the intended thought.

USE AN ACTIVE VERB FOR CONCISION

A common error among writers is the use of the passive verb when the use of an active verb would be clearer and more concise.

Example:

1. Angela is hoping to save enough for a trip to Europe, during which <u>the small village where her grandparents were born will be visited</u>.

Explanations for the example questions are included later in the chapter. Circle your answers now. Later when you reach the explanations at the end of the section, come back and check to make sure you answered the questions correctly.

   A. NO CHANGE
   B. the small village where her grandparents had been born will be visited
   C. she will visit the small village where her grandparents were born
   D. there will be a visit to the small village where her grandparents were born

Occasionally, an original sentence will be incorrect simply because it is needlessly wordy. Avoid needless repetition by selecting a choice that renders the thought most directly.

Example:

2. The speaker declared that <u>alternative ways of utilizing</u> waterfront land ought to be explored.

   F. NO CHANGE
   G. alternatives of use for
   H. alternative utilizations of
   J. alternate uses of

SUM IT UP - CONCISENESS

1. Correct answers will eliminate awkwardness.
2. Correct answers will almost always use active verbs.
3. Correct answers will eliminate wordiness.

CLARITY OF MEANING

The author's word choice should accurately and appropriately reflect what the author means. Use context clues to determine what word is most precise in the context of the given sentence.

Examples:

3. Using an infusion of capital and a clever idea for marketing computers, Eddie <u>enlarged</u> a small neighborhood store into a citywide chain of electronic boutiques.

   A. NO CHANGE
   B. transferred
   C. transformed
   D. enhanced

POWER TIP

Don't fear the unfamiliar. If you are confident that three of the answer choices are incorrect, don't shy away from the only remaining one just because you aren't sure what it means. Trust the process of elimination and choose the last choice confidently.

4. As the heir of the Samurai, the Japanese soldier had a worthy heritage, but the Allies initially underestimated the capabilities of the Japanese armed forces. Then, following early Japanese victories, the Allies overestimated them. Thus was born the myth of the Japanese super-soldier, a myth nurtured by Japanese propaganda and spread by <u>suspicious</u> war correspondents who wrote about their invincibility.

   F. NO CHANGE
   G. credulous
   H. credible
   J. callow

5. Deer are now more numerous than when the first European settlers arrived to this continent, and their <u>ghostly</u> forms are often glimpsed at dusk gliding by in the roadside brush.

   A. NO CHANGE
   B. spiritual
   C. deceased
   D. magical

Answers:

1. (C) avoids the awkward use of the passive voice.

2. The original version is wordy. (J) corrects the wordiness without introducing any new errors.

TEST SPECS

We've covered the highest value topics in this Style review. Less frequently tested topics include:

- Idiomatic Expression

Return to the pages below to review each item:
1. p. 58
2. p. 58
3. p. 58
4. p. 59
5. p. 59

3. The logical structure of the sentence says that the size of the merchant's business went from small to big. The target word must explain how a single, small store could become a large business. A single structure cannot be enlarged, transferred, or enhanced to become many stores. A small store could be "transformed," in a business sense, into many structures in a chain, so the correct answer is (C).

4. This item creates a contrast between the initial impression and the later impression of the Japanese soldiers. After initially underestimating the Japanese soldiers, the Allies overestimated them, and Japanese propaganda encouraged this belief. Propaganda is false, or at least exaggerated, and it is public, so the journalists who accepted this false information and reported it were "credulous," (G).

5. The writer likens the form of the deer at dusk to a ghost—it glides by the roadside and is hardly visible. The other choices may in other contexts be related to "ghostly," but here they are out of place, making (A) the correct answer.

POWER PRACTICE 5

> **DIRECTIONS:** Read the following statements and circle any errors in the underlined parts. Then select the correct answer. Answers are on p. 308.

1. Each year, the geese make their <u>annual migration</u> from Northern Canada to their winter habitats in the United States.

   A. NO CHANGE
   B. migration
   C. annually migration
   D. annual

2. Mardi Gras in Mobile is the annual Carnival celebration in Mobile, Alabama. In fact, it is the oldest annual Carnival celebration in the United States, having started in 1703, fifteen years before New Orleans was founded. However, <u>owing to the fact that it is better known,</u> the New Orleans celebration is more famous.

   F. NO CHANGE
   G. owing to the fact that it is best known,
   H. because of the fact that it is better known,
   J. DELETE the underlined part

3. With the evidence <u>accepted</u> from careful study of numerous x-rays, scientists are beginning to form a picture of the atomic structure of the cell.

   A. NO CHANGE
   B. gleaned
   C. enticed
   D. elicited

4. After two days of heavy fighting, the unit had been <u>truncated</u>. Of the original 50 soldiers, only 35 were still actively fighting when reinforcements arrived.

   F. NO CHANGE
   G. decimated
   H. fragmented
   J. detracted

5. <u>Finally and at long last</u>, the old dog opened his eyes and noticed the intruder.

   A. NO CHANGE
   B. Finally
   C. Yet at along last
   D. Finally and long lastingly

> **ACCELEPREP APPROACH**
>
> Check your answer (if it is not NO CHANGE) by re-reading the sentence and replacing the underlined phrase with your answer.

CHAPTER 3

Try It Out! English Practice

ACCELEPREP APPROACH

In Chapter 2, we covered the key question types one at a time with examples. In this chapter, you will practice with full-length passages. Consider each question and remember what you learned about that question type in Chapter 2.

DIRECTIONS: In the passages below, certain parts of the sentences have been underlined and numbered. In the right-hand column, you will find different ways of writing each underlined part; the original version is indicated by the "NO CHANGE" option. For each item, select the choice that best expresses the intended idea, is most acceptable in standard written English, or is most consistent with the overall tone and style of the passage.

There are also items that ask about a section of the passage or the passage as a whole. These items do not refer to an underlined portion of the passage; these items are preceded by statements that are enclosed in boxes.

Read the passage through once before you begin to answer the accompanying items. Finding the answers to certain items may depend on looking at material that appears several sentences beyond the item. So, be sure that you have read far enough ahead before you select your answer choice. Answers are on p. 308.

The Con Game Is No Game

[1]

Most people have a certain crime <u>that one</u> <u>believes</u> should be ranked as the worst of all crimes.

1.
  A. NO CHANGE
  B. that they believe
  C. which one believes
  D. that you believe

For some, <u>its'</u> murder; for others, it may be selling

2.
  F. NO CHANGE
  G. they are
  H. it's
  J. its

drugs to children. I believe, <u>moreover,</u> that the worst
                              3

of all crimes may be the confidence scheme.

[2]

The confidence scheme may seem an <u>odd</u>
                                        4

choice for the worst crime since con games are

usually <u>nonviolent. Although,</u> it is a crime that ranks
           5

high in heartlessness. Con artists are the most

devious, the most harmful, and the most disruptive

members of society because <u>they break</u> down
                                 6

<u>honesty, and trust, the</u> most important bonds of the
            7

social order.

[3]

The con games themselves are <u>simplistic</u>
                                    8

<u>almost infantile.</u> They work <u>on account of a con</u>
       8   9

<u>artist can</u> win complete confidence, talk fast enough
    9

to keep the victim slightly confused, <u>and dangling</u>
                                          10

enough temptation to suppress any suspicion or

skepticism.

3. A. NO CHANGE
    B. however
    C. further
    D. therefore

4. F. NO CHANGE
    G. obvious
    H. irrelevant
    J. apt

5. A. NO CHANGE
    B. nonviolent, though
    C. nonviolent, but
    D. nonviolent, and

6. F. NO CHANGE
    G. it breaks
    H. of its breaking
    J. of them breaking

7. A. NO CHANGE
    B. honesty, and trust the
    C. honesty and trust, the
    D. honesty and trust the

8. F. NO CHANGE
    G. simplistic; almost infantile
    H. simplistic, almost infantile
    J. simplistic, yet almost infantile

9. A. NO CHANGE
    B. on account of a con artist's ability to
    C. owing to a con artist's ability to
    D. because a con artist can

10. F. NO CHANGE
    G. and dangles
    H. and has dangled
    J. and dangle

[4]

Traditionally, the primary targets of these

criminals <u>will be</u> the elderly and <u>women. (And they</u>
     11   12

<u>prefer to work in large crowds.)</u>
        12

11. A. NO CHANGE
    B. to be
    C. are
    D. is

12. F. NO CHANGE
    G. women, and the con artists prefer to work in large crowds.
    H. women, preferring, of course, to work in large crowds.
    J. women (who prefer to work in large crowds).

Items #13–15 ask about the preceding passage as a whole.

---

13. Which of the following is most likely the author's opinion rather than a fact?

    A. The most disruptive members of society are con artists.
    B. The majority of con games are nonviolent.
    C. The targets of con games are mostly the elderly and women.
    D. The con artists succeed when they win the complete confidence of their targets.

14. What would be the most logical continuation of the essay?

    F. A description of some confidence games
    G. An account of the elderly as crime victims in society
    H. An account of the author's experience with con artists
    J. An explanation of crowd psychology

15. What would strengthen the author's assertion that con games rank first in heartlessness?

    A. Statistics to show the number of people who were taken in by the con artist
    B. A discussion of the way the police handle the problem
    C. An example that shows how the con artist breaks down honesty and trust
    D. An example to illustrate that con games are nonviolent and simple

Tradition Preservation During Meiji Restoration

Instead of casting aside traditional values during the Meiji Restoration of 1888, those who strove to dismantle feudalism and to modernize the country chose to preserve three traditions as the foundations <u>on which they could build a modern Japan upon</u>.
16

16. F. NO CHANGE
     G. on which they could be building a modern Japan upon
     H. upon which they could build a modern Japan
     J. upon which they someday could probably build a modern Japan

The oldest tradition and basis of the entire Japanese value system was <u>respect for and even worshipping</u> the emperor. During the early centuries
17

17. A. NO CHANGE
     B. respecting and even worshipping
     C. respect for and even worship of
     D. respect and even worship

of Japanese history, the Shinto cult, in which <u>the Imperial family traced its ancestry to the Sun Goddess</u>, became the people's sustaining faith.
18

18. F. NO CHANGE
     G. the Imperial family got its ancestry traced back to the Sun Goddess
     H. the Imperial family's ancestry was traced back to the Sun Goddess
     J. the Sun Goddess was considered to be the ancestor of the Imperial family

<u>Being later subordinated</u> to imported Buddhism and Confucianism, Shintoism was perpetuated in Ise and Izumo, the great shrines of the Imperial family, until the Meiji modernizers established it as a quasi-state religion to unify the people and restore the emperor as the symbol of national unity and the object of loyalty <u>to the Japanese</u>.
19   20

19. A. NO CHANGE
     B. Later subordinated
     C. Later subordinated,
     D. Subordinated later,

20. F. NO CHANGE
     G. the Japanese had
     H. by the Japanese
     J. for the Japanese

Another tradition was the hierarchical system of social relations based on feudalism. Confucianism

prescribed <u>a pattern by</u> ethical conduct between
₂₁

groups of people within a fixed hierarchy. Four of the

five Confucian relationships <u>(those between ruler</u>
₂₂

<u>and subject, husband and wife, father and son, and</u>
₂₂

<u>elder brother and younger brother)</u> were <u>vertical</u>
₂₂ ₂₃

<u>since they</u> required loyalty and obedience from the
₂₃

inferior toward the superior <u>and benevolence and</u>
₂₄

<u>protection from the superior to the inferior.</u> Only the
₂₄

fifth <u>relationship, that</u> between friend and friend—
₂₅

was horizontal.

A third tradition was respect for learning,

another basic <u>idea of Confucius.</u> In traditional
₂₆

Japan, study was the absolute duty of man. It was a

religious <u>mandate as well</u> as a social duty and was
₂₇

a means of promoting a harmonious and stable

21. A. NO CHANGE
B. patterns by
C. a pattern for
D. patterns with

22. Is the author's use of parentheses appropriate?

F. Yes, because the examples are irrelevant to the passage.
G. Yes, because although the information is relevant, the material is not part of the main development of the passage.
H. No, because the examples are relevant to the meaning of the sentence.
J. No, because the material is essential to the reader's understanding of the passage.

23. A. NO CHANGE
B. vertical, they
C. vertical, since it
D. vertical, being they

24. F. NO CHANGE
G. and also benevolence and protection from the superior to the inferior
H. with the benevolence and protection being from the superior to the inferior
J. and from the superior to the inferior, the benevolence and protection

25. A. NO CHANGE
B. relationship that
C. relationship—that
D. relationship

26. F. NO CHANGE
G. Confucius idea
H. idea of Confucianism
J. Confucianism idea

27. A. NO CHANGE
B. mandate as well as being
C. mandate as well,
D. mandate,

society. The individual's behavior was strictly

prescribed by law and custom. Only the samurai

had the right to retaliate with force if they were

displeased. But even his primary duty was to the

lord.

28. F. NO CHANGE
     G. An individual behavior
     H. Behavior by individual's
     J. The individuals behavior

29. A. NO CHANGE
     B. But even their
     C. Being that even their
     D. Because even their

Item #30 asks about the preceding passage as a whole.

---

30. The best description of the development of this essay would be:

     F. argument and rebuttal.
     G. a personal narrative.
     H. a three-part exposition.
     J. question and answer.

CHAPTER 4

Fast Track to Math Mechanics

DEMYSTIFYING THE MATH TEST

STRATEGY ALERT

You should always guess on questions you don't know how to solve, especially because you won't lose points for wrong answers. A blind guess has a 20% chance of being correct, whereas a blank answer has zero chance.

TEST SPECS

You must bring your own calculator (four-function, scientific, or graphing) to the test. What type of calculator is best? Well, the most important thing about your calculator is that you know how to use it.

There are certain restrictions on the types of calculators allowed during the test, though. Check that your calculator is permitted at www.actstudent.org/calculator-policy.html.

The ACT Mathematics Test consists of 60 multiple-choice items generally arranged in order of increasing difficulty. The time limit is 60 minutes and calculators are allowed.

The math test measures your knowledge of math skills typically learned in courses taken up to the beginning of 12th grade (pre-algebra, algebra, intermediate algebra, coordinate geometry, geometry, and trigonometry). The items on the test are pretty much the same kind of questions you'd see on a regular test—except they are multiple-choice questions, each with five answer choices.

You can do quite well on the math portion of the ACT test even if you're not exactly a math whiz. For example, for a very respectable score of 21 (above the national average), you need a raw score of about 33. That's just over half the questions on the test. So you could get almost half the questions wrong and still be above the national average.

You must bring your own calculator to the test; make sure you are familiar with its operations and functions. While the makers of the ACT state that every problem can be solved without a calculator, you may find one helpful for arithmetic calculations. Furthermore, since graphing calculators are allowed, you can use your calculator for graphing equations and solving quadratics.

ANATOMY OF THE MATH TEST

INSIDE THE DIRECTIONS

STRATEGY ALERT

Use your calculator. You should be doing almost no arithmetic by hand.

TEST SPECS

Figures are usually drawn to scale, even though the directions tell you not to count on that.

The directions below are similar to the directions that appear on the Math Test. On test day, don't waste any time reading the directions—you should know what you are expected to do.

MATH DIRECTIONS

DIRECTIONS: Solve each item and choose the correct answer choice. Calculator use is permitted; however, some items are best solved without the use of a calculator.

NOTES: All of the following should be assumed, unless otherwise stated.

1. Illustrative figures are NOT necessarily drawn to scale.
2. The word *average* indicates arithmetic mean.
3. The word *line* indicates a straight line.
4. Geometric figures lie in a plane.

There are two things to note about the directions. First, you can use a calculator, so use it! Use your calculator whenever you think it will save time, make a calculation easier, or prevent arithmetic errors. Second, the figures are not necessarily drawn to scale. However, in practice, figures are typically drawn to scale. We'll also return to this topic later in this chapter.

INSIDE THE ITEMS

The Math Test items are standard multiple-choice problems: the item stem includes any figures or graphs, additional information, and the question, followed by five answer choices. You must choose one of the five choices. There is no penalty for wrong answers. Always choose an answer to every problem, even if you have to guess.

Problems can be straightforward solution items, so solve the given problem and select the answer choice that matches your answer.

TEST SPECS

Wrong answers often correspond to errors in thinking. Notice that (A) is the value for *x* and (B) is the value for *y*. Always pay attention to what the question is asking, and rather than reworking your math to check your answers, ask yourself if your answer matches what the question is asking.

Example:

$$3x + 2y = 10$$
$$7x - 4y = -7$$

1. If (x,y) is a solution to the system of equations above, what is the value of $x + y$?

A. 1

B. $3\dfrac{1}{2}$

C. 4

D. $4\dfrac{1}{2}$

E. 7

Other problems depend on the answer choices for the solution.

Explanations for the example questions are included later in the chapter. Circle your answers now. Later when you reach the explanations at the end of the section, come back and check to make sure you answered the questions correctly.

Example: **2.** If s, t, and u are different positive integers and $\dfrac{s}{t}$ and $\dfrac{t}{u}$ are positive integers, which of the following CANNOT be a positive integer?

F. $\dfrac{s}{u}$

G. $\dfrac{u}{s}$

H. $(s)(t)$

J. $(s)(u)$

K. $(s + t)u$

The ACT Math Test items are generally arranged on a ladder of difficulty. The ladder of difficulty is an important feature of the Math Test. Given that the problems generally become more difficult as you proceed, it's important that you pace yourself accordingly and have a guessing strategy. We'll return to pacing and guessing tips later in this chapter.

PACING TIP

You will find easy problems at the beginning of the test, so finish those problems quickly to save time for the harder problems at the end.

INSIDE THE ANSWER CHOICES

Numerical answer choices are typically arranged from smallest to largest or vice versa. There are exceptions, such as items that ask, "Which of the following is the biggest?" This general arrangement makes it easier to find your answer in the list. It also means, as we'll discuss later, that you always start with (C) when testing the choices.

Numerical answer choices are also well defined. Wrong choices aren't usually close in value to the correct answer—they correspond to errors in thinking, not errors in arithmetic. Stop your calculations as soon as the correct choice is evident.

Example: 3. A pound of water is evaporated from 6 pounds of seawater containing 4% salt. What is the percentage of salt in the solution following evaporation?

A. 3.6%
B. 4.0%
C. 4.8%
D. 5.2%
E. 6.0%

Answers 1. The item stem presents two linear equations in two variables and asks for the sum of x and y if (x,y) is a solution to the system. Eliminate one variable by combining the two equations:

$$2\,(3x + 2y = 10)$$
$$\underline{+\ \ 7x - 4y = -7}$$
$$13x = 13 \Rightarrow x = 1$$

Use this value for x to find y from the first equation:

$3\,(1) + 2y = 10 \Rightarrow y = \dfrac{7}{2} = 3\dfrac{1}{2}$. The value of $x + y$ is $1 + 3\dfrac{1}{2} = 4\dfrac{1}{2}$.

Look at the answer choices to find a match: the answer is (D).

2. The words "which of the following" tell you to examine each of the answer choices to find the one that satisfies the stated conditions. First, determine what you can from the stem itself. Since $\dfrac{s}{t}$ is an integer, s must be greater than t. Likewise, $\dfrac{t}{u}$ is an integer, so t must be greater than u. The relationship among the three variables is

$s > t > u$. Consider the answer choices with this relationship in mind. Only $\dfrac{u}{s}$, (G), CANNOT be an integer because the denominator is bigger than the numerator.

3. The original 6 pounds of seawater contained 0.24 pounds of salt ($0.04 \times 6 = 0.24$). After evaporation, the remaining 5 pounds of seawater still contains the same 0.24 pounds of salt, so the question is really asking, "0.24 is what percentage of 5?" Use the "is-over-of" equation for percentages:

$\dfrac{is}{of} = \dfrac{\%}{100} \Rightarrow \dfrac{0.24}{5} = \dfrac{\%}{100} \Rightarrow \% = \dfrac{0.24}{5} \cdot 100 = 4.8\%$. Note that because

the answers are well defined, an exact calculation isn't even necessary. A glance at the answer choices is enough to determine the answer must be 4.8% ($24 \div 5$ is more than 4 but less than 5).

PACING FOR THE MATH TEST

STRATEGY ALERT

Practice makes perfect. Take a practice test or use the practice problems in the next chapter to work on your pace. If you can't quite solve every problem, don't forget to save time to guess. There's still a 1 in 5 chance you'll guess right.

Since the items are arranged generally according to a ladder of difficulty, you should move quickly through the easier items at the beginning of the test, saving time for the harder items at the end. The following guidelines illustrate how to adjust your timing per item as you work through the Math Test.

ITEM NUMBERS	TIME TO SPEND PER ITEM	TOTAL TIME SPENT
#1–10	36 seconds	6 minutes
#11–20	42 seconds	13 minutes
#21–30	54 seconds	22 minutes
#31–40	66 seconds	33 minutes
#41–50	72 seconds	45 minutes
#51–60	90 seconds	60 minutes

This table is a schedule for the best of all possible math worlds. It's intended to be a guide, not a rule. Try to stay on schedule, but be prepared to adjust your timing according to how many items you can realistically complete.

THE CAMBRIDGE GAME PLAN

STEP 1—PREVIEW THE QUESTION

Previewing the question means a lot of things, but it should all be familiar and automatic after a little practice. We'll go through each point in more detail, but for now here's a summary:

- Note the difficulty level of each item and tailor your solution appropriately.
- Read the question stem carefully.
- Identify what is being asked, organize the given information, and draw a figure if needed.
- Determine whether a calculator will be useful.

DIVIDE AND CONQUER

PACING TIP

Draw lines after questions 20 and 40 in your test booklet. You should be at about minute 13 when you finish question 20 and at minute 33 when you finish question 40. Make sure to draw these lines in your test booklet and not your answer sheet.

The multiple-choice items are arranged according to increasing difficulty. As you begin each math section, create three subsections: draw lines after problems 20 and 40, between the first third, second third, and last third of the multiple-choice items. These lines will remind you to tailor solutions to each item's difficulty level as you move through the section.

Easy problems are easy because they have easy solutions. Keep it simple when working on multiple-choice items in the first third of the section. If a solution seems too difficult, you've probably taken the wrong approach.

Hard problems are hard problems because a low percentage of test-takers answer them correctly. This is obvious, but what makes a problem difficult is not so obvious. The ACT can make an item difficult not only by testing challenging math concepts but also by including one or more attractive distractors in the answer choices. An attractive distractor is a wrong answer choice that cries out "Pick me, pick me!" Let's look at an example problem that could appear toward the end of the test.

Example:

STRATEGY ALERT

One type of attractive distractor is an answer choice that contains some or all of the values mentioned in the item stem. Spotting the matching values could lead a careless test taker to fall for this trap. This example shows how this type of distractor is used.

1. A professional chef knows that a certain food product loses 10 percent of its weight during cooking. If the chef wants the cooked product to weigh exactly 1 pound, what weight, in pounds, of uncooked product should be used?

A. $\frac{9}{10}$

B. $1\frac{1}{11}$

C. $1\frac{1}{10}$

D. $1\frac{1}{9}$

E. $1\frac{1}{8}$

READ THE QUESTION CAREFULLY

While some problems are simple and straightforward, others are more complex, particularly real-world story problems and applied geometry problems. The more complex the question, the easier it is to misread and set off down the wrong track. For long item stems, underline the key part of the question.

PACING TIP

This example demonstrates another type of common distractor: the partial answer. In this example, (D) is a partial answer; we had to calculate it on the way to solving for Lester's average speed, but it's not the final answer.

The moral: Make sure that the answer you select is the final answer, corresponding to the item stem.

Example: **2.** If Mark traveled 20 miles in 3 hours and Lester traveled twice as far in half the time, <u>what was Lester's average speed?</u>

F. $6\frac{2}{3}$ miles per hour

G. 26 miles per hour

H. $26\frac{2}{3}$ miles per hour

J. 40 miles per hour

K. 60 miles per hour

PAY ATTENTION TO UNITS

Some problems involve unit conversions, such as feet to inches or hours to minutes. The item stem states what units to use, and if the test-writer senses any possible confusion, the units for the answer choices will be emphasized—underlined, boldfaced, italicized, or capitalized. When you see an emphasized word, circle it and put a star beside it—it's very important.

Explanations for the example questions are included later in the chapter. Circle your answers now. Later when you reach the explanations at the end of the section, come back and check to make sure you answered the questions correctly.

Example **3.** A certain copy machine produces 13 copies every 10 seconds. If the machine operates without interruption, <u>how many copies will it produce in an hour?</u>

A. 780

B. 4,200

C. 4,680

D. 4,800

E. 7,800

PAY ATTENTION TO THOUGHT-REVERSERS

PACING TIP

When solving a math problem, start writing down given information and/or sketch the problem right away. This will get your brain started and get you moving in the right direction. In other words, don't sit idly and assume the answer will just "come" to you.

Thought-reversers such as "not," "except," or "but" turn a question inside out. Mark any thought-reversers to emphasize that the correct answer is the one that doesn't solve the item or can't be the solution.

Example:

4. There are 422 students at Emerson Elementary, and 20 percent of the fifth-graders bought a yearbook. If 18 fifth-graders bought yearbooks, how many students at Emerson Elementary are NOT fifth-graders?

F.   4
G.   43
H.   90
J.   332
K.   340

It's easy to make careless mistakes, so avoid these by underlining, circling, and marking with a star the key words and phrases in each item stem as you preview the problem. It takes almost no additional time and helps you stay focused on what the question asks.

USE, DISTORT, AND DRAW FIGURES

The directions for the Math Test specifically state that "Unless otherwise stated, assume…figures are NOT necessarily drawn to scale." However, the figures are intended to provide information that is useful in solving the items. It wouldn't make any sense for the test to distort figures in such a way as to mislead, as this would undermine the validity of the test.

In practice, the figures are almost always drawn to scale. Figures not drawn to scale will only be those for which measurements are irrelevant or not given, e.g., a triangle with sides a, b, and c is not necessarily drawn to scale.

Example:

5. In the figure below, what is the length of $\overline{AB} + \overline{CD}$?

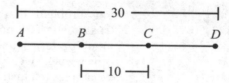

A.   5
B.   10
C.   15
D.   20
E.   40

On the other hand, since the items are NOT drawn to scale, you can practice distorting the figures (change the angle size or length of the lines to visualize comparative relationships in the figure when specific angle sizes or lengths aren't given). As long as the lines and points in a distorted figure are in the same position relative to each other as in the original, you'll be fine.

Example:

6. Which of the following must be true?

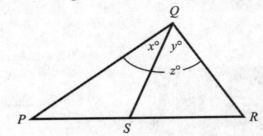

F. $\overline{PS} < \overline{SR}$
G. $z = 90$
H. $x > y$
J. $x + y < z$
K. $\overline{PR} > \overline{PS}$

STRATEGY ALERT

Distorting the figures is a more visual approach for exploring all logical possibilities. Depending on your strengths or weaknesses, you might work through this problem algebraically or you might distort the image and reason through the problem visually.

If an item doesn't provide a figure, you should draw one (as accurately as necessary). This is true for any question for which a drawing would help, not just geometry items. Drawing a picture is often the first step in solving a math problem.

Example:

7. A circle is inscribed in a square. If the area of the square is 4, what is the area of the circle?

A. $\dfrac{\pi}{4}$
B. $\dfrac{\pi}{2}$
C. π
D. 2π
E. 4π

USE YOUR CALCULATOR, BUT DON'T OVERUSE IT

For problems that you know how to solve, use your calculator to do the arithmetic if it's quicker than by hand. Never perform long division or multiply large numbers by hand. You can also use your calculator to get the right answer to questions you don't know how to solve. Here are some examples to illustrate the technique.

Example:

8. Photons travel at approximately 3×10^5 kilometers per second. How long does it take a photon to travel 12×10^{10} kilometers?

F. 2.5×10^{-6} seconds
G. 4×10^2 seconds
H. 4×10^5 seconds
J. 3.6×10^6 seconds
K. 36×10^{50} seconds

Example:

STRATEGY ALERT

Make sure to add the difference of squares to your bag of test day tricks. This is a "trick" because spotting it can save you precious time.

CLOSER LOOK

Solving with your calculator is a little more time consuming in this example, but it's a great alternative if you don't remember how to solve the problem algebraically.

Answers

Return to the pages below to review each item:
1. p. 76
2. p. 76
3. p. 76
4. p. 77
5. p. 77
6. p. 78
7. p. 78
8. p. 78
9. p. 79

9. If $x^2 = 3$, what is the value of $\left(\dfrac{2}{x} - x\right)\left(\dfrac{2}{x} + x\right)$?

A. $-\dfrac{5}{3}$

B. $-\dfrac{2}{3}$

C. $-\dfrac{3}{5}$

D. $\dfrac{\sqrt{3} - 2}{3}$

E. $\dfrac{2 - \sqrt{3}}{3}$

On the other hand, just because you have a calculator on one section doesn't mean you should use it to solve every problem. Assume you have to do the following arithmetic to get your answer: $\left(\dfrac{2}{3}\right)\left(\dfrac{7}{4}\right)\left(\dfrac{1}{6}\right)$. Since this involves single digit multiplication, it's easier to do the arithmetic by hand: $\left(\dfrac{\overset{1}{\cancel{2}}}{3}\right)\left(\dfrac{7}{4}\right)\left(\dfrac{1}{\underset{3}{\cancel{6}}}\right) = \dfrac{7}{12 \times 3} = \dfrac{7}{36}$.

1. This item tests proportions and percentages, not difficult concepts, so how could it be so high on the ladder of difficulty? Choice (C) is such an attractive distractor (it's wrong, but it just seems so right), that many test-takers will automatically pick it and move on. But think through the math. Create a proportion between the ratio of the pre-cooked to post-cooked weights and the ratio of the corresponding percentages, and solve for the pre-cooked weight: $\dfrac{1 \text{ pound}}{x \text{ pounds}} = \dfrac{90\%}{100\%} \Rightarrow x = \dfrac{100}{90} = \dfrac{10}{9} = 1\dfrac{1}{9}$ pounds. Therefore, the correct answer is (D).

2. The item stem states that Lester traveled twice as far as Mark in half the time, or 40 miles in 1.5 hours. The question asks for the <u>average speed</u>, so divide the total distance by the total time, using a calculator to avoid the arithmetic: $\dfrac{40 \text{ miles}}{1.5 \text{ hours}} = 26.66\overline{6} = 26\dfrac{2}{3}$ miles per hour, (H).

3. Create an expression of ratios that, after cancellation of like units, gives the number of copies produced in an <u>hour</u>:

$\dfrac{13 \text{ copies}}{10 \text{ \cancel{seconds}}} \cdot \dfrac{60 \text{ \cancel{seconds}}}{1 \text{ \cancel{minute}}} \cdot \dfrac{60 \text{ \cancel{minutes}}}{1 \text{ hour}} = 4{,}680$ copies/hour , (C).

4. The question asks, "how many students are...<u>NOT</u> fifth-graders?" The stem also says that there are 422 students, so determine how many students are fifth-graders. Since 18, or 20%, of the fifth-graders bought a yearbook, use this to find the number of fifth-graders. In other words, "18 is 20% of what?" Use the "is-over-of" equation:

$\dfrac{is}{of} = \dfrac{\%}{100} \Rightarrow \dfrac{18}{x} = \dfrac{20}{100} \Rightarrow x = \dfrac{18 \times 10\cancel{0}}{2\cancel{0}} = 90$. But don't be distracted

by choice (H): you are solving for how many students are NOT fifth-graders, so the correct answer is $422 - 90 = 332$, which is (J).

5. Although the figure is NOT necessarily drawn to scale, you can assume that points A, B, C, and D are on $\overline{AD}$ in the order shown. Therefore, regardless of the accuracy of the drawing, it can be deduced mathematically that the length of $\overline{AB} + \overline{CD}$ must be 20. If $\overline{AD}$ is 30 units long, and $\overline{BC}$ is 10 units long, the length of the other two segments together, $\overline{AB} + \overline{CD}$, must be 30 – 10 = 20, answer choice (D).

6. Although (F) and (G) appear true based on the figure as it is drawn, it is NOT necessarily drawn to scale. You could distort it to look as follows:

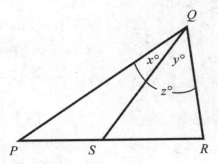

All the lines and points in this re-drawn figure are in the same position relative to each other as they are in the original. However, in this figure, it appears that the (G) and (H) statements are false. And the figure could be drawn such that (F) is clearly false. No matter how the figure is distorted, the combination of x and y must equal z, so (J) is always false. Therefore, by the process of elimination, (K) must be correct. Indeed, $\overline{PS}$ is only a part of $\overline{PR}$, so the length of $\overline{PS}$ must be less than the length of $\overline{PR}$.

7. Draw a picture of a circle inscribed in a square with sides of 2 (the area is 4, so $s^2 = 4 \Rightarrow s = 2$). Note what you are looking for: the area of the circle. Connect what you don't know with what you do: to get the area, you need the radius of the circle ($A_{circle} = \pi r^2$). Add all of this to your figure:

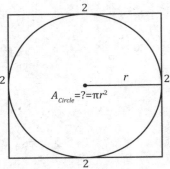

Now it's easy to see that the side of the square has the same length as

STRATEGY ALERT (( ))

Use your calculator if you can't find a direct solution or if it offers a time advantage, but don't assume automatically that every problem requires it.

the diameter of the circle, which is twice the radius. The diameter of the circle is 2, the radius is 1, and the area of the circle is $\pi(1)^2 = \pi$, (C).

8. Suppose you can't remember the rules for working with exponents and scientific notation. Use your calculator! It might even be quicker overall to start with your calculator in the first place. In this case, after entering 12 < EE > 10 ÷ 3 < EE > 5 = (or <EXP> depending on your calculator; be sure ahead of the exam to know how your particular calculator works), the display will read 400,000 if in Normal mode or 4E5 if in Scientific mode, which is equal to 4 followed by 5 zeros, or 4×10^5, answer choice (H).

9. You could solve this problem by recognizing that the given expression is the difference of two squares: $(a+b)(a-b) = a^2 - b^2$. Therefore,

$$\left(\frac{2}{x} - x\right)\left(\frac{2}{x} + x\right) = \left(\frac{2}{x}\right)^2 - x^2 = \frac{4}{3} - 3 = -\frac{5}{3}, \text{ (A). Or use the FOIL method}$$

to get to the last step.

If you don't see the algebra solution, use your calculator:

$$x^2 = 3 \Rightarrow x = \pm\sqrt{3} \approx \pm 1.73 \text{ and } \frac{2}{\pm\sqrt{3}} \approx \pm 1.15 \text{, so}$$

$$\left(\frac{2}{\sqrt{3}} - \sqrt{3}\right)\left(\frac{2}{\sqrt{3}} + \sqrt{3}\right) \approx (1.15 - 1.73)(1.15 + 1.73) =$$
$$(-0.58)(2.88) = -1.67.$$

And $\left(\frac{2}{-\sqrt{3}} + \sqrt{3}\right)\left(\frac{2}{-\sqrt{3}} - \sqrt{3}\right) \approx (-1.15 + 1.73)(-1.15 - 1.73) =$
$$(0.58)(-2.88) = -2.3.$$

Evaluate the choices: only (A) matches: $-\frac{5}{3} \approx -1.67$.

STEP 2—STRATEGIZE AND SOLVE

STRATEGY ALERT (( ))

Make sure you have the correct mindset when solving ACT math problems. The ACT Math Test is not a traditional, in-class math test that requires you to show your work. On the ACT test you are rewarded for a correct answer regardless of how you chose it.

The second step of the Game Plan is to pick a strategy and solve the problem. The strategy you choose depends on two factors: how best to solve the item *correctly* and *quickly*. The strategies in this section are designed with this in mind. The mathematical solution isn't always the fastest, or sometimes it bogs you down in variables, making a problem even harder.

We've already covered several techniques in Step 1 that always apply, such as reading carefully, organizing the given information, trusting figures, drawing figures when needed, and using your calculator. Now, we'll cover three additional strategies that are especially useful if you can't find the mathematical solution to an item. Even if you know how to solve a problem, these strategies can often be used to solve an item even faster.

USE THE ANSWER CHOICES

Answer choices are chosen and distributed according to certain test specifications. Use this feature to get leverage on the test. First, eliminate choices that can't possibly be an answer to the question being asked. And make sure your answer is a plausible answer to the question asked. Finally, the answers themselves can be used to double-check your calculations.

Even when you can't get the answer directly, common sense can help eliminate choices and improve your chances of guessing correctly. Sometimes, the answers include choices that, taken at face value, seem plausible, but really aren't.

Examples:

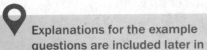

Explanations for the example questions are included later in the chapter. Circle your answers now. Later when you reach the explanations at the end of the section, come back and check to make sure you answered the questions correctly.

STRATEGY ALERT

Practice applying common sense in eliminating answer choices. With more practice, you will be able to do this quickly and under time pressure, so that you will improve your accuracy and ultimately your score.

1. In the figure below, if the length of the diagonal *QR* of rectangle *PQSR* is 5 and the circle with center *O* is tangent to *PQSR* at two points, what is the area of the shaded portion?

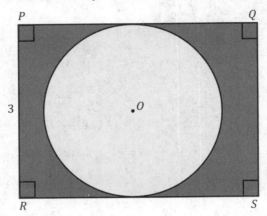

A. $12 - 9\pi$

B. $9 - 3\pi$

C. $9 - \dfrac{9\pi}{4}$

D. $12 - \dfrac{9\pi}{4}$

E. Cannot be determined from the information given

2. In the figure below, what is the sum of the indicated angles?

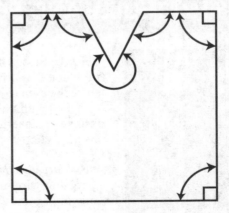

F. 540

G. 720

H. 900

J. 1,080

K. 1,200

ɔ

The answer choices can also help if you are stuck on a solution. One of the choices is the correct answer. Estimation and guessing based on the information provided in figures can be a great alternative strategy, especially when one of the choices backs up your intuition. When possible, use the answer choices to your advantage, as the next example illustrates.

Example:

STRATEGY ALERT

Be creative with how you use the figures to estimate. For example, if you're estimating how long one line segment is compared to another, instead of "eyeballing" it, use the edge of your test booklet or scratch paper to mark the length of one line and directly compare that to the other for a more accurate estimation.

3. In the figure below, *PQRS* is a rectangle, *T is* the midpoint of *PQ,* and $\overset{\frown}{TS}$ and $\overset{\frown}{TR}$ are arcs of circles with centers *P* and *Q*, respectively. If $PT = TQ = 1$, what is the area of the shaded area?

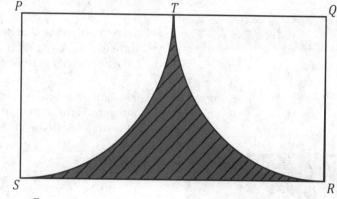

A. $2 - \dfrac{\pi}{4}$

B. $\dfrac{\pi}{4}$

C. $2 - \dfrac{\pi}{2}$

D. $1 - \dfrac{\pi}{4}$

E. $4 - \pi$

Answer choices function as a feedback loop on the accuracy of your calculations. Don't waste time double-checking your calculations. If you finish your calculations and an answer choice matches your results, do NOT check your arithmetic. The possibility that you did the arithmetic, made a mistake, and still got a number that matches an answer choice is too remote to consider. On the other hand, if you don't find a choice that matches your calculation, then you'd better check both your set-up and your arithmetic to find the error.

PLUG-AND-CHUG

Algebra is usually harder than arithmetic because it deals with variables while arithmetic deals with numbers. You can turn a problem with variables into an arithmetic problem and make it easier.

STRATEGY ALERT

Always read a problem carefully before plugging in values. For example, if a problem involves an equation that only holds true when *x* is positive, then choose a positive value for *x*.

Examples:

4. What is the total value, in cents, of *x* dimes and *x* + 6 nickels?

F. 2*x* + 6

G. 5*x* + 10

H. 11*x* + 15

J. 15*x* + 6

K. 15*x* + 30

5. If the value of r in the equation $Q = 3\pi r^2$ is doubled, the value of Q is multiplied by what value?

    A. $\dfrac{1}{4}$

    B. 2

    C. 3

    D. 4

    E. 6

TEST-THE-TEST

For every multiple-choice item, you're given the right answer. Of course, you have to find it, but with some questions, it's just a matter of time. Test the answer choices until you find the right one.

Example:

6. The sum of m and n is evenly divisible by 5, where m and n are integers. If the sum of m and 4 is three times as large as n, which of the following CANNOT be the value of n?

    F. 6
    G. 8
    H. 11
    J. 16
    K. 21

PACING TIP

If you have answered all questions and have time remaining, use that time to double-check any answers that you may have guessed and after that, double-check calculations on problems.

If the answers are arranged in order and the stem doesn't include a thought-reverser, start with the middle choices, (C) or (H). If that choice works, you've found the right answer. If it doesn't work, decide whether it is too large or too small, and test the next smaller or larger choice. Whether that one works or not, you're done. If it does work, that's your answer. If it doesn't work, the answer is the next larger or the next smaller number, and you don't have to bother testing it. This way, you have to test, at most, two choices, often making this approach faster than the math solution. (If an item includes a thought-reverser, you have to test, at most, four.)

Example:

7. Cyd received a gift of money for her birthday and spent one-fourth of it on books and one-third of what remained on music. If Cyd still had $60, what was the original amount of the gift?

    A. $30
    B. $70
    C. $80
    D. $100
    E. $120

STRATEGY ALERT

The Test-the-Test method works well to solve certain problems but not every problem. With practice, it will become clear to you when to use Test-the-Test. In example #7, think about why Test-the-Test works well. What qualities of the problem hint that Test-the-Test is ideal? In contrast, look back at previous examples and find one where Test-the-Test would not work well.

Return to the pages below to review each item:

Answers

1. The shaded area is the difference between the area of the rectangle and the area of the circle—it doesn't matter where the circle is located inside the rectangle or that the figure isn't drawn to scale. The rectangle is comprised of two 3-4-5 right triangles, so its length is 4, the area of the rectangle is 12, and the shaded area is

    $$12 - \pi\left(\frac{3}{2}\right)^2 = 12 - \frac{9\pi}{4}$$, answer choice (D).

    What if you didn't see the geometry solution? Before guessing, eliminate any choices that don't make sense. Since π is slightly more than 3, (A) and (B) are negative numbers and cannot possibly be the area. You've narrowed your odds of guessing correctly to 1 out of 3. A little more common sense should be enough to convince you that the shaded area can be found, so eliminate (E). Now, your odds are 50/50!

2. The ACT wants you to use the formula for the total number of degrees in a polygon, where n is the number of angles: $180(n-2) = 180(5) = 900$. You can also divide the figure into triangular regions. There are five triangles in the polygon, so the total number of degrees in the polygon is $5(180) = 900$.

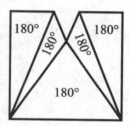

    What if you don't remember the formula and don't see how to derive it from the figure (as the second solution above does)? Use what you do know to eliminate wrong answers. For example, you know that every right angle measures 90° and there are 360° in a square. In the figure, the arrows mark four right angles, plus two angles measuring slightly more than 90°, and one angle measuring slightly less than 360°. Estimate the sum of the angles: $4(90°) + 2(>90°) + (<360°) = 360° + (<360°) + (>180°) = (<720°) + (>180°) \approx 900°$. The answer must be (H).

3. The ACT wants you to look at the answer choices and think the geometry solution is the only approach to solving this item. The unshaded area is one-half of a circle with radius 1 and area $\pi r^2 = \pi$. The entire circle would be inscribed in a square with sides of length 2 and an area of 4. The shaded area is equal to one-half the difference between the area of the square and the area of the circle:

    $$A_{shaded} = \frac{A_{square} - A_{circle}}{2} = \frac{4-\pi}{2} = 2 - \frac{\pi}{2}.$$

    But that's not the only approach, and it's not necessarily the fastest, depending on your geometry skills. You can use estimation and the answer choices to your advantage. Take a second look at the figure: $PQRS$ is a rectangle, and $\widehat{TS}$ and $\widehat{TR}$ are quarter circles, each with a radius of 1. The stem asks, "What is the area of the shaded area?" The rectangle has a width of 1 and a length of 2, so the area of the rectangle is 2. Recall that figures are drawn to scale unless otherwise noted, so you can trust the proportions in the figure: the shaded area looks about one-half of the entire rectangle, or $\frac{2}{4} = \frac{1}{2}$. Estimate the answer choices using $\pi \approx 3$. (C) is the closest: $2 - \frac{\pi}{2} \approx 2 - \frac{3}{2} = \frac{1}{2}$.

4. The ACT wants you to get confused by the variable x. This is not a hard item, just potentially more confusing and time-consuming. The total value is $x \; \cancel{dimes} \times \frac{10 \text{ cents}}{\cancel{dime}} + (x + 6 \; \cancel{nickels}) \times \frac{5 \text{ cents}}{\cancel{nickel}} = 10x + 5x + 30 = 15x + 30$ cents.

    Instead, avoid the variables. If there was 1 dime, there were $1 + 6 = 7$ nickels. The total value is $1(10) + 7(5) = 45$ cents. Test the answer choices. Only (K) equals 45: $15x + 30 = 15(1) + 30 = 45$.

5. Replace the variable r with a value, say 2. This makes the second problem much easier to solve. Evaluate the expressions: $3\pi(2)^2 = 12\pi$ and $3\pi(1)^2 = 3\pi$. Since 12π is four times as large as 3π, the answer is (D).

6. The correct answer is the one that doesn't meet the conditions. Test each choice starting with the second condition: $m + 4 = 3n \Rightarrow m = 3n - 4$. If $n = 6$, $m = 3(6) - 4 = 14$ and $m + n = 14 + 6 = 20$, which is divisible by 5, so eliminate (F). If $n = 8$, $m = 3(8) - 4 = 20$ and $m + n = 20 + 8 = 28$, which is not divisible by 5, so (G) must be the answer. Indeed, 11, (H), 16, (J), and 21, (K), are all possible values for n: if $n = 11$, $m = 3(11) - 4 = 29$ and $m + n = 29 + 11 = 40$, which is divisible by 5. If $n = 16$, $m = 3(16) - 4 = 44$ and $m + n = 44 + 16 = 60$, which is divisible by 5. And if $n = 21$, $m = 3(21) - 4 = 59$ and $m + n = 59 + 21 = 80$, which is divisible by 5.

7. If x is the original amount of the gift, after buying books, Cyd had $\frac{3}{4}(x)$ left. After buying music, she had $\frac{2}{3}\left(\frac{3x}{4}\right) = \frac{6x}{12} = \frac{x}{2}$, which the stem states is equal to $60: \frac{x}{2} = \$60 \Rightarrow x = \$120$, answer choice (E).

    Testing the choices may be a faster approach. After buying books, Cyd had three-fourths of the original amount left, and after buying music, she had two-thirds of what remained left. Start with (C): three-fourths of $80 is $60, and two-thirds of $60 is $40, which is less than the $60 stated in the stem. The gift must have been larger than $80. Test (D): three-fourths of $100 is $75, and two-thirds of $75 is $50, which is still less than $60. The answer must be (E).

STEP 3—CHECK YOUR ANSWER

The final step of the Game Plan is to check your answer before bubbling it on your answer sheet or confirming it on the computer. This doesn't mean double-check your calculations—the answer choices do this for you. Rather, check that your answer actually answers the question asked. Always double-check the units if units are involved.

> **SUM IT UP – MATH GAME PLAN**
>
> **Step 1—Preview the Question**
> • Divide and Conquer
> • Read the Question Carefully
> • Pay Attention to Units and Thought-Reversers
> • Use, Distort, and Draw Figures
> • Use Your Calculator, but Don't Overuse It
>
> **Step 2—Strategize and Solve**
> • Use the Answer Choices
> • Plug-and-Chug
> • Test-the-Test
>
> **Step 3—Check Your Answer**

POWER PRACTICE 1

DIRECTIONS: Solve the problems in this drill using the Game Plan. The problems increase in difficulty with increasing item number. Circle your answers.

1. The TSA agents at a regional airport select for inspection by hand 9 carry-on bags out of every 750 bags that are inspected by x-ray. At this rate, how many carry-on bags will be inspected by hand out of 10,000 bags that are x-rayed?

   A. 12
   B. 85
   C. 120
   D. 130
   E. 150

2. If the sum of five consecutive odd integers is 685, what is the largest of these integers?

   F. 133
   G. 137
   H. 141
   J. 145
   K. 146

3. Which of the following is equivalent to $\dfrac{1}{10^{25}} - \dfrac{1}{10^{26}}$?

   A. 10

   B. $\dfrac{9}{10^{25}}$

   C. $\dfrac{1}{10^{25}}$

   D. $\dfrac{9}{10^{26}}$

   E. $-\dfrac{9}{10^{25}}$

4. If $-1 < x < 0$, which of the following expressions is the largest?

    F. -1
    G. x
    H. $2x$
    J. x^3
    K. $x - 1$

5. In the function $f(x,y) = \dfrac{xy}{x-y} + b$, b is a constant. If $f(1,2) = 4$, what is the value of $f(f(6,3),6)$?

    A. 18
    B. 10
    C. 8
    D. 6
    E. 4

BMI	Weight Classification
Below 18.5	Underweight
18.5 – 24.9	Healthy Weight
25.0 – 29.9	Overweight
30.0 – 34.9	Obese
35.0 – 39.9	Severely Obese

6. The body mass index (BMI) is a measure of a person's health based on their height and weight. The table above shows how BMI relates to weight classifications. BMI is defined as a person's weight, in kilograms, divided by the square of their height, in meters. For a person 1.6 meters tall, what is the smallest number of kilograms of weight gain required to change their weight classification from healthy to obese?

    F. 5
    G. 8
    H. 10
    J. 13
    K. 15

7. If a law firm needs x legal pads each week for each paralegal, and if there are p paralegals at the law firm, for how many weeks will c packs of legal pads last if there are 6 pads per pack?

    A. $\dfrac{xc}{6p}$
    B. $\dfrac{xp}{6c}$
    C. $\dfrac{6c}{xp}$
    D. $\dfrac{6cp}{x}$
    E. $\dfrac{6xp}{c}$

8. In the figure below, the area of the smaller rectangle is 12. What is the area of square $PQRS$?

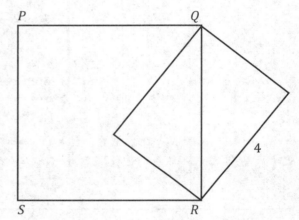

    F. 5
    G. 15
    H. 16
    J. 25
    K. 35

9. The figure below represents the graph of $y = f(x)$ in the coordinate plane. Which of the following is the graph of $y = f(x - 1)$?

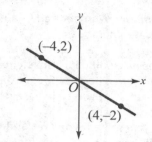

A.

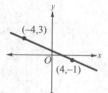

B.

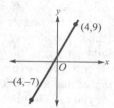

C.

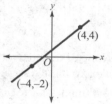

D.

E.

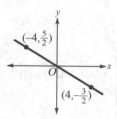

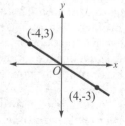

10. In the xy-plane, a circle is centered on the origin and points A and B lie on the circumference of the circle. If the coordinates of point B are $(2,0)$ and $\angle AOB = \dfrac{\pi}{4}$, which of the following ordered pairs (x,y) corresponds to point A?

F. $\left(1, \dfrac{\sqrt{2}}{2}\right)$

G. $\left(\dfrac{\sqrt{2}}{2}, \dfrac{\sqrt{2}}{2}\right)$

H. $(\sqrt{2}, \sqrt{2})$

J. $(2, 2)$

K. $(2, \sqrt{2})$

ANSWERS

1. **(C)** *Mathematics/Number and Quantity/Rates and Proportions*

Preview the question. The item stem asks for the number of bags inspected by hand out of 10,000 bags, so this is a proportion problem. It's an easy problem, so the direct approach is probably the fastest. Use your calculator for the arithmetic.

Strategize and solve. Set up a direct proportion between two ratios to find the number inspected out of the total number: $\frac{9}{750} = \frac{x}{10,000}$. Use your calculator for the arithmetic: $x = (9 \times 10000) \div 750 = 120$.

Check your answer. The number of inspected bags out of 10,000 is 120, (C).

2. **(H)** *Mathematics/Number and Quantity/ Properties of Numbers*

Preview the question. The item stem asks for the <u>largest</u> of five <u>consecutive odd</u> integers that total 685. Use your calculator on this item.

Strategize and solve. A calculator means that you can test-the-test quickly on this item. Start with (G): if 137 is the largest of the five consecutive odd integers, the remainder includes 135, 133, 131, 129: $137 + 135 + 133 + 131 + 129 = 665$, which is less than the given sum 685. Test the next largest value, 141: $141 + 139 + 137 + 135 + 133 = 685$, which matches the sum 685.

This approach is easier, and probably faster, than the algebra solution. Translate the given information into an equation and solve for the largest odd integer:
$n + (n + 2) + (n + 4) + (n + 6) + (n + 8) = 685 \Rightarrow$
$5n = 685 - (2 + 4 + 6 + 8) \Rightarrow$
$n = (685 - 20) \div 5 = 133$. The largest of the integers is $n + 8 = 133 + 8 = 141$.

Check your answer. The largest integer is 141, so the answer is (H).

3. **(D)** *Mathematics/Number and Quantity/Basic Arithmetic Manipulations*

Preview the question. The item stem asks for the difference between two rational expressions with exponents of base 10 in each denominator.

Strategize and solve. If you are comfortable working with exponents, simplify the expression:
$$\frac{1}{10^{25}} - \frac{1}{10^{26}} = \frac{1}{10^{25}}\left(\frac{10}{10}\right) - \frac{1}{10^{26}} = \frac{10}{10^{26}} - \frac{1}{10^{26}} = \frac{9}{10^{26}}.$$

If you are not comfortable with the rules of exponents, use your calculator! You may even use it simply because it may be a faster method, depending on the calculator. Whichever method is fastest and less prone to error is the one you should choose. How fractions and exponents are entered in a calculator depends on the calculator—make sure you are familiar with yours and the required order of key entries. The final readout should be 9^{-26} or 9E-26, which is the same as 9×10^{-26}.

Check your answer. None of the answers have the format of negative exponents, so rewrite 9×10^{-26} with the exponent on the bottom: $9 \times 10^{-26} = \frac{9}{10^{26}}$. This form now matches choice (D).

4. **(J)** *Mathematics/Number and Quantity/ Properties of Numbers*

Preview the question. The item stem states that x is some negative value between -1 and 0, which makes x a negative fraction. There are two approaches to this problem: reason based on the properties of negative fractions or use the strategy of plug-and-chug. Use the method that is fastest and least error prone for you.

Strategize and solve. You can reason through the problem an answer choice at a time. (G) represents the variable in $-1 < x < 0$, so

(G) is clearly larger than (F). Since (H) is double the value of (G), which is negative, (G) is also larger than (H). (G) is larger than (K) because when 1 is subtracted from either a positive or negative value, the result is always less than the original value. However, if a negative fraction is raised to an odd power, then the resulting value, though smaller in absolute value, is negative and therefore larger than the original. So, (J) is larger than (H).

It's probably even faster to use the "plug-and-chug" approach. Substitute a negative fractional value for x, such as $x = -\dfrac{1}{2}$, and evaluate the answer choices:

F. -1

G. $x \Rightarrow -\dfrac{1}{2}$

H. $2x \Rightarrow 2\left(-\dfrac{1}{2}\right) = -1$

J. $x^3 \Rightarrow \left(-\dfrac{1}{2}\right)\left(-\dfrac{1}{2}\right)\left(-\dfrac{1}{2}\right) = -\dfrac{1}{8}$

K. $x - 1 \Rightarrow -\dfrac{1}{2} - 1 = -\dfrac{3}{2}$

Since all of the answer choices yield negative values, the largest value is the one that is closest to zero: $-\dfrac{1}{8}$.

Check your answer. Either method shows that x^3, (J), is the largest expression for a negative fractional value for x.

5. **(A)** *Mathematics/Algebra and Functions/ Evaluating, Interpreting, and Creating Algebraic Functions/Function Notation*

Preview the question. This is a medium difficulty item. You can use your calculator on this item, but the math is so simple it's probably faster to do the arithmetic by hand.

Strategize and solve. The item tests understanding of function math, so the best approach is to plug in the given values for x and y and evaluate the functions. Work through the item a step at a time. Determine the value of b from the given value of the function for $x = 1$ and $y = 2$: $f(1,2) = \dfrac{xy}{x-y} + b = \dfrac{1 \times 2}{1-2} + b = 4 \Rightarrow$

$b = 4 - \dfrac{2}{-1} = 4 + 2 = 6$. The function

$f(x,y)$ is $\dfrac{xy}{x-y} + 6$. Determine the value of

$f(6,3)$: $f(6,3) = \dfrac{6 \times 3}{6-3} + 6 = \dfrac{18}{3} + 6 = 12$.

Determine the value of $f(12,6)$: $\dfrac{12 \times 6}{12-6} + 6 =$

$\dfrac{72}{6} + 6 = 12 + 6 = 18$.

Check your answer. The question asked for $f(f(6,3),6)$, and $f(6,3) = 12$, so the item stem asked for $f(12,6)$, which is 18, (A).

6. **(J)** *Mathematics/Algebra and Functions/ Manipulating Algebraic Expressions/Basic Algebraic Manipulations and Statistics and Probability/Data Representation/Tables*

Preview the question. The table gives the weight classifications for five BMI ranges and the item stem describes the equation for BMI and asks for the change in weight required to take a person 1.6 meters tall from a healthy BMI to an obese BMI. According to the table, a 24.9 BMI is healthy and a 30.0 BMI is obese.

Strategize and solve. This problem is straightforward, so use the algebra solution. Translate the given information into an equation for BMI, where w is the weight and h is the height, and solve for the weight:

$$\text{BMI} = \frac{w\,(\text{kilograms})}{h\,(\text{meters})^2} \Rightarrow w = (\text{BMI})\,h^2. \text{ The}$$

change in weight that accompanies a change in BMI of $30.0 - 24.9 = 5.1$, for a person 1.6 meters tall, corresponds to a weight change of $5.1 \times 1.6^2 = 13.056$ kilograms.

Check your answer. Choice (J) is the closest to 13.056.

7. **(C)** *Mathematics/Algebra and Functions/ Evaluating, Interpreting, and Creating Algebraic Functions*

Preview the question. The item requires you to translate the given information into an expression with units of weeks.

Strategize and solve. The algebra approach may be faster, depending on your algebra skills. You'll have to decide which strategy works best for you. The algebra solution uses ratios and cancellation of units:

$$\text{weeks} = \frac{\text{week}}{\dfrac{x\,\text{pads}}{\text{paralegal}} \times p\,\text{paralegals}} \times \frac{6\,\text{pads}}{\text{pack}} \times$$

$$c\,\text{packs} = \frac{6c}{xp}.$$

You can also arrive at this answer by reasoning through the steps: 1) each week, the firm needs x legal pads for each of p paralegals, or xp pads; 2) each of c packs contains 6 pads, so there are

$6c$ packs; 3) the $6c$ packs will last $\dfrac{6c}{xp}$ weeks.

While the test-the-test method is likely slower than the algebra solution, it's a viable approach if you're stuck. Replace the variables with easy numbers. If the firm needs 2 legal pads per paralegal, and if there are 3 paralegals, the firm needs 6 pads each week. If they have 4 packs, that's 24 pads. The pads will last 4 weeks. Check the answer choices to find the one that equals 4 for $x = 2$, $p = 3$, and $c = 4$. Also, use your number sense so you don't perform needless

calculations. (A) becomes $\dfrac{xc}{6p} = \dfrac{2 \times 4}{6 \times 3}$, which is

less than 1. (B) becomes $\dfrac{xp}{6c} = \dfrac{2 \times 3}{6 \times 4}$, which is

also less than 1. Test (C): $\dfrac{6c}{xp} = \dfrac{6 \times 4}{2 \times 3} = \dfrac{24}{6} = 4$,

so the answer is (C).

Check your answer. Double-check the units in the

algebra approach. The final expression $\dfrac{6c}{xp}$ has

units of weeks, so (C) is the correct choice.

8. **(J) Mathematics/Geometry/Rectangles and Squares**

Preview the question. The problem asks for the area of a square, no units are given, and the figure is not necessarily drawn to scale. The answer choices are well defined.

Strategize and solve. If the area of the smaller rectangle is 12, the missing side length of the smaller rectangle must be 3. And comparing the

two sides of the smaller rectangle, the figure appears to be drawn to scale. Skip the geometry solution and solve the item using estimation— it's the fastest solution given the differences between the answer choices. Comparing the given length of 4 with QR, QR must be close to 5 units. That would make the area of $PQRS$ 25.

Alternatively, use the properties of triangles. The side QR of the square is the same as the diagonal of the smaller rectangle. The area of the smaller rectangle is 12, the width of the rectangle is 3, and each of the smaller triangles are 3-4-5 triangles. The length of QR, a side of the square, is 5, and the area of the square is $5^2 = 25$.

Check your answer. Even in the estimation approach, a quick glance at the answer choices is enough to determine that the answer must be (J).

9. **(D) Mathematics/Algebra and Functions/ Coordinate Geometry/Transformations and Their Effects on Graphs of Functions**

Preview the question. This is a difficult item due to the tested concept: transformations and their effects on graphs of functions. Before performing a transformation, you must first determine the equation of the line plotted in the figure.

Strategize and solve. Calculate the slope of the line from the two points given in the

figure: $\dfrac{-2-2}{4-(-4)} = -\dfrac{1}{2}$. Since the y-intercept,

b, is 0, the original equation of the line is

$y = mx + b = -\dfrac{x}{2}$. Replace x with $x - 1$ in the

original equation: the transformed line equation

is $y = f(x-1) = -\dfrac{x-1}{2} = -\dfrac{x}{2} + \dfrac{1}{2}$. Solve for

$x = 4$ and $x = -4$: $y(4) = -\dfrac{4}{2} + \dfrac{1}{2} = -\dfrac{3}{2}$, and

$y(-4) = -\dfrac{-4}{2} + \dfrac{1}{2} = \dfrac{5}{2}$.

Check your answer. The graph in (D) is the only

one to include points $\left(4, -\dfrac{3}{2}\right)$ and $\left(-4, \dfrac{5}{2}\right)$, so

(D) is the correct choice.

10. (H) *Mathematics/Geometry/Circles* and *Algebra and Functions/Coordinate Geometry/The Coordinate System*

Preview the question. This is a difficult item—don't look for easy answers. A figure is not included, so you should draw one. The question asks for the coordinates of point *A*, which have to be derivable from the given information since a calculator is not allowed.

Strategize and solve. Draw a picture of what is known:

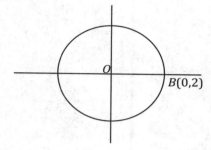

To determine which quadrant *A* is in, use $\angle AOB = \dfrac{\pi}{4}$. Since 2π equals $360°$,

$$\frac{\frac{\pi}{4}}{2\pi} = \frac{\angle AOB}{360°} \Rightarrow \angle AOB = \frac{360° \times \frac{\pi}{4}}{2\pi} = \frac{90°}{2} = 45°.$$

Construct a $45°$-$45°$-$90°$ triangle that describes

the position of *A* in terms of its sides *x* and *y*, which are equal :

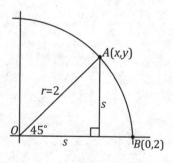

Since it's a $45°$-$45°$-$90°$ triangle, the *x*- and *y*-coordinates are equal. Use the Pythagorean theorem to solve for *x* and *y*: $2^2 = s^2 + s^2 \Rightarrow 4 = 2s^2 \Rightarrow s = \sqrt{2}$. The coordinates of *A* are $(\sqrt{2}, \sqrt{2})$. (You can also solve for the sides of the isosceles triangle using the ratio of the sides as given in the reference section of the directions, but this method is longer.)

Check your answer. The question asked for the coordinates of *A*, $(\sqrt{2}, \sqrt{2})$, so the answer is (H).

CHAPTER 5
HyperPrep Math

WORD PROBLEMS

ACCELEPREP APPROACH

This HyperPrep covers the problem types that appear most often on the ACT test. We concentrate on alternative strategies— techniques that are common sense and avoid cumbersome math procedures. If the strategies taught in this chapter help you to answer just 10 more questions right (out of a total of 60), your ACT math score will be 5 or even 6 points higher.

As you'd expect, some math questions are word problems that require addition, subtraction, multiplication, and division.

Example: **1.** A restaurant chef can order lettuce from Purveyor A or Purveyor B. Purveyor A sells a case with 30 heads of lettuce for $36. Purveyor B sells a case with 48 heads of lettuce for $60. Which purveyor's price, per head of lettuce, is cheaper and by how much?

   A. A, $0.05 cheaper per head
   B. A, $1.20 cheaper per head
   C. They are the same price
   D. B, $0.05 cheaper per head
   E. B, $1.25 cheaper per head

Since this type of problem doesn't require any advanced math, you'll probably find it toward the beginning of the math section. Just do the arithmetic.

AVERAGES

Word problems also use averages, percentages, ratios, and proportions.

Example: **2.** Marty received the following scores on the five tests given during the semester: 82, 88, 96, 92, and *x*. If his average on the five tests was 90, what was his score on the fifth test?

   F. 82
   G. 90
   H. 91
   J. 92
   K. 96

STRATEGY ALERT

You can solve this first algebra example using a running total: 82 is –8 from the average of 90; 88 is –2; 96 is +6; and 92 is +2. That's a total of –2. So to make the average 90, the last test has to be +2, or 92.

Explanations for the example questions are included later in the chapter. Circle your answers now. Later when you reach the explanations at the end of the section, come back and check to make sure you answered the questions correctly.

PERCENTAGES

Many percent problems fall into one of two categories:
- This is what percent of that?
- What was the percent change?

Here is an example from the first category.

Example:

3. A shirt that normally sells for $25 is on sale for $5 off. The sale price is what percent of the normal selling price?

   A.   5%
   B.   20%
   C.   25%
   D.   30%
   E.   80%

STRATEGY ALERT

Easy does it. Problems near the beginning of the math section are the easy ones. Just do the arithmetic.

Of course, a problem might be dressed up with a lot of words to make it seem difficult, but if you can locate the key words, it becomes easy.

Example:

4. Oxygen is carried in human blood by attaching to hemoglobin molecules. Oxygen saturation is a measure of how much oxygen the blood is carrying as a percentage of the maximum it could carry. One hemoglobin molecule can carry a maximum of four molecules of oxygen. Thus, a hemoglobin molecule carrying three molecules of oxygen is carrying $\frac{3}{4}$ or 75% of the maximum amount of oxygen it could carry. If a test shows that 100 hemoglobin molecules are carrying 380 oxygen molecules, what is the oxygen saturation of the blood?

   F.   2.6%
   G.   38%
   H.   95%
   J.   97.4%
   K. 105%

CLOSER LOOK

Use key words to set up an is/of equation to represent the percentage.

The other type of percent question asks about percent change.

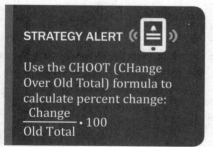

STRATEGY ALERT

Use the CHOOT (CHange Over Old Total) formula to calculate percent change:
$$\frac{\text{Change}}{\text{Old Total}} \cdot 100$$

Example:

5. The 2000 census shows that the population of Muhlenberg County was 36,331. The 2010 census shows that the population of the county was 33,299. What was the approximate percentage change in the population from 2000 to 2010?

   A.   An increase of 8%
   B.   An increase of 11%
   C.   A decrease of 3%
   D.   A decrease of 11%
   E.   A decrease of 8%

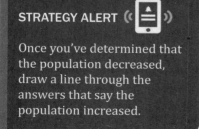

STRATEGY ALERT

Once you've determined that the population decreased, draw a line through the answers that say the population increased.

PROPORTIONS

Simply put, a proportion is a statement that two fractions are equal.

Example:

$$\frac{2}{4} = \frac{6}{12}$$

Since $\frac{2}{4}$ equals $\frac{1}{2}$ and $\frac{6}{12}$ equals $\frac{1}{2}$, we know the above statement is true.

One of the amazing things about the world is that many situations can be described using proportions:

Example:

Lourdes uses 3 gallons of gas to drive 105 miles. How much gas will she use to drive 315 miles? (The farther Lourdes drives, the more gas she uses.)

Hector is building a wall. If 12 bricks weigh 40 pounds, how many bricks are there in a stack that weighs 60 pounds? (The more bricks there are in a stack, the more the stack weighs.)

Joseph has planted 60 acres of corn that he needs to fertilize. If a tanker truck of liquid fertilizer is used for 12 acres, how many tanker trucks of liquid fertilizer will Joseph need? (The more acres to be fertilized, the more truckloads are required.)

Each of these situations can be represented with a proportion. Set up a proportion to calculate how much gas Lourdes needs to drive 315 miles:

$$\frac{\text{Gas Used}_1}{\text{Miles Driven}_1} = \frac{\text{Gas Used}_2}{\text{Miles Driven}_2}$$

$$\frac{3 \text{ gal}}{105 \text{ miles}} = \frac{x \text{ gal}}{315 \text{ miles}}$$

Just solve for x (by cross-multiplying and dividing):

$105x = 3(315)$
$x = 9$

Now calculate how many bricks are in a stack that weighs 60 pounds:

$$\frac{12 \text{ bricks}}{40 \text{ pounds}} = \frac{x \text{ bricks}}{60 \text{ pounds}}$$

$40x = 720$

$x = 18$

Finally, calculate how many tanker trucks Joseph will need:

$$\frac{1 \text{ truck}}{12 \text{ acres}} = \frac{x \text{ trucks}}{60 \text{ acres}}$$

$12x = 60$

$x = 5$

REVIEW

Proportions represent a similar change in a given relationship:

More Input, More Output
Less Input, Less Output

STRATEGY ALERT

A proportion is a comparison of two ratios. Typically a question stem will give you enough information to complete one ratio. The second ratio will have a missing element, x. After you have set these ratios equal to one another, check that the units of the two numerators match and that the units of the two denominators match.

Examples:

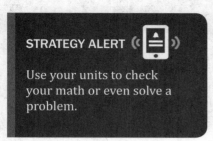

STRATEGY ALERT

Use your units to check your math or even solve a problem.

6. Researchers have determined that 12 out of every 50 persons in a population have genetic marker EXL, which triggers an allergic dermatological reaction in response to contact with the leaves of *Toxicodendron vernix*. In a population of 1,500 persons of similar genetic make-up, approximately how many can be expected to have EXL?

   F. 36
   G. 40
   H. 125
   J. 360
   K. 750

7. A swimming pool with a capacity of 25,000 gallons is being filled by a water pipe that flows at a constant rate. At 9:00 a.m., the pool contains 5,500 gallons, and at 1:00 p.m. the pool contains 17,500 gallons. If no water is drained from the pool, at what time will the pool be filled to capacity?

   A. 2:30 p.m.
   B. 3:30 p.m.
   C. 4:00 p.m.
   D. 7:00 p.m.
   E. 8:40 p.m.

USING UNITS TO CHECK SOLUTIONS

One of the most powerful common-sense test-taking strategies that is available to you is using the given units to check your solution. Now, how many times have you solved a problem by multiplying when you should have divided or by dividing when you should have multiplied? Yes, we are all guilty. But a really slick way of avoiding the mistake is to put the units into the solution. Let's start with a simple example.

Example:

8. The EPA highway mileage estimate for a certain vehicle is 32 miles per gallon of gasoline. If the estimate is correct, how far, in miles, will the vehicle travel on 8 gallons of gasoline?

   F. 4
   G. 24
   H. 40
   J. 250
   K. 256

Now let's look at a more complicated example.

Example:

9. What is the total cost of 3.5 pounds of asparagus at $2.80 per pound and 3.5 pounds of leeks at $2.66 per pound?

   A. $1.86
   B. $2.57
   C. $9.31
   D. $9.80
   E. $19.11

USING UNITS TO AVOID ALGEBRA

You can even use units to solve problems.

Example:

10. A printer operating at a constant rate produces *x* pages every *t* minutes. How long, in minutes, will it take the printer to produce *p* pages?

F. pxt

G. $p(t+x)$

H. $\dfrac{px}{t}$

J. $\dfrac{x}{pt}$

K. $\dfrac{pt}{x}$

The value of this strategy cannot be overstated. You may be able to solve fairly difficult algebra problems without any mathematical calculations.

Answers

Return to the pages below to review each item:
1. p. 96
2. p. 96
3. p. 97
4. p. 97
5. p. 97
6. p. 99
7. p. 99
8. p. 99
9. p. 99
10. p. 100

1. Purveyor A's price per head is $\dfrac{\$36}{30 \text{ heads}} = \dfrac{\$1.20}{\text{head}}$.

Purveyor B's price per head is $\dfrac{\$60}{48 \text{ heads}} = \dfrac{\$1.25}{\text{head}}$.

Now determine the difference in the prices per head: $1.25 - 1.20 = 0.05$. So Purveyor A's price is cheaper by $0.05 per head, (A).

2. Again, we have an item that doesn't require advanced math, just the concept of "average":

$$\text{Avg} = \frac{82 + 88 + 96 + 92 + x}{5}$$

$$90 = \frac{358 + x}{5}$$

$$450 = 358 + x$$

$$x = 92, \text{ (J)}.$$

3. Focus on the grammar used in the question. You'll see that there is a prepositional phrase "of the normal selling price." "Normal selling price" is a number, 25. There is a second number in the question, "sale price," 25 – 5 = 20. The way to answer a percent question that has the structure "What percent of this is that?" is to create a fraction with "of this" as the denominator and "that" as the numerator: $\dfrac{20}{25} = \dfrac{4}{5}$. Convert $\dfrac{4}{5}$ to a percent: $\dfrac{4}{5} = 0.80 = 80\%$, (E).

4. In this case, the "of" phrase is "of the maximum" and the other number is "how much oxygen the blood is carrying." So the problem is just $\dfrac{\text{carrying}}{\text{of maximum}}$. If one hemoglobin molecule can carry four molecules of oxygen, 100 hemoglobin molecules can carry 400 molecules of oxygen. So $\dfrac{\text{carrying}}{\text{of maximum}} = \left(\dfrac{380}{400}\right) \cdot 100 = 95\%$, (H).

5. A percent change can be easily calculated using the "CHOOT" formula (Remember, since the answer only requires an approximation, just round the numbers to make the calculations easier):

$$\frac{\text{Change}}{\text{Old Total}} \cdot 100 = \text{Percent Change}$$

Use the CHOOT formula to solve:

$$\frac{\text{Population}_{2010} - \text{Population}_{2000}}{\text{Population}_{2000}} \cdot 100 \approx \frac{33,000 - 36,000}{36,000} \cdot 100 =$$

$$\frac{-3}{36} \cdot 100 = -8\%.$$

The negative value indicates a decrease, so (E) is correct.

6. The larger the pool of people, the more with EXL:

$$\frac{12}{50} = \frac{x}{1,500}$$

$$50x = 12(1,500)$$

$$x = 12(30) = 360, \text{ (J)}.$$

7. There are several routes to the correct answer, so we'll pick one. Water flows in at the rate of 17,500 gal – 5,500 gal = 12,000 gallons every 4 hours, and it will take another 25,000 – 17,500 = 7,500 gallons to fill the pool completely.

$$\frac{12,000 \text{ gal}}{4 \text{ hours}} = \frac{7,500 \text{ gal}}{x \text{ hours}}$$

$$12,000x = 30,000$$

$$x = 2\frac{1}{2} \text{ hours} = 2 \text{ hours and } 30 \text{ minutes.}$$ And 2 hours and 30 minutes after 1 p.m. is 3:30 p.m., (B).

8. A common mistake here would be to divide rather than multiply: $\dfrac{32}{8} = 4$. And (F) is available as a wrong answer for this mistake. But put in the units associated with the calculation:

$$\frac{32 \text{ mi/gal}}{8 \text{ gal}} = 4 \text{ mi/gal}^2$$

In other words, a gallon-unit multiplied by a gallon-unit, just like a number, would be gallon². And mi/gal² is not a unit that answers the question "How far?" Now multiply instead:

$$\frac{32 \text{ mi}}{\text{gal}} \cdot 8 \text{ gal} = 256 \text{ miles, (K)}.$$

9. To avoid dividing when you ought to be multiplying, be sure to include your units:

$$3.5 \, \cancel{lbs} \cdot \frac{\$2.80}{\cancel{lb}} + 3.5 \, \cancel{lbs} \cdot \frac{\$2.66}{\cancel{lb}} = \$9.80 + \$9.31 = \$19.11 \, , \, (E).$$

Notice that your "lb" units cancel. And your final answer is expressed in units of "dollars," which is exactly how you would answer the question "What is the total cost?"

10. Since you are asked, "How long, in minutes, will it take the printer to produce p pages," your final answer should be in terms of minutes. But do you multiply, add and multiply, or multiply and divide—and using what values? Watch what happens if we use units:

F. pxt = (pages)(pages)(minutes) = (pages^2)(minutes)

That is not a unit that makes any sense. You'd never, ever say to someone, "Give me three pages-squared-minutes." What about (G)? You run into the same problem. And (H)? You'd have $\dfrac{(\text{pages})(\text{pages})}{\text{minutes}}$. Nonsense. Look at (J): $\dfrac{\text{pages}}{(\text{pages})\text{minutes}}$. Here, "pages" cancels out and you are left with $\dfrac{1}{\text{minutes}}$. Is $\dfrac{1}{\text{minutes}}$ an answer to the question "How long?" Obviously not. The correct answer must be (K). Indeed, $\dfrac{(\text{pages})\text{minutes}}{\text{pages}} = \text{minutes}$. The "pages" in the numerator and "pages" in the denominator cancel, leaving only "minutes." And the question asks, "How many minutes?" so we have found our answer.

POWER PRACTICE 1

DIRECTIONS: Solve each problem. Circle your answers. Answers are on p. 309.

1. The high temperatures for 5 days were 82°F, 86°F, 91°F, 79°F, and 91°F. What is the average of these temperatures?

   A. 79°F
   B. 82°F
   C. 85.8°F
   D. 86°F
   E. 91°F

2. If the price of candy increases from 5 pounds for $7 to 3 pounds for $7, how much less candy (in pounds) can be purchased for $3.50 at the new price than at the old price?

   F. $\frac{2}{7}$
   G. 1
   H. $1\frac{17}{35}$
   J. 2
   K. $3\frac{34}{35}$

Year	2011	2012	2013	2014	2015	2016
Monthly Daycare Fee	$1,349	$1,391	$1,432	$1,475	$1,519	$1,565

3. The table above summarizes the monthly fee for enrolling one child into a certain daycare. What is the percent increase in the monthly daycare fee from 2011 to 2016?

   A. 9
   B. 13
   C. 16
   D. 32
   E. 216

4. Motorcycle A averages 40 kilometers per liter of gasoline, while Motorcycle B averages 50 kilometers per liter. If the cost of gasoline is $2 per liter, what will be the difference in cost of operating the two motorcycles for 300 kilometers?

   F. $3
   G. $6
   H. $12
   J. $15
   K. $20

5. The recommended daily dosage of an antibiotic for treatment of a certain infection is 200 milligrams per kilogram of patient body weight administered in 6 equal doses. If a patient weighs 175 pounds, which of the following can be used to calculate how much of the antibiotic, in milligrams, the patient should receive in a single dose?

   (Note: 1 kilogram = 2.2 pounds)

   A. $\frac{200(2.2)}{175(6)}$
   B. $\frac{200(175)}{2.2(6)}$
   C. $\frac{175(2.2)}{200(6)}$
   D. $\frac{175(6)}{200(2.2)}$
   E. $\frac{175(200)(2.2)}{6}$

ALGEBRAIC OPERATIONS

SUBSTITUTE AND SOLVE

You may be asked to evaluate or manipulate algebraic expressions, solve equations, and even create equations. Many of these items are fairly straightforward and can be answered using the basic algebraic procedures that you learned in math class.

Example: **1.** If $x = -2$, what is the value of $x^2 + 2x + 1$?

> A. −4
> B. −2
> C. 0
> D. 1
> E. 2

STRATEGY ALERT

If you are given a value, substitute and solve.

Now let's look at an item that is a bit more difficult. It is more challenging because it uses function notation, but the procedure is the same.

Example: **2.** If $f(x) = x + 3$ and $g(x) = 2x - 5$, what is the value of $f(g(2))$?

> F. −2
> G. 0
> H. 2
> J. 4
> K. 10

Explanations for the example questions are included later in the chapter. Circle your answers now. Later when you reach the explanations at the end of the section, come back and check to make sure you answered the questions correctly.

Let's call this process of plugging in the values given in the item stem "Substitute and Solve." Substitute and Solve is a good approach for items where a value is provided for you to test. But what if there is no specific value?

PLUG-AND-CHUG

If you are not given a specific value, Plug-and-Chug. Choose your own values to test. Calculate the solution for the expression given in the item stem, then test the answer choices using the value(s) you chose. The correct answer choice will return a numerical value that is <u>equal</u> to that returned by the expression in the question stem. It's actually easier to demonstrate.

Examples:

3. Which of the expressions shown below is equivalent to $\dfrac{x^2-1}{x+1}$?

A. $x-1$
B. $x+1$
C. x^2
D. x^2-2x-1
E. x^2+2x-1

STRATEGY ALERT

Plug-and-Chug. To understand an algebraic expression, substitute various numbers to see how they behave.

4. If $y=x-2$, then $(y-x)^2=$

F. -16
G. -4
H. 0
J. 4
K. 16

STRATEGY ALERT

A word about substituting the number 1: It's fast, but can be tricky. You have two options concerning 1. First, you can avoid 1 altogether, since it can lead to ambiguous or duplicate results. Or second, you can use 1 carefully, making sure to check duplicate or ambiguous answers with another number (this is our preference because of its speed).

5. Which of the following expressions is equivalent to
$4a+3b-(-2a-3b)$?

A. $2a$
B. $12ab$
C. $2a+6b$
D. $6a+6b$
E. $8a+9b$

6. If neither x nor y is 0, which of the expressions below is equivalent to
$\dfrac{9\left(x^2y^3\right)^6}{\left(3x^6y^9\right)^2}$?

F. 1
G. 3
H. x^2y^3
J. $3x^2y^3$
K. $9x^2y^3$

You may also be asked to create an equation.

Examples:

7. An airplane takes off from the Metro County Airport and ascends at a constant rate of 1,000 feet per minute until it reaches its cruising altitude of 28,000 feet above sea level. If the airport is 750 feet above sea level, which of the following equations, where m is minutes since take-off, can be used to find the altitude of the plane above sea level during its ascent?

A. $A=28,000-1,000m+750$
B. $A=28,000-1,000m-750$
C. $A=1,000m-28,000+750$
D. $A=1,000m+750$
E. $A=1,000m-750$

8. The cost of making a call using a phone card is $0.15 for dialing and $0.04 per minute once connected. Which of the following equations could be used to find the cost, in dollars, of a call with a connection time of x minutes long?

F. $y = x(0.04 + 0.15)$
G. $y = 0.04x + 0.15$
H. $y = 0.04 + 0.15x$
J. $y = 0.15 - 0.04x$
K. $y = 0.04 - 0.15x$

Plug-and-Chug can also be useful for solving some of the more difficult "specialty" items that test a particular math concept such as absolute value.

Example:

STRATEGY ALERT

Solve absolute value problems by assuming numerical values for variables.

9. For all nonzero values of a and b, which of the following expressions is *always* positive?

A. $|-a| + b$
B. $a + |b|$
C. $-|a| + |b|$
D. $-|a| - |b|$
E. $|-a| + |-b|$

TEST-THE-TEST

STRATEGY ALERT

Test-the-Test. The correct answer to any item is always one of five given choices. To Test-the-Test, plug the answer choices back into the item until a choice returns a true statement, or check each answer choice against any stated conditions.

Another alternative strategy that also uses the multiple-choice structure of the test is Test-the-Test.

Some problems involving variables ask you to choose a numerical value as an answer.

Examples:

10. If $2x - 3 = 7x - 5$, then $x =$

F. $-\dfrac{5}{2}$

G. $-\dfrac{2}{5}$

H. -1

J. $\dfrac{2}{5}$

K. $\dfrac{5}{2}$

CLOSER LOOK

When to use Test-the-Test:

1. Test-the-Test if you are unsure of how to directly solve the item from the information given in the item stem.
2. Test-the-Test if it is the fastest or easiest approach.

11. Which of the following is a solution for the equation $x^2 - 16 = 0$?

    A. 32
    B. 16
    C. 8
    D. 4
    E. −2

12. Chelsea's current height is 150 cm and her growth is averaging 0.5 cm per month. Travis's current height is 140 cm and his growth is averaging 0.75 cm per month. If Chelsea and Travis continue to grow taller at these constant rates, in approximately how many months will Chelsea and Travis be the same height?

    F. 2
    G. 20
    H. 40
    J. 60
    K. 80

Answers

Return to the pages below to review each item:
  1. p. 104
  2. p. 104
  3. p. 105
  4. p. 105
  5. p. 105
  6. p. 105
  7. p. 105
  8. p. 106
  9. p. 106
 10. p. 106
 11. p. 107
 12. p. 107

1. This item specifically asks you to evaluate an algebraic expression at a particular value, so test the value:

$$(-2)^2 + 2(-2) + 1 = 4 - 4 + 1 = 1, \text{ (D)}.$$

2. $g(2) = 2(2) - 5 = 4 - 5 = -1$

$$f(-1) = -1 + 3 = 2$$

Therefore (H) is correct.

3. Just assume a value for x, say $x = 2$, and substitute 2 for x in the expression given in the stem:
$$\frac{x^2 - 1}{x + 1} = \frac{2^2 - 1}{2 + 1} = \frac{3}{3} = 1$$

Now substitute 2 for x in each answer choice, and the correct answer will return the value 1:

    A. $x - 1 = 2 - 1 = 1$ (Correct)
    B. $x + 1 = 2 + 1 = 3$ (Wrong)
    C. $x^2 = 2^2 = 4$ (Wrong)
    D. $x^2 - 2x - 1 = 2^2 - 2(2) - 1 = -1$ (Wrong)
    E. $x^2 + 2x - 1 = 2^2 + 2(2) - 1 = 7$ (Wrong)

4. Here you have two variables, so assume values for both. If $x = 2$, then $y = 2 - 2 = 0$, and $(0 - 2)^2 = 4$. Therefore, the value of the expression is 4, (J).

5. Assume some numerical values for the variables in the question stem, say $a = 1$ and $b = 1$. Using these values, the numerical value of the expression in the question stem is calculated as:

$$4(1) + 3(1) - (-2(1) - 3(1)) = 4 + 3 - (-2 - 3) = 12$$

Now test those same values in the choices. The correct choice will return the value 12:

$2(1) = 2$ (Wrong)
$12(1)(1) = 12$ (Correct?)
$2(1) + 6(1) = 8$ (Wrong)
$6(1) + 6(1) = 12$ (Correct?)
$8(1) + 9(1) = 17$ (Wrong)

We've eliminated three choices that are definitely wrong, but both (B) and (D) returned the value 12. Do we have two right answers? No. Since $(1)(n) = n$, two choices returned the same value—a coincidence. Just use two more values, say $a = 1$ and $b = 0$:
$4(1) + 3(0) - (-2(1) - 3(0)) = 4 + 0 - (-2 - 0) = 6$

B. $12(1)(0) = 0$ (Wrong)
D. $6(1) + 6(0) = 6$ (Correct)

6.   You can use the rules for working with exponents to simplify the

expression: $\dfrac{9\left(x^2 y^3\right)^6}{\left(3x^6 y^9\right)^2} = \dfrac{9(x^{2(6)})\left(y^{3(6)}\right)}{3^2 (x^{6(2)})\left(y^{9(2)}\right)} = \dfrac{9x^{12}y^{18}}{9x^{12}y^{18}} = 1$.

Or you can Plug-and-Chug. Let's say $x = 1$ and $y = 1$. On that assumption, since 1 to any power is just 1, the complicated expression in the question stem becomes $\dfrac{9}{9} = 1$. If you substitute 1 for both x and y in the choices, the correct choice will return the value 1:

F.   1 (Correct?)
G.   3 (Wrong)
H.   1 (Correct?)
J.   3 (Wrong)
K.   9 (Wrong)

We have two seemingly right choices. Why? Because $1(1) = \dfrac{1}{1}$, duplicates are possible. So we just pick another pair of values: $x = 1$ and $y = 2$. On those assumptions, the complicated expression in the question stem becomes 1 (use your calculator), and of (F) and (H), only (F) returns the value 1.

7.   At take-off, the plane is already 750 feet above sea level. Climbing at 1,000 feet per minute, it will attain an additional altitude of $1,000m$ feet. So after m minutes, the plane has attained an altitude of $1,000m + 750$, (D).

Want to avoid all that? Then Plug-and-Chug. Pick a numerical value for m. Say $m = 1$, which is to say 1 minute after take-off. At that point, the plane will be 1,000 feet higher than the airport, and since the airport is 750 feet above sea level, the plane will be a total of $1,000 + 750 = 1,750$ feet above sea level. Substitute 1 for m in the answer choices. The correct choice will return the value 1,750:

D. $A = 1,000m + 750 = 1,000(1) + 750 = 1,750$

8. Just Plug-and-Chug. Choose a value for *x*, say 4. What is the cost of a call lasting exactly 4 minutes? The cost of dialing is $0.15, and the cost of the connection time is 4($0.04) = $0.16. So the total cost is $0.15 + $0.16 = $0.31. Now substitute 4 for *x* into the answer choices. The correct answer will return the value $0.31:

F. $y = 4(0.04 + 0.15) = 0.76$
G. $y = 0.04(4) + 0.15 = 0.31$
H. $y = 0.04 + 0.15(4) = 0.64$
J. $y = 0.15 - 0.04(4) = -0.01$
K. $y = 0.04 - 0.15(4) = -0.56$

9. Solve this problem by assuming some numerical values for *a* and *b*. You may have to try a couple of different values, but the method is very reliable. For example, try $a = -1$ and $b = -1$:

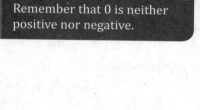

CLOSER LOOK

Remember that 0 is neither positive nor negative.

A. $|-a| + b = |-(-1)| + (-1) = 0$ (Not positive, so wrong)
B. $a + |b| = -1 + |(-1)| = 0$ (Not positive, so wrong)
C. $-|a| + |b| = -|-1| + |-1| = 0$ (Not positive, so wrong)
D. $-|a| - |b| = -|-1| - |-1| = -2$ (Not positive, so wrong)
E. Correct by the process of elimination:
   $|-a| + |-b| = |-(-1)| + |-(-1)| = 2$ (Positive in this case, so check)

10. You can most certainly use the procedures for manipulating the equation to solve for *x*. But there is another alternative: Test-the-Test. One of those five choices is the value of *x*, so just plug the choices into the question and do the arithmetic until you find the correct one.

F. $2\left(-\dfrac{5}{2}\right) - 3 = 7\left(-\dfrac{5}{2}\right) - 5$

$-5 - 3 = -\dfrac{35}{2} - 5$

$-8 = -\dfrac{45}{2}$ (Wrong)

The first plug-in returns a false statement, so (F) is wrong. If you do the arithmetic for (G) and (H), you'll find that those choices also return false statements and must be wrong. Then you would try (J):

J. $2\left(\dfrac{2}{5}\right) - 3 = 7\left(\dfrac{2}{5}\right) - 5$

$\dfrac{4}{5} - 3 = \dfrac{14}{5} - 5$

$-\dfrac{11}{5} = -\dfrac{11}{5}$ (Correct)

Since the value for *x* given in (J) returns a true statement, (J) is the right answer.

11. Just Test-the-Test:

A. $32^2 - 16 = 0$ (Wrong)
B. $16^2 - 16 = 0$ (Wrong)
C. $8^2 - 16 = 0$ (Wrong)
D. $4^2 - 16 = 0$ (Correct)

So (D) is the correct answer.

12. One way of approaching this item is to create an equation to model the situation:

$$150 + 0.5m = 140 + 0.75m$$

But you can also Test-the-Test. What is the situation at the end of two months (choice F)?

Chelsea: $150 + 0.5(2) = 151$
Travis: $140 + 0.75(2) = 141.5$

The two would not be the same height, so (F) is wrong. What would be the situation at the end of 20 months, (G)?

Chelsea: $150 + 0.5(20) = 160$
Travis: $140 + 0.75(20) = 155$

Again the two are not equal, so (G) is wrong. What would be the situation at the end of 40 months, (H)?

Chelsea: $150 + 0.5(40) = 170$
Travis: $140 + 0.75(40) = 170$

Bingo. They will be the same height after about 40 months, (H).

POWER PRACTICE 2

DIRECTIONS: Solve each problem and circle your answer. Answers are on p. 309.

1. If $\dfrac{x}{x+3} = \dfrac{3}{4}$, and $x \neq -3$, then $x = ?$

   A. 3
   B. 4
   C. 5
   D. 7
   E. 9

2. Y years ago, Paul was twice as old as Bob. If Bob is now 18 years old, how old is Paul today in terms of Y?

   F. $36 + Y$
   G. $18 + Y$
   H. $18 - Y$
   J. $36 - Y$
   K. $36 - 2Y$

3. A merchant increased the original price of an item by 10%. If she then reduces the new price by 10%, the final price, in terms of the original price, is equal to which of the following?

   A. a decrease of 11%
   B. a decrease of 1%
   C. no net change
   D. an increase of 1%
   E. an increase of 11%

4. If $\dfrac{12}{x+1} - 1 = 2$, and $x \neq -1$, then $x = ?$

   F. 1
   G. 2
   H. 3
   J. 11
   K. 12

5. Which of the following is the factorization of $6x^2 + 4x - 2$?

   A. $(6x+1)(x-3)$
   B. $2(x+2)(3x-2)$
   C. $2(3x-1)(x-1)$
   D. $2(x+1)(3x-1)$
   E. $3(2x+1)(x-1)$

GEOMETRY

STRATEGY ALERT

A picture is worth a point. The test directions say that the figures are not necessarily drawn to scale. But in practice, they are drawn to scale whenever possible. This means that you can often solve a geometry problem using the picture that comes with it.

You probably know a lot of geometry formulas such as:

$$\text{Perimeter}_{\text{triangle}} = s_1 + s_2 + s_3$$
$$\text{Area}_{\text{circle}} = \pi r^2$$

And these may be useful for solving problems on the test.

But what if you don't quite remember how to use the formula? Or can't remember at all? We have some super strategies to use to get points just from the pictures.

GUESSTIMATING

Sometimes it is possible to arrive at a correct answer simply by making a rough approximation, or "guesstimating." For example, if the angles below weren't labeled, could you determine their approximate degree measure just by eyeballing?

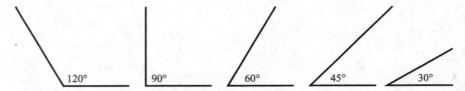

If you can visualize these angles successfully, you can accurately approximate almost any angle on the test (except in those special cases where figures are not drawn to scale).

Examples:

1. If the measure of an angle is 42.5°, what is the measure of its supplement? (Shown below)

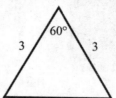

A.   17.5°
B.   47.5°
C.   67.5°
D.   137.5°
E.   Cannot be determined from the information given

Explanations for the example questions are included later in the chapter. Circle your answers now. Later when you reach the explanations at the end of the section, come back and check to make sure you answered the questions correctly.

2. What is the perimeter of the triangle shown below?

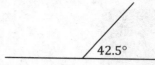

F. $3\sqrt{2}$
G.   6
H.   7.5
J.   9
K.   15

YOU CAN MEASURE

"Guesstimating" is a useful technique, but often it will not be enough to accurately determine the correct answer. In these situations, measure. While you aren't allowed to bring a protractor or a ruler to the test, you will have something that does both jobs: the answer sheet.

The answer sheet has four right angles—one at each corner. If you have trouble visualizing angles, the answer sheet will help; you can use any corner of the answer sheet to measure angles. This will immediately reveal whether an angle is larger than, smaller than, or exactly 90°.

Example:

3. In the figure below, *x* = ?

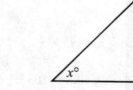

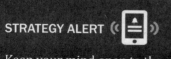

STRATEGY ALERT

Keep your mind open to the possibilities for measurement shortcuts.

A.   30
B.   45
C.   60
D.   75
E.   90

4. The chord in the figure below is 16 units long and 6 units from the center of circle O. What is the radius of circle O?

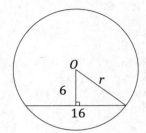

REVIEW

In a right triangle, the square of the longest side (the hypotenuse) is equal to the sum of the squares of the other two sides (the legs):

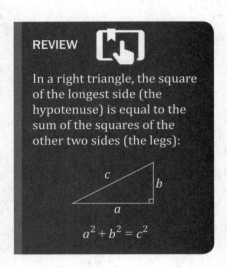

$$a^2 + b^2 = c^2$$

F.   5
G.   10
H.   12
J.   14
K. 10π

Here's a problem that looks very difficult but becomes easy when you measure.

Example:

5. The figure below shows the structural elements of a barn. What is the distance, in feet, from the floor of the barn to the peak of the roof?

REVIEW

45°-45°-90° triangles are right isosceles triangles with a hypotenuse equal to the length of either side multiplied by $\sqrt{2}$.

In a 30°-60°-90° triangle, the leg opposite the 30° angle equals the hypotenuse length multiplied by $\frac{1}{2}$; the leg opposite the 60° angle equals the hypotenuse length multiplied by $\frac{\sqrt{3}}{2}$.

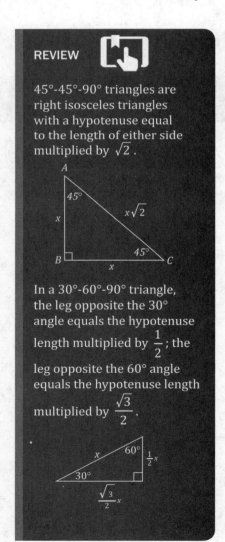

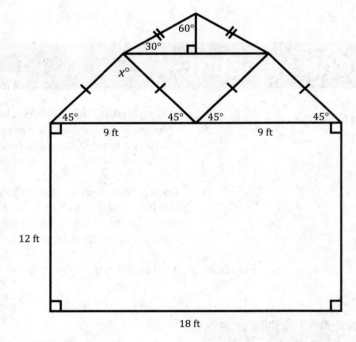

A.   6.75
B.   12
C.   18.75
D. $18 + \dfrac{3\sqrt{3}}{2}$
E. $12 + 9\sqrt{2} + \dfrac{3\sqrt{3}}{2}$

MEASTIMATING

"Meastimating" is a combination of "guesstimating" and measuring. The idea is to approximate measurements based on the information that is provided in the figure.

Example: **6.** In the figure below, what is the area of square *ABCD*?

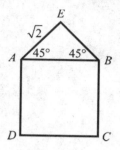

F. 2
G. $2\sqrt{2}$
H. 4
J. $4\sqrt{2}$
K. 8

MATCH THE GRAPH TO THE EQUATION

Two or three math problems will probably involve graphs, and the test-writers tend to ask you to match the information given in a graph to an equation.

Example: **7.** Which of the following is the equation for the line shown in the coordinate (*x,y*) plane below?

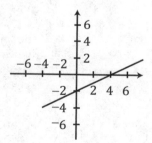

STRATEGY ALERT

If you plug in the point (0,–2), you will return two true statements. When this happens, pick another point and test it for just those two answer choices.

A. $y = \dfrac{x}{2} + 4$

B. $y = \dfrac{x}{2} - 2$

C. $y = x + 1$

D. $y = 2x + 2$

E. $y = 2x - 2$

Answers

Return to the pages below to review each item:
1. p. 113
2. p. 113
3. p. 113
4. p. 114
5. p. 114
6. p. 115
7. p. 115

1. You should be able to answer this item with just a quick glance. The "big" angle is the supplement to the angle which measures 42.5°. And the "big" angle is certainly greater than 90°, probably greater than 120°. So only (D) is a possible answer.

2. The angles opposite equal sides of a triangle are also equal. This is possible for the given triangle only if each of the three angles equals 60°. Therefore, the triangle is an equilateral triangle and each side is 3 units long. The perimeter of the triangle is: $3 + 3 + 3 = 9$, (J).

   If you aren't able to make this deduction to determine the unknown length, assume the drawing is approximately accurate: all three sides seem to be equal in length, so the perimeter must be approximately $3 \cdot 3 = 9$.

3. If you cannot see that the answer is (B), place the corner of a piece of paper next to the angle in question and fold back the corner:

   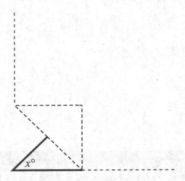

   The angle seems to be about half of the right angle formed by the page, so $x = 45$.

   To be sure, the answer sheet does not have marked inches or centimeters, but then again, you won't need them. Relative measurements—based on lengths provided in the figure accompanying an item stem—will be enough to draw basic conclusions regarding lengths.

4. The "official" way to solve this problem is to use the Pythagorean theorem. The vertical line from the center of the circle, O, and perpendicular to the chord of length 16 bisects the chord. So you have a right triangle with sides of 6, 8, and r. You can use the Pythagorean theorem to find r:

   $$r^2 = 6^2 + 8^2$$
   $$r = \sqrt{100}$$
   $$r = 10$$

   So what do you do if that insight escapes you? Measure r. No, you don't have a ruler, but you do have an answer sheet. And your answer sheet can be used as a straight-edge. Using very light tics, mark off the length of r on your answer sheet. Compare it to the length of the chord: r is a bit more than half the chord and so a bit more than 8, roughly 10, choice (B).

If you still aren't sure of your answer, measure the chord (16) and take away the segment from the chord to O (6) so that you are left with 10. Now measure r: 10.

5. You can solve this problem by using the special properties of 45°-45°-90° and 30°-60°-90° triangles. Or you can just measure. There's no line to measure, but you're supposed to find the distance from the peak of the roof to the floor, so just use your answer sheet as a straight edge. Mark the distance from the peak to the floor. Then convert that distance to a number by comparing the marked distance with known quantities on the drawing. You can see that the distance from the roof to the floor is very similar to the length of the barn, 18 feet, so (C) must be correct.

6. Mark off the length of $\overline{AE}$ on a piece of paper—this length is $\sqrt{2} \approx 1.4$. Compare this length of $\overline{AE}$ to one side of the square—the side is about 1.5 times as long as $\overline{AE}$, or 2 units. Thus, the area of the square is approximately $2^2 = 4$, so (H) appears correct. Double-check the answer choices on both sides of (H). (G) is approximately 2.8; (J) is approximately 5.6. Therefore, (H) is correct.

7. The "official" math approach to this problem is to use the information given in the graph to derive the equation for the line:

$$\text{Slope} = m = \frac{\text{rise}}{\text{run}} = \frac{0-(-2)}{4-0} = \frac{2}{4} = \frac{1}{2}$$

The equation of a line can be written as $y = mx + b$, so plug in the given values:

$$-2 = b$$

Therefore, $y = \dfrac{x}{2} - 2$, (B).

If you can remember this procedure, great! But if you're a little fuzzy on the details, just remember that one of those five answer choices IS the equation for the line. Pick a pair of (x,y) points from the graph and substitute those values into the answer choices. For example, we can see from the diagram that $(4,0)$ is a point on the line. We can substitute $x = 4$ and $y = 0$ into each answer choice:

A. $0 = \dfrac{4}{2} + 4 \Rightarrow 0 = 6$ (Wrong)

B. $0 = \dfrac{4}{2} - 2 \Rightarrow 0 = 0$ (Correct)

C. $0 = 4 + 1 \Rightarrow 0 = 5$ (Wrong)

D. $0 = 2(4) + 2 \Rightarrow 0 = 10$ (Wrong)

E. $0 = 2(4) - 2 \Rightarrow 0 = 6$ (Wrong)

POWER PRACTICE 3

DIRECTIONS: Solve each problem and circle your answer. Answers are on p. 309.

1. In the figure below, x = ?

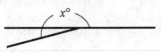

A. 120
B. 150
C. 180
D. 210
E. 240

2. What is the degree measure of the smaller of the two angles formed by the line and the ray shown in the figure below?

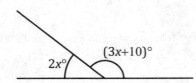

F. 25°
G. 30°
H. 48°
J. 68°
K. 142°

3. In the figure below, what is the length of $\overline{AC}$?

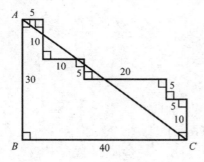

A. $30\sqrt{2}$
B. 50
C. 75
D. $60\sqrt{2}$
E. 100

4. In the triangle below, the measure of $\angle BAC$ is 30° and the length of $\overline{AB}$ is 2. Which of the following best approximates the length of $\overline{AC}$?

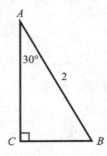

F. $\dfrac{\sqrt{3}}{2}$
G. 1
H. $\sqrt{3}$
J. $\dfrac{3\sqrt{3}}{2}$
K. $2\sqrt{3}$

5. The figure below is the graph of which of the following equations?

A. $x + 2y = 6$
B. $2x + y = 6$
C. $x + \dfrac{y}{2} = 6$
D. $\dfrac{x}{2} + y = 2$
E. $x - 3y = 2$

POWER PRACTICE 4

DIRECTIONS: Solve each problem and circle your answer. Answers are on p. 309.

1. A map is hanging on the wall of your classroom. You measure the distance between New York City and Los Angeles as $9\frac{1}{2}$ inches. The map's legend says "1 inch = 250 kilometers." What is the approximate distance between the two cities in kilometers?

   A. 2,375
   B. 2,600
   C. 3,450
   D. 3,800
   E. 6,000

2. Most motor gasoline is a blend of ethanol and gasoline. The blends are categorized as "E" for "ethanol" followed immediately by a two-digit number indicating the percentage of the blend that is ethanol. For example, E85 designates an ethanol-gasoline blend that is 85% ethanol and 15% gasoline. If 12 gallons of an ethanol-gasoline blend contain 3 gallons of ethanol, the blend should be categorized as:

   F. E3
   G. E10
   H. E15
   J. E25
   K. E85

3. For all pairs of real numbers M and N such that $M = 4N - 2$, $N =$

   A. $\dfrac{M}{2}$

   B. $\dfrac{M+2}{4}$

   C. $4(M+2)$

   D. $\dfrac{M}{4}+2$

   E. $8M$

4. Which of the following describes all of the values of x that satisfy the inequality $x + 2 > x + 6$?

   F. Zero only
   G. All positive numbers only
   H. All non-negative numbers only
   J. All negative numbers only
   K. There are no values of x that satisfy the inequality.

5. If $f(x) = x^2 + 3$, then $f(x+y) =$

   A. $\left(x^2 + y^2\right) + 3$

   B. $3\left(x^2 + y^2\right)$

   C. $x^2 + 2xy + y^2 + 3$

   D. $x^2 + y^2 + 9$

   E. $(x+y+3)^2$

6. Milk is sold by dairy farmers to dairy packing plants by the hundred weight, or 100 pounds of milk, abbreviated cwt, for $18 per cwt. The average dairy cow produces 6 gallons of milk daily, and a gallon of milk weighs approximately 8.6 pounds. If a farmer is milking 90 cows, approximately how much money, in dollars, can the farmer expect to receive for 3 days of milk production?

   F. $40
   G. $280
   H. $800
   J. $1,600
   K. $2,500

7. Flight 110 has just begun its approach to land at Metropolitan Airport from the south and is descending at the rate of 1,000 feet per minute from a cruising altitude of 30,000 feet. Flight 220 has just taken off to the north from Metropolitan Airport and is climbing to its cruising altitude of 31,000 feet at the rate of 1,500 feet per minute. After how many minutes will the two planes pass through the same altitude?

   A. 6 minutes
   B. 12 minutes
   C. 20 minutes
   D. 24 minutes
   E. 40 minutes

8. The figure below represents a sequence of numbers in which the difference between each larger number and the number immediately preceding it is always the same. Which of the following pairs of numbers represents the second and third elements of the sequence, respectively?

   78, ----, ----, 114

   F. 79, 80
   G. 83, 88
   H. 84, 90
   J. 90, 102
   K. 112, 113

9. Given circles O and P, circle P is tangent to circle O at point R. The diameter of circle P is 6. What is the area of the shaded region in the figure?

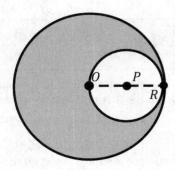

   A. 6
   B. 36
   C. 6π
   D. 27π
   E. 36π

10. In the figure below, the sine of angle C is equal to $\frac{3}{5}$. What is the approximate length of AB?

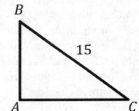

   F. 5
   G. 6
   H. 9
   J. 12.5
   K. 25

CHAPTER 6
Try It Out! Math Practice

DIRECTIONS: Solve each item and choose the correct answer choice. Use any available space for scratch work. Calculator use is permitted; however, some items are best solved without the use of a calculator. Answers are on p. 309.

Notes: All of the following should be assumed, unless otherwise stated.

1. Illustrative figures are NOT necessarily drawn to scale.
2. The word *average* indicates arithmetic mean.
3. The word line indicates a straight line.
4. Geometric figures lie in a plane.

1. A normal dozen contains 12 items, and a baker's dozen contains 13 items. If x is the number of items that could be measured either in a positive whole number of normal dozens or in a positive whole number of baker's dozens, what is the minimum value of x?

   A. 1
   B. 12
   C. 13
   D. 25
   E. 156

2. Starting from points that are 20 kilometers apart, two cyclists travel toward each other on a straight stretch of highway. If one cyclist travels at 14 kilometers per hour and the other travels at 16 kilometers per hour, how much time, in hours, will elapse before the cyclists meet?

   F. $\frac{1}{3}$

   G. $\frac{1}{2}$

   H. $\frac{2}{3}$

   J. $\frac{3}{4}$

   K. 1

3. A student begins heating a certain substance with a temperature of 50°C over a Bunsen burner. If the temperature of the substance will rise at a constant rate of 20°C for every 24 minutes it remains over the burner, what will be the temperature of the substance, in degrees Celsius, after 18 minutes?

   A. 52
   B. 56
   C. 60
   D. 65
   E. 72

Team Expenses

Transportation	$240	■
Lodging	$360	▨
Meals	$120	☐

4. Which of the following pie charts represents the data shown above?

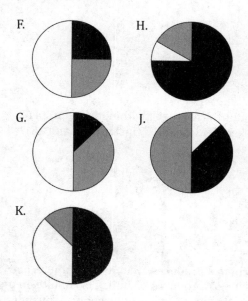

F.

H.

G.

J.

K.

5. At a recreation center, it costs $3 per hour to rent a ping pong table and $12 per hour to rent a bowling lane. At the same cost as renting a bowling lane for 2 hours, for how many hours is it possible to rent a ping pong table?

A. 4
B. 6
C. 8
D. 18
E. 36

6. The average weight of three boxes is $25\frac{1}{3}$ pounds. If each box weighs at least 24 pounds, what is the greatest possible weight, in pounds, of any one of the boxes?

F. 25
G. 26
H. 27
J. 28
K. 29

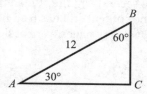

7. In the figure above, what is the length of $\overline{BC}$? $\left(\sin 30° = \frac{1}{2}\right)$

A. 2
B. $2\sqrt{3}$
C. 3
D. $3\sqrt{3}$
E. 6

8. If $x^2 + 3x - 18 = 0$ and $2m = x$, which of the following could be a value of m?

F. −3
G. 1
H. 3
J. 6
K. 9

9. Which of the following is the complete solution set for $|2x + 4| = 12$?

   A. $\{-8,4\}$
   B. $\{-4,8\}$
   C. $\{0,8\}$
   D. $\{4,8\}$
   E. $\{6,8\}$

10. On the first day after being given an assignment, a student read $\frac{1}{2}$ the number of pages assigned, and on the second day, the student read 3 more pages. If the student still has 6 additional pages to read, how many pages were assigned?

    F. 15
    G. 18
    H. 24
    J. 30
    K. 36

11. If $x = 6 + y$ and $4x = 3 - 2y$, what is the value of x?

    A. 4
    B. $\frac{11}{3}$
    C. $\frac{5}{2}$
    D. $-\frac{2}{3}$
    E. $-\frac{7}{2}$

12. What is the perimeter of the rectangle below?

    F. $10a - 6$
    G. $10a - 3$
    H. $6a - 3$
    J. $5a - 6$
    K. $5a - 3$

13. If n subtracted from $\frac{13}{2}$ is equal to n divided by $\frac{2}{13}$, what is the value of n?

    A. $\frac{2}{3}$
    B. $\frac{13}{15}$
    C. 1
    D. $\frac{13}{11}$
    E. 26

14. What is the average (arithmetic mean) of all integers 6 through 15 (including 6 and 15)?

    F. 6
    G. 9
    H. 10.5
    J. 11
    K. 21

15. Machine X produces 15 units per minute, and Machine Y produces 12 units per minute. In one hour, Machine X will produce how many more units than Machine Y?

    A. 90
    B. 180
    C. 240
    D. 270
    E. 360

16. If the ratio of apples to oranges in a fruit salad made of only those two fruits is 8 to 7, what fraction of the salad is oranges?

F. $\dfrac{1}{56}$

G. $\dfrac{1}{15}$

H. $\dfrac{1}{7}$

J. $\dfrac{7}{15}$

K. $\dfrac{8}{7}$

17. If $2a = 3b = 4c$, then what is the average (arithmetic mean) of a, b, and c, in terms of a?

A. $\dfrac{13a}{18}$

B. $\dfrac{4a}{3}$

C. $\dfrac{13a}{9}$

D. $2a$

E. $\dfrac{8a}{3}$

18. Maggie has to inventory her employer's collection of books. There are three categories of books. Historical novels account for one-fourth of the books. Classics comprise $\dfrac{1}{6}$ of the remaining books and there are 30 travel books. How many books does she have to inventory?

F. 30
G. 36
H. 48
J. 64
K. 96

19. In the figure below, what is the slope of line *l*?

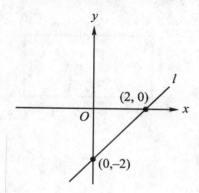

A. 1

B. $\dfrac{1}{2}$

C. 0

D. $-\dfrac{1}{2}$

E. -1

20. If Yuriko is now twice as old as Lisa was 10 years ago, how old is Lisa today if Yuriko is now *n* years old?

F. $\dfrac{n}{2} + 10$

G. $\dfrac{n}{2} - 10$

H. $n - 10$

J. $2n + 10$

K. $2n - 10$

21. If the rectangle below has an area of 72, then
$x = ?$

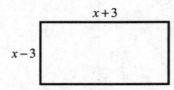

A.   3
B.   4
C.   6
D.   8
E.   9

22. If $\dfrac{x}{x+3} = \dfrac{3}{4}$, and $x \neq -3$, then $x = ?$

F.   3
G.   4
H.   5
J.   7
K.   9

23. If $12 + x = 36 - y$, then $x + y = ?$

A.   −48
B.   −24
C.   3
D.   24
E.   48

24. A jar contains 5 blue marbles, 25 green marbles, and x red marbles. If the probability of drawing a red marble at random from the jar is $\dfrac{1}{4}$, what is the value of x?

F.   25
G.   20
H.   15
J.   12
K.   10

	Old Scale	New Scale
Minimum Score	0	120
Minimum Passing Score	60	?
Maximum Score	100	180

25. The table above shows a teacher how to convert scores for a test from the Old Scale to the New Scale. If both the Old Scale and the New Scale are linear, what is the Minimum Passing Score on the New Scale?

A.   124
B.   136
C.   156
D.   164
E.   208

26. If each of the dimensions of a rectangle is increased by 100%, by what percent is the area increased?

F.   100%
G.   200%
H.   300%
J.   400%
K.   500%

27. In the figure below, what is the length of $\overline{AC}$?

$$\left(\sin \angle ABD = \frac{\sqrt{7}}{4}\right)$$

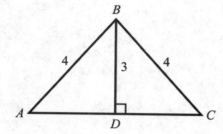

A. 5
B. $2\sqrt{7}$
C. $4\sqrt{3}$
D. 7
E. 10

28. Tommy has blue, green, and red marbles. The number of blue marbles and green marbles combined total 25. The number of blue and red marbles combined total 30. There are twice as many red marbles as green marbles. How many green marbles does Tommy have?

F. 5
G. 10
H. 15
J. 20
K. 25

29. If the average (arithmetic mean) of a, b, and c is z, which of the following is the average of a, b, c and d?

A. $\dfrac{z + d}{3}$

B. $\dfrac{z + d}{4}$

C. $\dfrac{3z + d}{3}$

D. $\dfrac{3z + d}{4}$

E. $\dfrac{3(z + d)}{4}$

30. If $x - y = 7$ and $x^2 - y^2 = 35$, what is $x + y$?

F. 5
G. 7
H. 10
J. 28
K. 42

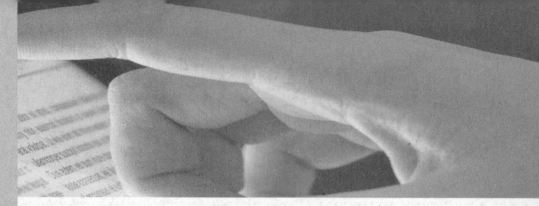

CHAPTER 7

Fast Track to Reading Mechanics

DEMYSTIFYING THE READING TEST

TEST SPECS

- 35 minutes long
- 40 multiple-choice questions
- Four sections (three single passages with 10 questions each and a pair of passages with 10 questions)
- Passages range from 700–800 words

At first glance, the Reading test looks simple: just read some passages and answer some questions about them. In fact, you're probably thinking, "No problem! That's what we do in school all the time." However, the Reading test is completely unlike school.

First of all, the Reading test is open book. You can look at the passages as many times as you want while you're answering the questions, which should make you suspicious. After all, if you had an open-book test in history in school, you wouldn't be worried about taking the test and you'd probably get a pretty good score.

You're right to be suspicious. The Reading test has developed a well-deserved reputation for being difficult. There are two main reasons why:

Reason #1. The passages can discuss just about anything. Also, they exhibit the difficulty level and kind of material you would encounter as a first-year college student. As a result, there's no way to prepare for specific topics, and you'll be reading some reasonably difficult material.

Reason #2. Even though you get a two- or three-line introduction, you often feel like you're plunging headfirst into the middle of a lecture on an unfamiliar topic.

However, don't let these features of the test intimidate you. If you start to think you can't do it, you won't be able to. Just remember two things:

1. The ACT writers intentionally make the Reading test extra difficult. You're supposed to have trouble with it.

2. Everyone else is in the same boat. Anyone who tells you that they breezed through the Reading test is either exaggerating or just didn't show up for the test.

Now, are you ready to learn more about the Reading test? Then let's go.

ANATOMY OF READING

At its most basic, the Reading test consists of directions, a brief introduction to each passage, the passage itself, and a set of multiple-choice questions. Let's take a look at each part of the test.

INSIDE THE READING DIRECTIONS

DIRECTIONS: Each passage or pair of passages below is followed by a set of items. Read the passage or pair of passages and choose the best answer for each item. You may refer to the passages as often as necessary to answer the items.

Notice that the directions instruct you to choose your answer based on what is stated or implied in a passage. Outside knowledge isn't tested; everything you need to answer the questions is in the passage.

So you've read the directions, which are pretty basic (read this and answer the items). Now, you can ignore them. Don't waste time reading them on test day.

INSIDE THE READING PASSAGES

Read the sample passage below, looking for differences between this passage and other readings you might do. Note that this passage is shorter than the passages you will see on test day; the passages you encounter then will be 700–800 words long.

Example: **Items #1–4 are based on the following passage.**

Social Science: This passage is adapted from a government publication about the history of alcohol abuse.

ACCELEPREP APPROACH

We recommend reading the short introduction that precedes every passage because 1) it should only take a few seconds to read and 2) it gives you a glimpse of what the passage is about before you even begin reading.

The movement to prohibit alcohol began in the early years of the nineteenth century with the formation of local societies in New York and Massachusetts to promote temperance in the consumption of alcohol. Many of the temperance societies were affiliated with Protestant evangelical denominations and met in local churches. As time passed, most temperance societies modified their goal to call for complete abstinence from all alcoholic beverages.

In 1919, largely in response to the lobbying efforts of the Anti-Saloon League, the Eighteenth Amendment to the Constitution was passed

5

CLOSER LOOK

This passage is about a topic you may have studied in school. However, even if you've written a paper about Prohibition, that doesn't mean the questions will be easy. The test writers ask about the main idea and details of this particular passage, not about Prohibition in general.

10 banning the production, transportation, and sale of all alcoholic beverages. The Amendment, also known as the Prohibition Amendment, provided for concurrent enforcement by both federal and state law. By January 1920, in addition to the federal Volstead Act, which was enacted to carry out the Eighteenth Amendment, the nation had laws in thirty-three states 15 prohibiting alcohol entirely.

Prohibition, however, proved unworkable as bootleggers and speakeasies quickly organized to satisfy the public's continuing thirst for alcohol. Thirteen years later, the "Noble Experiment," doomed by the impracticality of enforcement, ended with the repeal of the Prohibition 20 Amendment.

You may have noticed a few key features of the passage. First, the passage includes an introductory sentence telling you about the source of the passage. These notes can provide a helpful orientation to the passage topic, so make sure to read them.

Second, think about how the passage is organized. Every passage is a little different, and noticing the structure of the passage will help you find the answers to the questions. In this case, the passage is organized chronologically; it begins with the origins of the Prohibition movement, then discusses the Eighteenth Amendment, and ends by explaining the failure of the movement.

INSIDE THE READING QUESTIONS

Next, let's look at the questions that go along with this passage. Answer the questions below.

Examples:

1. The passage is primarily concerned with the:

    A. social problems caused by alcohol abuse.
    B. founding of anti-alcohol temperance societies.
    C. origins of Prohibition and its subsequent failure.
    D. efforts to enforce Prohibition legislation.

2. According to the passage, in the early nineteenth century, temperance societies originally:

    F. encouraged moderation in alcohol use.
    G. demanded the repeal of the Eighteenth Amendment.
    H. supported efforts to enforce the Volstead Act.
    J. refused to align with religious groups.

3. In line 12, the word "concurrent" means:

    A. unsuccessful.
    B. shared.
    C. practicable.
    D. intermittent.

4. The passage implies that Prohibition failed because:

    F. religious organizations withdrew their support for the program.
    G. the repeal of the Eighteenth Amendment was only experimental.
    H. too many states passed laws prohibiting the sale of alcohol.
    J. widespread demand for alcohol made enforcement impossible.

Answers

1. The first question is a common type of Reading item: the item asks you to identify the main idea of the passage. The passage discusses the origins and failure of Prohibition, and the answer is (C).

2. The second question asks about something that is specifically stated in the passage. The author clearly states that the temperance societies were originally founded to "promote temperance" rather than promote the complete prohibition of alcohol, so (F) is correct.

3. The third question asks you for the definition of a term in the context of the passage. The passage states that the federal government and the states were given "concurrent" authority and that the states, as well as the federal government, passed laws against alcohol. So, "concurrent" must mean something like "joint" or "shared," (B).

4. This item requires that you read between the lines of the passage. In the third paragraph, the author does not specifically say why Prohibition failed, but you can figure it out from what's said: people simply refused to quit consuming alcohol, even if it was illegal, (J).

POWER TIP

Use line numbers to refer back to the exact line and surrounding lines and find context clues. Do not fall into the trap of relying solely on cited lines though; understanding the larger context of the passage can point you to a word's meaning when the specific line may not. For example, this passage discusses legislation regarding a nationwide issue: alcohol consumption. We could gather from this passage that mass legislation was required to enforce Prohibition and that it probably would have involved more than one authority (i.e., been a shared responsibility).

c

PACING

PACING TIP

Should you speed read? No, and here's why.

First, the Reading test rewards comprehension, not raw speed. You need to focus on understanding the passage content, development, and organization.

Second, it's possible to move quickly without speed reading. Just stay on task as you read, and don't get bogged down answering a single question. If you don't know the answer, guess and move on.

We've noticed that as soon as students learn that a test is timed, they immediately ask two questions: "How much time do I have?" and "How fast should I go?" When it comes to the Reading test, the answer to the first question is easy enough: 35 minutes. And the answer to the second question is, "Well, that depends. Go as fast as you can—while still answering questions correctly."

Now you're probably thinking that this isn't very helpful advice at all. You want some solid, concrete numbers to work with so that you can make sure you're on track while you're taking the test. Well, there are four passages (one of which is a pair of passages) with 10 questions each, so you should spend eight minutes and 45 seconds on each passage—about two-and-a-half minutes reading the passage and the rest of the time answering the items. We've even put together a little table:

TASK	ALLOTTED TIME	REMAINING TIME
Read the first selected passage	2.5 minutes	32.5 minutes
Answer the accompanying items	6.25 minutes*	26.25 minutes
Read the second selected passage	2.5 minutes	23.75 minutes
Answer the accompanying items	6.25 minutes*	17.5 minutes
Read the third selected passage	2.5 minutes	15 minutes
Answer the accompanying items	6.25 minutes*	8.75 minutes
Read the fourth selected passage	2.5 minutes	6.25 minutes
Answer the accompanying items	6.25 minutes*	0 minutes

Approximately 38 seconds per item

You should remember that these pacing guidelines are just that—guidelines. No one's going to be standing over you with a stopwatch and yelling at you if you spend a little more time on one or two items or finish reading a passage faster than expected. The guidelines are flexible in that regard. However, the guidelines also show that you absolutely must not get bogged down on any one particular item. That could kill your score. You should be willing to abandon an item when it's taking too much time to answer, making an educated guess if you can. Bottom line: you should work quickly but accurately and not obsess about time.

POWER PRACTICE 1

Now it's time for some fun. To help you get a feel for just how fast time goes when you're taking the Reading test, we've put together a time trial—just a little passage and a couple of items for you to take under timed conditions. Try answering the three questions below with a 5-minute time limit.

> **DIRECTIONS:** The passage below is followed by a set of items. Choose the best answer to each question based on what is stated or implied in the passage. Give yourself 5 minutes to complete this exercise.

Items #1–3 are based on the following passage.

Natural Science: This passage is an excerpt from an essay about the possible reasons for the extinction of salmon runs in New England rivers.

Folklore holds that Atlantic salmon were once so abundant in New England rivers that early colonists walked across the backs of the fish as they ran up the rivers in spring. Then, according to
5 the received wisdom, at the turn of the nineteenth century, increasing pollution in the rivers and the construction of large dams across rivers caused salmon to become severely depleted. If this theory were accurate, then there should be ample
10 archaeological evidence that salmon played a major role in the diets of the aboriginal peoples of New England. But in site after site, although bones of many other fish species have been recovered, no salmon bones have been found. It's more likely that
15 the accounts of salmon were embellished by early writers.

In fact, salmon did not begin to colonize in New England streams until a period of climatic cooling known as the Little Ice Age (C.E. 1550–1800). At
20 the end of this period, the climatic warming created less favorable environmental conditions for salmon. Thus, their range retracted. The idea that initial colonization did not occur until this time, and then only as a temporary range expansion, explains the
25 lack of salmon in prehistoric sites and the depletion of the fish at the end of the eighteenth century.

While authorities such as D. W. Lufkin have stated that "the circumstances leading to the demise of *Salmo salar* are relatively simple to identify" and
30 have cited dams, pollution, logging practices, and overfishing, causes behind its demise are more complex, with ecological and climatological bases. If pollution and dams were the major cause of

the extinctions, then why were the runs not made
35 extinct on the Penobscot, a heavily dammed and polluted river in Maine? Why did salmon runs become extinct downstream of the dams on the Connecticut River? The general lack of success in salmon restoration programs over the last two
40 centuries suggests a fundamental ecological cause for impoverished salmon runs in New England rather than an anthropogenic one.

1. The primary purpose of the passage is to:

   A. propose a long-term plan for restoring salmon runs to the rivers of New England.
   B. undermine the theory that human activity caused the extinction of salmon runs in New England rivers.
   C. demonstrate that anthropogenic factors are often more powerful than natural ones in shaping the environment.
   D. provide evidence that the disappearance of *Salmo salar* was caused by the damming and pollution of the rivers.

2. The author cites the lack of salmon bones in archaeological digs as evidence that:

   F. the salmon population in New England rivers declined sharply after the end of the Little Ice Age.
   G. aboriginal Americans, who consumed other fish species, refused to eat the abundant salmon.
   H. salmon were not available to aboriginal Americans before the arrival of the first colonists.
   J. anthropogenic factors were largely responsible for the extinction of the salmon runs.

STRATEGY ALERT

You can write in your test booklet, so mark up the passage and cross out wrong answers as you go.

3. It can be inferred that D. W. Lufkin would most likely:

A.   agree with the author that the primary causes of the depletion of salmon stocks are climatological.

B.   accept the author's contention that early reports about the abundance of salmon were greatly exaggerated.

C.   reject the author's thesis and insist that the causes of salmon extinction are anthropogenic.

D.   disagree with the author that salmon stocks have declined precipitously since the end of the eighteenth century.

PACING TIP

- Read the passage quickly but carefully. Give yourself between two and three minutes to read a single passage or pair of passages.

- Read the passage for important themes such as the main point, the purpose of individual paragraphs, or the author's intention.

- Don't memorize details. Instead, try to remember the most important points and where things are located so you can refer back to the passage if necessary.

ANSWERS

1.   (B) *Reading/Key Ideas and Details/Main Idea*

This item asks about the main idea of the passage. The burden of the argument is that it was not pollution or dams that caused the salmon to disappear but a change in climate. The author further states that the change in climate over 300 years first allowed the salmon to move into the New England rivers and then caused the retraction of their range. From this, the author concludes that "big" causes, such as climate change, may better account for some phenomena than would anthropogenic, or human-related, causes. (A) is wrong because the author apparently believes that the salmon are permanently gone because they can't survive where it is too warm. (C) and (D) are wrong because they are the opposite of the thesis developed by the author.

2.   (H) *Reading/Integration of Knowledge and Ideas/Development*

This item asks about the use of evidence in the passage, that is, the structure or development of the argument. The author notes that salmon bones are not found among the fish bones at sites where aboriginal Americans lived. Apparently, they did not eat salmon. Why not? The author says it was because there were no salmon in the rivers for them to catch and eat,

as (H) states. (F) is a point made by the author, but it is not the explanation offered for the lack of salmon bones in archaeological digs. (G) appears to be a good choice until it says that the aboriginals wouldn't eat the salmon—this conclusion is not offered in the passage. Finally, (J) is wrong because the author insists that it was not human-related factors that caused the collapse of the salmon stocks.

3.   (C) *Reading/Key Ideas and Details/Implied Idea*

This item asks for an idea that is implied, rather than stated, in the passage. Lufkin is an authority who offered the thesis that dams and pollution caused the collapse of the salmon stocks. Thus, we can infer that Lufkin believes the causes to be anthropogenic, as (C) states. (A) and (B) are wrong because Lufkin and the author differ on this key point. Finally, (D) is wrong, not because Lufkin would deny that the stocks collapsed, but because Lufkin insists that the cause was human related.

THE CAMBRIDGE GAME PLAN

Okay, so you've learned the basics of the Reading test. Now you're ready to develop a game plan to use as you continue on your Reading journey. Remember, however, that these are suggestions, not hard-and-fast rules. If you don't want to use some of them, that's fine. Pick what works for you and discard the rest.

BEGIN IN PREVIEW MODE

When you go to the theater to watch a movie, you'll inevitably see a number of previews for upcoming movies. Each preview tells you the genre of the movie, who the actors are, and some of the movie's key moments. The preview prepares you to watch the movie. In the same way, previewing a passage on the test prepares you for what you will read in the passage.

PREVIEW THE INTRODUCTORY NOTES

Passages will include an introductory note telling you where the passage comes from and maybe some other information. Sometimes, this information is useful for getting a better understanding of the passage. Therefore, before starting on a passage and items, always read any introductory notes.

PREVIEW THE KEY SENTENCES

Before you begin reading a passage, you should take fifteen to thirty seconds to preview the key sentences.

Why are key sentences so important? Well, they're likely to express the most important ideas of the passage and to key you in to the passage's development. First sentences are often topic sentences, so reading a series of topic sentences will tell you what the author is trying to say.

Here are the key sentences from our Social Science passage:

Examples:
The movement to prohibit alcohol began in the early years of the nineteenth century with the formation of local societies in New York and Massachusetts to promote temperance in the consumption of alcohol.

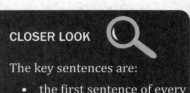

CLOSER LOOK

The key sentences are:

- the first sentence of every paragraph

- the last sentence of the last paragraph

In 1919, largely in response to the lobbying efforts of the Anti-Saloon League, the Eighteenth Amendment to the Constitution was passed to ban the production, transportation, and sale of all alcoholic beverages.

Prohibition, however, proved unworkable as bootleggers and speakeasies quickly organized to satisfy the public's continuing thirst for alcohol.

The first sentence tells you that the topic will be about various attempts to prohibit alcohol, starting with the temperance movement. The second tells you about the next historical phase; it begins in 1919 and results in passage of the Eighteenth Amendment. The final sentence tells you the whole idea was a bust. So the three sentences, even when isolated from the details of the passage, tell the bigger story.

PREVIEW THE ITEM STEMS

Additionally, before reading a particular passage, you may find it helpful to preview the item stems. If an item stem mentions a key word or phrase, make a mental note and look for it as you read the selection.

Here are the item stems from our Social Science passage:

Examples:

The passage is primarily concerned with the:

According to the passage, in the early nineteenth century, temperance societies originally:

In line 12, the word "concurrent" means:

The passage implies that Prohibition failed because:

The first item stem could be applied to any passage at all, so you don't need to make any mental notes about it. The second stem mentions temperance societies, so make a mental note to watch for any information about those societies and mark any such references as you read. The third stem mentions a specific line, so circle that word in the passage. Finally, the fourth stem asks about the reason Prohibition failed, but it says the passage implies this reason (rather than stating it directly). So watch for any references to the failure of Prohibition as you read. You may need to come back to this question.

POWER PRACTICE 2

To show just how well these reading techniques work, this exercise doesn't have a passage, just some key sentences. Preview the key sentences and then go to the questions. You may actually be able to answer one or two questions, or at least come close. On the others, try to think about what you would have to do to find the answer.

DIRECTIONS: The passage below is followed by a set of items. Choose the best answer to each question based on what is stated or implied in the passage.

Items #1–4 are based on the following passage.

Natural Science: This is an excerpt from a government report on the significant health risks of oral use of smokeless tobacco.

Tobacco use in the United States has gone through many stages.

* * *

The changing social acceptance of the manufactured cigarette, together with the use of
15 milder, blended tobaccos, beginning around 1913, allowed tobacco users to absorb nicotine more quickly and efficiently through inhalation than via absorption through the oral mucosa.

* * *

The 1920s and 1930s saw a major increase
30 in the number of male smokers, with the 1940s and 1950s characterized as the beginning of this country's lung cancer epidemic.

* * *

Social norms have played a major role in the history of tobacco use.

* * *

45 Paradoxically, it was the heightened awareness of smoking hazards in the 1970s and early 1980s that prompted some people, looking for a safe alternative to cigarettes, to begin using a product that the industry labeled "smokeless" tobacco....
50 Millions of consumers succumbed to this faulty logic, and the use of spitting tobacco (chewing tobacco and snuff) spread rapidly.

1. The author's primary concern is to:

   A. outline the history of the use of smokeless tobacco in the United States.
   B. detail the health hazards posed by excessive use of smokeless tobacco.
   C. enumerate the social norms that have played an important role in tobacco use.
   D. announce that the government may further curtail the use of tobacco products.

2. According to the passage, the Native Americans who knew of tobacco before the arrival of the Europeans:

   F. preferred spitting tobacco to smoking tobacco.
   G. relied on tobacco as a trading commodity.
   H. used tobacco only in religious ceremonies.
   J. smoked tobacco in pipes on a routine basis.

3. In line 18, "oral mucosa" means:

   A. instrument for smoking.
   B. tissues in the mouth.
   C. smokeless tobacco.
   D. mouth cancer.

4. Based on information provided in the passage, which of the following is most probably the year in which sales of smoking tobacco exceeded the sales of spitting tobacco?

   F. 1913
   G. 1919
   H. 1929
   J. 1934

ANSWERS

1. **(A)** And you can probably get this just from the key sentences.

2. **(H)** But you would need the rest of the information in paragraph one.

3. **(B)** You might or might not be able to get this without the rest of the passage.

4. **(H)** You would definitely need the rest of paragraph three.

PRACTICE BIG PICTURE READING

After doing a preview, you should read the passage. However, you're not going to be reading the passage like you would read any old text for school. When you study for an exam in school, you are reading for content. You underline, outline, and take notes to help you remember the important points you're likely to be tested on. These are good study habits for school but will kill you on the ACT test. On the ACT test, read the provided passages for the big picture, in the same way you would read a map. Read for organization and reference, not for details.

Remember that this is an open-book test. You don't have to memorize the details. If you need to find any information, you can just locate it in the text. Additionally, focusing on organization can help you discover the main point or theme of the passage, as well as how the paragraphs develop that theme as a whole.

ANSWER THE ITEMS

You've previewed. You've read the passage. Now it's on to the items.

LOOK FOR THE BEST OF THE REST

When you take a test in school, you're graded on your ability to recall facts. So you get test questions such as:

What is the title of Herman Melville's novel about Captain Ahab's search for a killer white whale?

There's only one right answer for this question. (It's *Moby-Dick*, in case you wanted to know.) But the directions for the Reading test don't talk about right and wrong answers. The directions say, "Choose the *best* answer." So the question above, written ACT-test style, would be something like:

Example:

Q Which of the following is the best title for the novel you have just read?

    A.   A History of the Whaling Industry
    B.   A Madman's Pursuit of a Killer White Whale
    C.   A Typical Day on Captain Ahab's Boat
    D.   Ishmael's Holiday Cruise

A The "best" answer is (B). Of course, (B) is not the real title of the book, so the "best" answer is wrong. It's best not because it is correct, but because it's better than any of the other answers.

ANSWER THE RIGHT QUESTION

When you read "answer the right question," you probably said, "Duh!" But you'd be surprised how many times students don't answer the question that's being asked. Sometimes students read the item carelessly and answer the "wrong" question—what they think they read rather than what is actually on the page. Wrong ACT test answers typically include a lot of words that sound like the passage, but when you read carefully, you realize that the meaning of the answer choice is not the same as the meaning presented in the passage. So read carefully, and make sure you answer the right question.

Let's look at #2 of the Social Science passage as an example.

Example:

Q According to the passage, in the early nineteenth century, temperance societies originally:

    F.   encouraged moderation in alcohol use.
    G.   demanded the repeal of the Eighteenth Amendment.
    H.   supported efforts to enforce the Volstead Act.
    J.   refused to align with religious groups.

A With only a quick read, all of the answer choices sound at least plausible. There are key words in each that are mentioned in the passage: "alcohol use," "Eighteenth Amendment," "Volstead Act," and "religious groups." Of course, that's what you'd expect, right? The test writers wouldn't give you wrong answer choices that talked about the history of the modern piano; that would make your job entirely too easy.

If all the answer choices sound plausible, you need to make sure you read the item itself carefully. If you only do a quick read of the item, you might completely skip the part about "in the early nineteenth century." And if you miss that, you may start to think that (H) is a good answer choice—after all, it makes sense that temperance societies would support efforts to enforce a law that prohibits alcohol. But the time reference is key to getting the right answer for this item. As mentioned in the first paragraph, in the nineteenth century, temperance societies wanted temperance (or moderation) in alcohol use, which makes (F) the correct answer.

WATCH OUT FOR THOUGHT-REVERSERS

Another type of item that can throw you off is the type that uses thought-reversers, or words such as "not," "cannot," and "except." These words turn the question inside out. What would be a right answer to an ordinary item would be a wrong answer to a negative item and vice versa. Typically, thought-reversers are capitalized, but it always pays to read the items carefully so that you answer the question that's being asked.

To give you an idea of what to look for, here are some examples of thought-reverser items:

Examples:

Q According to the passage, Hamilton hoped to exploit all of the following features of the political situation EXCEPT:

Q Which of the following claims is NOT supported by the graph?

Q All of the following are true of the comparison drawn in the third paragraph of Passage 2 EXCEPT:

LOOK OUT FOR FAULTY SYNONYMS

This part of the Game Plan relates specifically to Vocabulary items. Vocabulary items typically fall into one of two categories: those that test unfamiliar words and those that test familiar words with multiple meanings. For both types, you need to use context clues to figure out the correct meaning, but for the second type (familiar words, multiple meanings), the ACT test-writers usually throw a devious twist in: they'll include a contextually incorrect common meaning of the word just to throw you off.

Example:

Q The new film was a <u>pale</u> copy of the expertly crafted and highly acclaimed original.

The word "pale" most nearly means:

A. early.
B. white.
C. weak.
D. fixed.

A "Pale" could mean white, (B), or weak, (C). In this context, a film would be a weak copy, not a white copy, so (B) is a faulty synonym.

POWER PRACTICE 3

DIRECTIONS: The provided passage is followed by a set of items. Choose the best answer to each question based on what is stated or implied in the passage.

Items 1–10 are based on the following passage.

Natural Science: This passage is an excerpt from an article describing the four types of mass wasting.

Soil, sand, and rock remain in place on a slope so long as the frictional forces keeping the material in place are greater than gravitational forces. When the gravitational force acting on a slope exceeds its
5 resisting force, a geomorphic process called mass wasting occurs. Different types of mass wasting are distinguished according to the time elapsed—from years to just seconds—and include creep, flows, falls, and slides. Mass wasting occurs on both terrestrial
10 and submarine slopes and has even been observed on other planets, including Mars and Venus.

Creep is a long-term process and happens when small, downslope movements of soil and rock occur in many directions. The steeper the slope,
15 the faster the creep; but, in general, soil creep is not observable to the naked eye. A landslide, on the other hand, is the rapid, often sudden, downslope movement of a large mass of earth and rocks. A mudslide is the most rapid (up to 80 kilometers
20 per hour) and fluid type of downhill mass wasting. Mudslides are caused by unusually heavy rain or a sudden thaw. They consist mainly of mud, water, and fragments of rock and other debris, which cause them to behave like a flood.

25 The world's largest historic landslide occurred during the 1980 eruption of Mount St. Helens, a volcano in the Cascade Mountain Range in the State of Washington. Spirit Lake was directly in the path of the mass of moving material. Today, the bottom of
30 Spirit Lake is 100 feet above its original surface and the lake has two and a half times more surface area than it did before the eruption. During the eruption, the water temperature was raised instantly from about 5°C to nearly 38°C.

35 The world's largest prehistoric landslide discovered to date took place in southwestern Iran and had a volume of about 20 cubic kilometers,

a depth of 300 meters, a travel distance of 14 kilometers, and a width of 5 kilometers. This means
40 that about 50 billion tons of rock moved in this single event.

The largest prehistoric underwater slide was an enormous submarine landslide 60,000 years ago that produced the longest flow of sand and mud
45 yet documented on Earth. The massive submarine flow traveled 1,500 kilometers—the distance from London to Rome—before depositing its load.

Although these cataclysmic events caused extensive geomorphic changes, there was very
50 little damage in human terms. However, every year, events of less magnitude account for more than 6,000 deaths worldwide, killing more people than typhoons, hurricanes, and cyclones combined.

The largest recent event in terms of lives lost
55 was the Zhouqu landslide in China on August 8, 2010, which killed 1,765 people. Other very large events were the Morro do Bumba landslide in Niterói, Brazil, which resulted in 196 deaths; the debris flows in Leh, India, which caused 234 deaths;
60 and the landslide in Wasior, Indonesia, which killed 145 people. In the United States, landslides and debris flows result in 25 to 50 deaths each year.

Landslides have grown worse in recent years because of agriculture and development. The areas
65 most likely to experience landslides or mudslides are those where wildfires or human modification of the land (such as the construction of buildings and roads) have destroyed vegetation and channels along streams and rivers.

1. The author's primary purpose is to:

   A. describe the causes and effects of landslides.
   B. report the number of lives lost annually to landslides.
   C. recommend ways to minimize the chance of a landslide.
   D. advocate changes in human behavior that affect vegetation.

2. According to the passage, the greatest loss of life due to a landslide occurred in:

F. Leh, India.
G. Niterói, Brazil.
H. Wasior, Indonesia.
J. Zhouqu, China.

3. It can be inferred that creep is not visible to the naked eye because it:

A. occurs deep in the ocean.
B. takes place very slowly.
C. is seen only on other planets.
D. is triggered suddenly.

4. The author mentions that the distance from London to Rome is 1,500 kilometers in order to:

F. give the reader some appreciation for the distance covered by the underwater landslide.
G. explain how a large landslide could take place beneath the surface of the ocean.
H. prove that landslides can be costly in terms of the loss of human lives.
J. explain why neither Rome nor London has experienced a massive landslide in recent history.

CLOSER LOOK

Reading passages are drawn from a variety of sources. Some are current, like this passage, and some were published more than 100 years ago. The older the passage, the more students often struggle to understand the passage and answer the questions. If you have trouble with older passages, consider saving those for last. Also, remember that other test-takers are likely struggling too.

5. According to the passage, mass wasting begins when:

A. gravitational forces exceed the frictional forces holding a slope in place.
B. the resisting force of the slope is greater than the downward gravitational pull.
C. moving earth material encounters an obstacle that changes the direction of movement.
D. subsurface water flows into a lake, raising the water level significantly.

6. It can be inferred from the context in which the word is used that "cataclysmic" (line 48) means:

F. ancient.
G. predictable.
H. catastrophic.
J. lethal.

7. Which fact mentioned in paragraph three is NOT used by the author to illustrate the magnitude of the Mount St. Helens' landslide?

A. The water temperature in Spirit Lake rose sharply.
B. Mount St. Helens is located in the Cascade Mountain Range.
C. A nearby lake was filled in, raising the surface level significantly.
D. The landslide changed the shape of a lake to make it over twice as large.

8. In context, the word "submarine" (line 10) is used by the author to mean:

F. undetectable.
G. underwater.
H. directionless.
J. buoyant.

9. It can be inferred that landslides would be most likely to occur in regions:

A. remote from human habitation such as forest preserves.
B. protected by law from significant development.
C. where agriculture has resulted in the removal of vegetation.
D. in close proximity to large bodies of water such as lakes or oceans.

10. In paragraph seven, the author's primary goal is to:

F. warn about the consequences of uncontrolled land development.
G. prove that landslides can occur anywhere, including on other planets.
H. list areas of the world where landslides are likely to occur in the future.
J. illustrate the danger that landslides pose to human populations.

ANSWERS

1. **(A)** *Reading/Key Ideas and Details/Main Idea*

You might first ask yourself which of the first words of each answer choice are not descriptive of the author's approach. In this way, you can eliminate (C) and (D). Then examine (A) and (B) more carefully. The author does report the number of lives lost annually in line 52, but this is a detail, not the main point. The main purpose is to describe both causes and effects of landslides.

2. **(J)** *Reading/Key Ideas and Details/Explicit Detail*

This item requires a comparison of the loss of the figures provided by the author in the seventh paragraph.

3. **(B)** *Reading/Integration of Knowledge and Ideas/Implied Idea*

The passage states that creep is a long-term process, so it can be inferred that the process is very slow and not really noticeable.

4. **(F)** *Reading/Key Ideas and Details/Development*

This is a development or "how details are used" question. The question is not: "How far is it from London to Rome" or "Which cities does the author mention?" Instead, the question asks why the author includes the note. And the answer is that it dramatizes the magnitude of the surface landslide—all the way from London to Rome, 1,500 kilometers.

5. **(A)** *Reading/Key Ideas and Details/Explicit Detail*

The answer to this item is found in lines 3–6.

6. **(H)** *Reading/Craft and Structure/Vocabulary*

The "cataclysmic" events are enormous, "catastrophic" landslides.

7. **(B) *Reading/Key Ideas and Details/Development***

    First, you should notice that the stem includes a thought-reverser, the NOT. Some students will miss this question because they overlook this point. Then, note that three of the details illustrate the magnitude of the changes caused by the eruption and consequent landslide. (B), the location of Mount St. Helens, is a fact that is mentioned, but this point is not used by the author to dramatize the magnitude of the landslide.

8. **(G) *Reading/Craft and Structure/Vocabulary***

    In lines 9–10, the author says mass wasting occurs on "terrestrial and submarine slopes." If you know "terrestrial" means "land," you might reason that "submarine" means "underwater," (G). Or you could reason that the slopes the author is describing must be physical places, since the author states that wasting has also been observed on other planets. And the only answer that describes a physical place is (G).

9. **(C) *Reading/Key Ideas and Details/Implied Idea***

    The author explains in the last paragraph that landslides are more likely to occur in areas where humans have altered conditions, such as by removing vegetation.

10. **(J) *Reading/Key Ideas and Details/Main Idea***

    This is a main idea question that asks about a particular paragraph. In the seventh paragraph, the author lists significant landslide events along with the death toll from each. (H) may seem correct, but the author is only reporting where landslides *have* occurred, not saying where they are "likely to occur in the future."

CHAPTER 8
HyperPrep Reading

PACING TIP

If you're feeling especially motivated, grab a timer and see if you can preview and read the passages in two-and-a-half minutes.

In the previous chapter, you learned the basics about the Reading test. Now it's time to break down the test by learning about each of the ACT item-types.

Before we begin, take a couple of minutes to read through the following paired passages. We'll be using them to learn about the seven item-types.

Ready . . . go!

DIRECTIONS: Each passage or pair of passages is followed by a set of items. Read the passage or pair of passages and choose the best answer for each item. You may refer to the passage(s) as often as necessary to answer the items.

Natural Science: These passages are excerpted from articles discussing research on Colony Collapse Disorder in honeybee populations.

Passage A

Honey bees are essential crop pollinators, and are responsible for more than $15 billion in increased crop value each year. Recently, honey bees have been under serious pressure from
5 a mystery problem: Colony Collapse Disorder (CCD). Beekeepers have reported losses of 30 to 90 percent of their hives. While colony losses are not unexpected, especially over the winter, this magnitude of loss is unusually high. The main
10 features of CCD are very low numbers of adult bees in the hive, a live queen, honey still in the hive, and the presence of immature bees.

According to a study from Harvard's School of Public Health, the probable cause of
15 CCD is pesticides, specifically two widely used neonicotinoids: imidacloprid and clothianidin. The research was conducted by Dr. Chengsheng Lu, associate professor of environmental exposure biology at Harvard, and the results were published
20 in the *Bulletin of Insectology.*

Dr. Lu studied 18 bee colonies in three locations. Researchers separated the six colonies at each location into three groups—one treated with imidacloprid, one with clothianidin, and one
25 untreated. The result was that in 6 of the 12 colonies that were treated with neonicotinoids, bees died at elevated rates and fled the hives, exhibiting symptoms of Colony Collapse Disorder.

There was a steady decline in the size of all
30 of the colonies during the beginning of winter, a decline that is typical among hives during the colder months in New England. Beginning in January, bee populations in the control colonies began to increase as expected, but populations in the neonicotinoid-
35 treated hives continued to decline. By April, 6 out of 12 of the neonicotinoid-treated colonies were lost, with abandoned hives that are typical of CCD. Only

one of the control colonies was lost, apparently to an infestation of *Nosema ceranae*, a common intestinal
40 parasite.

Exposure to imidacloprid and clothianidin affected the winterization of healthy colonies and subsequently led to CCD. This observation suggests that the impairment of honey bee neurological
45 functions—specifically memory, cognition, or behavior—is the result of chronic sub-lethal neonicotinoid exposure.

Passage B

Honey bees, which are a critical link in US agriculture, have been under serious pressure from
50 a mystery problem: Colony Collapse Disorder (CCD). Following the collapse of the colony, a live queen remains with honey in the hive and immature bees are still present, but no adult bees are left, only dead bee bodies. CCD is only one of several major dangers
55 threatening honey bees, but the syndrome captured the imaginations of certain elements of the press following the announcement that a connection had been made between CCD and pesticides. *The Boston Globe, The New Yorker, Motherjones, The Guardian,*
60 *Salon* and others ran stories citing the research conducted by Dr. Chensheng Lu under the auspices of the Harvard School of Public Health, in which neonicotinoids are blamed for CCD. As one writer put it, neonicotinoids were the "smoking gun" that
65 killed the bees.

A more careful examination of Lu's research shows that there was a rush to judgment. In the first place, Dr. Lu himself is not an expert on insects—much less bees—and many reputable
70 journals in the United States declined to publish his findings. The paper was finally printed in an obscure Italian journal called the *Bulletin of Insectology,* a publication of little importance. There are many more expert researchers who have reached far more
75 conservative conclusions who might have been cited, but the press was excited by the dramatic story line that evil manufacturers were killing innocent bees with nasty chemicals for their own profits, and a thin scientific veneer that dressed up the simplistic story
80 line made it perfect for public consumption.
One of the central problems with Lu's conclusion—and much of the reporting—is that despite the colony problems, the global bee population has remained remarkably stable since the widespread
85 adoption of neonicotinoids in the late 1990s. The United Nations reports that the number of hives has actually risen over the past 15 years to more than 80 million colonies, a record, as neonicotinoids usage has soared.

90 Then, a closer examination of Lu's methodology shows striking flaws in the experimental setup. Bees are ordinarily fed a supplemental diet of high fructose corn syrup, and Lu spiked their diet with either imidacloprid or clothianidin in hopes of
95 mimicking field conditions. In reality, Lu fed his bees concentrations of chemicals that were 135 parts per billion compared with concentrations found in ordinary applications of 1 to 3 parts per billion. Given the strength of this toxic cocktail, it
100 is a wonder that Lu's bees survived as long as they did. What Lu proved was only something we have known all along: you can kill bees using a sufficiently powerful poison.

KEY IDEAS AND DETAILS

TEST SPECS

One of the Reading assignments in each test will be a pair of passages. The pair together is roughly the same length as a single passage.

Key Ideas and Details includes four question types: Main Idea, Explicit Detail, Implied Idea, and Application. These questions focus on the content of the passage. Main Idea questions will ask you about the theme of a passage, while Explicit Detail and Implied Idea questions will ask about specific points that are explicitly stated or can be inferred. Application questions will challenge you to apply information to new situations. Let's go through each type in more detail.

MAIN IDEA

Main Idea items ask about central themes—what unifies the passage(s). They're usually pretty easy to identify, too, asking questions such as:

- The primary purpose of the passage is to:
- The author is primarily concerned with:
- This passage is mainly about the relationship between:

The questions may also ask about the main idea of a particular section or paragraph of the passage.

POWER TIP

We call this the Goldilocks Principle: the correct answer is neither too big nor too little, but just right.

The best answer for a Main Idea item will be one that fully summarizes the main points in the passage or section of the passage in question. "Fully" is an important word to remember here. The ACT test writers will try to trick you by giving you answer choices that mention parts of the main idea but will be either too narrow (they don't mention all of the main points) or too broad (they refer to things that aren't mentioned in the passage).

Examples:

Explanations for the example questions are included later in the chapter. Circle your answers now. Later when you reach the explanations at the end of the section, come back and check to make sure you answered the questions correctly.

1. The primary purpose of Passage A is to:

   A. convince readers that scientific research proves the need to limit the use of neonicotinoids as pesticides.
   B. present evidence that honey bees are economically important to the agricultural sector of the economy.
   C. report on an experiment that seems to establish that neonicotinoids cause honey bee Colony Collapse Disorder.
   D. praise Dr. Lu for research that discovered the "smoking gun" that has caused the death of honey bee colonies.

2. Paragraph 4 of Passage A primarily describes the:

   F. scientific methodology of Dr. Lu's experiment.
   G. results of Dr. Lu's scientific experiment.
   H. political implications of Dr. Lu's experiment.
   J. importance of using the scientific method.

3. The main point of the final paragraph of Passage B is that:

   A. several publications incorrectly reported Dr. Lu's findings.
   B. Dr. Lu's experimental setup was fatally flawed.
   C. CCD can be triggered by small dosages of neonicotinoids.
   D. field conditions are very difficult to simulate in a laboratory setting.

POWER TIP

Why should you learn all the item types you will see on test day? Once you recognize each type of item, you can use strategies specific to each type to power through the Reading test.

EXPLICIT DETAIL

STRATEGY ALERT

Take advantage of locator words and phrases to help track down the answer. These include:

- "In line(s) x..."
- "In paragraph x..."
- "In passage x..."
- "In the beginning..."
- "At the end..."

Explicit Detail items ask you to locate details that are mentioned clearly and specifically in the passage. They often provide helpful locator words (such as particular phrases or ideas actually mentioned in the passage) to help you find the necessary information. Some examples of Explicit Detail items include:

- The author mentions which of the following?
- According to paragraph . . . ?
- In the last paragraph, the author writes that:

It's important to remember that the correct answer will be one that is specifically stated in the passage. The only exception to this is if the Explicit Detail item has a thought-reverser (such as "NOT"), in which case the correct answer will be the only one NOT specifically stated in the passage. Thought-reversers turn the question inside out. Either way, you'll be looking for details clearly mentioned in the passage.

Example:

4. According to Passage A, a decrease in the number of bees in colonies during the start of winter cold is:

   F. proof that neonicotinoids are harmful.
   G. typical of the life cycle of the hive.
   H. a sign that disease agents are present.
   J. unusual except in regions of New England.

POWER TIP

Thought-reversers turn the question inside out. The best way to proceed if you are stuck on a thought-reverser question is by finding and eliminating answer choices that ARE mentioned in the passage.

IMPLIED IDEA

Now it starts to get tricky. Both of the previous two item-types were fairly straightforward: identify main ideas and find some details. Implied Idea items are a little more complicated. For these items, you have to figure out what can be logically inferred from details in the passage.

Let's say a passage states that a certain organism (X) is only found in the presence of another organism (Y). An Implied Idea item might ask: "If organism Y isn't present, what can be inferred?" Since the passage explicitly states that X is to be found only in the presence of Y, we can infer that the correct answer is "X is not present."

Some examples of Implied Idea question stems are:

- The passage implies that:
- The author uses the phrase " . . . " to mean:
- It can be inferred from the passage that:
- Which of the following can be inferred from the passage?

Unlike Explicit Detail items, the answer to an Implied Idea item will NOT be explicitly stated. Instead, it will be strongly suggested or implied by the passage and will be consistent with all of the other details of the passage, but you will have to use your critical thinking skills to logically answer the question.

Example: **5.** In lines 66–80, the author of Passage B implies that:

   A. scientists in the field of public health generally have a reputation for producing questionable research.
   B. the reputation of a professional scientific journal is a measure of the quality of research it chooses to publish.
   C. scientific research conducted in Italy is not as good as that done by the scientific community in the United States.
   D. conservative researchers are more likely to be published in scientific journals than researchers who take a controversial position.

APPLICATION

POWER TIP

Application items really test your comprehension of the main idea of the passage or a particular part of the passage. It's a good idea to reread the section in question, quickly, to enhance/refresh your understanding and then try to answer the question.

If Implied Idea items were tricky, Application items go one step further. Instead of simply inferring ideas from details in the passage, now you have to take what you've learned from the passage and apply it to a new situation. For example, a passage might ask you:

- With which of the following statements would the author most likely agree?
- The author would probably consider which of the following a good example of his or her theory?
- The passage is most likely taken from which of the following sources?

For Application items, you have to be able to identify and understand the author's point of view or opinions expressed in the passage. Having a good handle on the author's point of view will help you find the best answer to an Application item.

Example:

6. Given the definition of CCD provided in the first paragraph of Passage A, Dr. Lu's findings, as reported in paragraphs three and four, show the hives exhibited:

F. all of the symptoms associated with CCD.
G. some but not all of the symptoms associated with CCD.
H. none of the symptoms associated with CCD.
J. all but one of the symptoms associated with CCD.

ACCELEPREP APPROACH

The answers to Implied Idea and Application questions are not explicitly mentioned in the passage, so these questions may appear to have more than one correct answer. Notice that the words "most likely," "probably," and "a good example" are nonrestrictive. One answer choice will be stronger than all the rest. Give yourself permission to choose it, ignore the runner-up, and move on.

Answers

Return to the pages below to review each item:
1. p. 150
2. p. 151
3. p. 151
4. p. 151
5. p. 152
6. p. 153

1. This is a Main Idea question that asks about the theme of Passage A. Passage A begins by defining CCD, and then the author cites the main conclusion of Lu's research followed by a description of the methodology used. The fourth paragraph provides the results of the experiment, and then in the last paragraph the author draws the conclusion explicitly that the neonicotinoids caused the CCD. (C) best describes this development. (A) goes beyond the scope of the passage. To be sure, the idea promoted by (A) is one that the author (or another writer) might go on to make using Passage A, but it does not describe Passage A as written. The same is true for (D). The author may admire Dr. Lu for his work and think that the research deserves recognition, but the author does not take on that burden in the passage as written. Finally, (B) is a minor point mentioned in the passage, not the main theme.

2. This is a Main Idea type question that asks about a specific part of the passage. Paragraph 4 of Passage A gives detail on what Dr. Lu's studies showed, so (G), the results of the experiment, is the correct answer.

3. This is a Main Idea question that asks about the final paragraph of Passage B. The opening sentence of the paragraph tells you the main point: the methodology was fatally flawed, (B).

4. This an Explicit Detail question asking about the specific information contained in paragraph four of Passage A. According to that part of Passage A, a decline in the bee population with the onset of cold winter is expected. Normally, the population would then increase, (G).

5. This is an Implied Idea question that asks what inference can be drawn from the author's remarks in lines 66–80. There the author is criticizing Lu's research and notes that several reputable journals declined to publish his findings. This indicates that the reputable journals function as arbiters of good and bad research, that is, the journals won't publish articles that are weak. (A) takes a swing at the pitch but misses. The author is targeting Lu, not researchers in public health in general. (C) misconstrues the author's point. The author considers the one journal, the *Bulletin of Insectology*, to be weak, not Italian scientific journals in general. And (D) is simply a misreading of that part of the passage that uses the word "conservative." The US journals refused to publish Lu's research, on the author's view, because they found its conclusions to be shaky, which leaves (B) as the correct answer.

6. The definition of CCD provided in the first paragraph includes: (1) few adult bees, (2) live queen, (3) honey, and (4) immature bees. The results of Dr. Lu's research, as reported by Passage A, showed few adult bees (the bees either had died or fled). That is only the first element of the definition of CCD. In other words, Dr. Lu's research, even taken at face value, does not show CCD as the cause of the problems of the hive studied, making (G) the best answer.

SUM IT UP - KEY IDEAS AND DETAILS

Information and Ideas items test your general understanding of the passage, your understanding of specific details or words in the passage, and your ability to evaluate the passage.

1. **Main Idea** items ask about the central theme that unifies the passage(s). The first sentence of a paragraph—often the topic sentence—may provide a summary of the content of that paragraph. Also, the last sentence of a paragraph usually provides concluding material that may also be helpful in understanding the general theme of the passage(s).

2. **Explicit Detail** items ask about details that are specifically mentioned in the passage. Explicit details are points provided by the author in developing the main idea of the passage. These questions often provide "locator words" that identify the required information in the passage so you know where to locate the information.

3. **Implied Idea** items don't ask about what is specifically stated in the passage, but about what can be logically inferred from what is stated in the passage. Since this type of item generally builds on a specific detail, "locator words" for identifying information in the passage are often provided in the item stem.

4. **Application** items are similar to Implied Idea items, but they go one step further: examinees must apply what they have learned from the passage to a new situation.

POWER PRACTICE 1

DIRECTIONS: The passage below is followed by a set of items. Read the passage and choose the best answer for each item. You may refer to the passage as often as necessary to answer the items. Answers are on p. 310.

Items #1–5 refer to the following passage.

Natural Science: This passage is excerpted from an article about lichens.

Lichens ("lie-kins") are life forms that can grow on surfaces in some of the most extreme environments on earth—from the frozen arctic tundra and scorching hot deserts, to rainforests and
5 steep cliff faces.

Lichens are a combination of two organisms living together in a relationship called "symbiosis." The two partners are algae, such as stoneworts, seaweed, or pond scum, and fungi, such as molds,
10 rusts, or mushrooms.

How these two elements form a lichen is one of the great puzzles in biology. But their partnership is a successful one, as there are as many as 30,000 lichen species worldwide. Many of these species
15 are quite beautiful and colorful, their appearance looking much like crystals under a microscope. Once joined together, an alga begins using sunlight to make sugars as food for both itself and its fungal partner. The fungus' job includes protecting them
20 both from intense sunlight and other stresses.

This partnership is a very efficient way to get nutrients—up to 20 percent of fungus species live in a lichen partnership. The algal or cyanobacterial cells are photosynthetic, and, as in plants, they
25 reduce atmospheric carbon dioxide into organic carbon sugars to feed both the fungus and the alga. Both partners gain water and mineral nutrients, mainly from the atmosphere, through rain and dust. The fungal partner protects the alga by retaining
30 water and serving as a larger capture area for mineral nutrients. This system has worked for thousands of years, as lichens have fine-tuned their feeding mechanisms.

Although lichens had been recognized as
35 organisms for quite some time, it was not until 1867, when Swiss botanist Simon Schwendener proposed

his dual theory of lichens that the true nature of the lichen association began to emerge. Schwendener's hypothesis, which at the time lacked experimental
40 evidence, arose from his extensive analysis of the anatomy and development in lichens, algae, and fungi using a light microscope. Many of the leading lichenologists at the time rejected Schwendener's hypothesis because the consensus was that all living
45 organisms lived independently. Other prominent biologists were not so quick to reject Schwendener's ideas and the concept soon spread into other areas of study. When the complex relationships between pathogenic microorganisms and their hosts were
50 finally identified, Schwendener's hypothesis began to gain popularity.

Lichens play an important role in our environment, and they are a valuable tool for scientific study. The chemicals produced by
55 lichens have been used to make all sorts of products, including dyes, cosmetic ingredients, and homeopathic medicines. Scientists also use lichens to gauge the effects of pollutants in air or water. Because lichens are vulnerable to environmental
60 disturbances, they are used to study the effects of air pollution, ozone depletion, and metal contamination. They help break down material that keeps soil healthy, and they provide food and shelter for all sorts of creatures—big and small.

1. The passage mentions all of the following as being functions of the fungal component of a lichen EXCEPT:

   A. protecting the lichen from stressful conditions.
   B. using sunlight to produce sugars to be used for food.
   C. retaining water for use by both organisms.
   D. providing a surface area for capturing mineral nutrients.

2. According to the passage, lichens are particularly useful in the scientific study of environmental issues because they are:

   F. sensitive to environmental changes.
   G. used in manufacturing various products.
   H. observable underneath a microscope.
   J. found in the most extreme conditions.

3. It can reasonably be inferred that the discovery of complex relationships between pathogenic microorganisms and their hosts:

   A. proved conclusively that lichens comprise mutually dependent organisms.
   B. undermined confidence in the theory that all organisms live independently.
   C. provided a counter-example to the claim that all lichens were two organisms.
   D. prompted scientists to ask whether or not lichens might have practical uses.

4. In the final paragraph, the author is primarily concerned with showing that lichens are:

   F. useful.
   G. algae and fungi.
   H. fragile.
   J. readily available.

5. The primary purpose of the passage is to:

   A. describe the important characteristics of lichens and the value they hold.
   B. credit Schwendener with the discovery of the dual nature of lichens.
   C. criticize contemporaries of Schwendener for their failure to give credit to his theory.
   D. show that lichens are important organisms that are threatened by change.

PASSAGE DEVELOPMENT

Explanations for the example questions are included later in the chapter. Circle your answers now. Later when you reach the explanations at the end of the section, come back and check to make sure you answered the questions correctly.

In this section, we will cover the three Passage Development question types: Development, Vocabulary, and Voice. These questions test your ability to understand the structure and tone of a passage. Development questions ask about the sequence of events or the organization of a passage. Vocabulary questions test your understanding of a word or phrase in context. Voice questions ask about the author's attitude and tone.

DEVELOPMENT

Development items ask about the sequence or structure of the passage. However, the test-writers don't simply ask "What comes next?" They're a little bit more devious than that. Although they may ask questions about the passage's or a part of the passage's overall structure, they can also ask about the relationship between one part of the passage and the whole passage or about details and the logical roles those details play. Some examples of Development question stems include

POWER TIP

While there's no way for you to actually know what the author intended, or why he or she made a specific decision, you can deduce what the best answer would be based on logic. The best question to ask yourself when dealing with these items is, what is the most reasonable reason?

- The author develops the passage primarily by:
- The author proceeds primarily by:
- The author mentions . . . in order to:
- Which of the following best explains why the author introduces . . . ?

One of the keys to answering Development items correctly is asking why— why did the author make a specific decision? Why did he or she choose to include a specific example at that specific point? Being able to give a good, logical answer to questions like these could put you well on your way to finding the correct answers to Development items.

Example:

ACCELEPREP APPROACH

These questions refer back to the passages on pages 148–149.

7. The author of Passage A mentions *Nosema ceranae* in order to:

A. explain the loss of the colony that was not treated with nicotinoids.
B. show that the losses due to CCD are greater than those normally expected.
C. refute the suggestion that CCD is caused by exposure to nicotinoids.
D. identify a fatal flaw in the design of Dr. Lu's experiment on the cause of CCD.

VOCABULARY

REVIEW

Remember the advice in Chapter 7 about looking out for faulty synonyms. Just because you recognize the word in question, don't assume the most common meaning of that word is the correct answer. The correct answer must be correct in context, and the test writers will include common definitions that could trip you up if you're not careful.

Vocabulary items test your understanding of a word or phrase in context. The wording of Vocabulary items is usually pretty easy to identify; an item will ask you something like:

- The word ------ in line ## means:
- In line ##, what is the best definition of the word ------?
- In context, the word ------ in line ## means:

There are two keys to answering Vocabulary items correctly. First, the correct answer will make perfect sense if it's substituted for the word for which you're trying to find the meaning. Second, if you remember your Reading Game Plan, you should be familiar with less commonly known meanings of certain words. For example, consider the word "politic." If you see this word on the test, you might assume the correct answer has something to do with government or politics. However, "politic" can also mean "prudent" ("Although I did not want to attend my friend's party, it was the politic thing to do"). You *have* to use context clues in order to figure out the correct answer.

Examples:

8. As it is used in line 78, "thin" most nearly means:

    F.   flimsy.
    G. narrow.
    H. emaciated.
    J.   slim.

9. As it is used in line 61, "auspices" means:

    A. influence.
    B. control.
    C. sponsorship.
    D. opinion.

10. In context, "sub-lethal" (line 46) means:

    F.   not sufficient to kill.
    G. ineffective amount.
    H. insignificant quantity.
    J.   extremely concentrated dosage.

VOICE

Voice items ask about the author's attitude toward a particular detail or about the overall tone of the passage. Some examples include:

- The tone of the passage can best be described as:
- The author regards . . . as:
- Which of the following best describes the author's attitude toward . . . ?

Once again, key words are usually big clues in determining the correct answer to a Voice item. There might be specific words or phrases that convey a negative versus a positive attitude or a casual versus a scholarly tone. When you finish reading the passage and are summarizing it in your own words, think of a couple of words that you might use to describe the tone, even if it's nothing more specific than, "That seemed positive," or "The author didn't seem to like that idea very much."

Example: **11.** The attitude of the author of Passage B toward the authors of the articles on CCD that appeared in the publications listed in lines 58–60 can best be described as one of:

   A. contempt.
   B. sympathy.
   C. indifference.
   D. compassion.

Answers

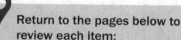

Return to the pages below to review each item:
  7. p. 157
  8. p. 158
  9. p. 158
  10. p. 158
  11. p. 159

7. This is a Development question. In reporting the results of Lu's experiment, the author has to acknowledge that there was one colony that died that was not treated with the pesticides. To avoid the implication that Lu made a mistake, the author needs to account for that seeming anomaly. And the explanation given is that some other agent killed that colony, (A).

8. "Thin" could have any of the meanings given, depending on the context. In this case, "thin" is used in the phrase "a thin scientific veneer." A "veneer" is a decorative covering, so (H) doesn't make sense in context. As for the other choices, the author says the veneer "dressed up the simplistic story line." If the thin scientific veneer is a dressing, it is better described as "flimsy" rather than "narrow" or "slim." Therefore, the correct answer is (F).

9. "Under the auspices of" means under the guidance or sponsorship of, (C). The phrase does not imply that the sponsor has direct control of the project but only that the sponsor has authorized the project be undertaken and is associated with its name. The sponsor may also provide funding for the project.

10. The context in which "sub-lethal" appears makes it clear that the word means "not deadly," (F). The passage, for example, specifically states that the dosage adversely affected various functions such as memory but did not kill the bees.

11. This is a Voice question that asks for a description of the author's attitude toward the publications mentioned. The passage contains several verbal clues to help you understand the author's position that the media coverage is not very scholarly, including the observation that Dr. Lu is not himself an expert, the note that the *Bulletin of Insectology* is not widely respected, the statement that there was a "rush to judgment," and the sarcastic phrase "smoking gun" in quotation marks, so (A) is the correct answer.

SUM IT UP - PASSAGE DEVELOPMENT

Passage Development items test your ability to understand the underlying structure and tone of the passage(s). Since this is an "open-book" test, returning to the selection is always an option. Therefore, if something is highly technical or difficult to understand, do not dwell on it for too long—come back later if necessary.

1. **Development** items ask about the overall structure of the passage or about the logical role played by a specific part of the passage.

2. **Vocabulary** items test your understanding of a word or phrase in context.

3. **Voice** items ask about the author's attitude toward a specific detail or the overall tone of the passage.

POWER PRACTICE 2

DIRECTIONS: The passage below is followed by a set of items. Read the passage and choose the best answer for each item. You may refer to the passage as often as necessary to answer the items. Answers are on p. 310.

Items #1–5 refer to the following passage.

Social Science: This passage is adapted from an essay on nutrition in the Republic of Senegal.

Ironically, despite being a major producer of cereal in the Republic of Senegal, Africa, the region of Seno Palel has extremely high rates of malnutrition. As many as 22 percent of the children
5 living in Seno Palel are underweight and nearly 18 percent suffer from stunted growth. Due to the harsh climate, there's not much to eat apart from staple grains. The few vitamin-rich fruits and vegetables that are cultivated locally are expensive and rarely
10 become a regular part of villagers' diets. With the help of scientists and aid workers, a group of local Senegalese women have developed a vitamin-enriched flour that meets the nutritional needs of children by blending regular corn flour with other
15 pulverized, vitamin-rich ingredients like black-eyed peas, peanuts, millet, jujube, and baobab. This flour can be found in larger urban areas, but not in rural areas where the high cost of transportation makes its regular use by villagers too expensive.

20   To help get this enriched flour to villagers, 225 women of Seno Palel have established an enterprise known as *Jab Gollade*, which means, "The Working

Women." Using enriched flours to combat moderate and chronic malnutrition is not a new phenomenon.
25 However, typically these flours have been provided by humanitarian agencies like the World Food Program. This is the first time that a local group has been responsible for distributing this life-saving flour.

30   Although the most popular flour is used to create porridge that is fed to infants and young children, adults are now modifying it for use in their own morning *lakh*, a local cereal made of yogurt, cereal flour, and sugar. Binta Diafara Daff, a local
35 mother, has been using the flour since December 2012, when she took her fifteen-month-old son, Dewel Boucoum, to the local clinic and found out that, at thirteen pounds, he was malnourished and at risk for long-term health problems. Daff began
40 feeding Dewel one hundred grams of the flour mix three times a day. Within three months, Dewel had gained more than five pounds, bringing him up to the normal weight for his age. "I don't have to take him to the hospital so often," Daff said. "He isn't sick
45 as much as he was, and that means I'm spending less than half of what I used to in doctor's fees."

      Dewel's case is part of a larger trend. The Senegalese Committee for the Struggle Against Malnutrition recently conducted surveys that
50 showed a significant drop in the number of cases of moderate and acute malnutrition in the villages around Seno Palel—from thirty cases in 2011 to ten in 2012.

"The example of Seno Palel points the way
55 forward for nutrition interventions because it is
an example of a social enterprise that generates
revenue for these women, but also provides a range
of health dividends for the entire community," said
project director Todd Crosby. "It is a sustainable
60 solution that at once improves the community's
health and increases its wealth, which ensures that
these beneficial products will be around for a long
time to come." The women of *Jab Gollade* are making
a significant difference in the lives of Senegalese
65 children by providing them with this nutritious
alternative to single grain cereal.

1. In the passage, the author mentions the
experience of Binta Diafara Daff in order to:

   A. demonstrate that it is economically feasible
   to make enriched flour.
   B. raise questions about the ability of *Jab
   Gollade* to provide a regular supply of
   enriched flour.
   C. prove that Dewel's case is an example of a
   trend in the Seno Palel region.
   D. show that the enriched flour mixture can
   solve malnutrition and improve health.

2. The passage uses the word "sustainable" (line
59) to mean that:

   F. the revenue produced by the sale of the
   flour will continue to support *Jab Gollade*.
   G. humanitarian organizations like the World
   Food Program will provide additional
   enriched flour.
   H. health benefits from the consumption of
   enriched flour last as long as the flour is
   eaten on a regular basis.
   J. agriculture in the region of Seno Palel does
   no extensive damage to the cultivated fields.

3. The author uses the word "ironically" (line 1) to
describe the contrast between:

   A. the health benefits of the enriched cereal
   with the cost of obtaining it.
   B. *Jab Gollade* as a business with its
   humanitarian mission of improving health.
   C. Seno Palel as a major cereal producer with
   high rates of malnutrition.
   D. the experience of one family with the
   general trends in the area's population.

4. It can be inferred that the population of Seno
Palel suffers high rates of malnutrition because:

   F. the cost of grain produced by Seno Palel
   farmers is beyond the means of most of the
   residents.
   G. a single-cereal diet is lacking in the vitamins
   required to ensure adequate nutrition.
   H. the climate of Seno Palel is too
   unpredictable to permit regular planting
   and harvesting.
   J. Seno Palel is a rural area that is not
   serviced by international humanitarian aid
   organizations.

5. The author is primarily concerned with
discussing:

   A. a philosophy of sustainability and how to
   implement it.
   B. the concept of self-sufficiency and a specific
   example.
   C. a historical event and changes it has caused.
   D. the cause of a problem and a possible
   solution.

PAIRED PASSAGES

One set of questions on the test will be based on a pair of passages. You'll need to understand both passages separately and then be able to compare them with each other. (The question below continues our discussion of the paired passages on pp. 148–149.)

Example:

12. Which of the following best describes the differences in tone between Passage A and Passage B?

F.   The author of Passage A criticizes Lu's study, while the author of Passage B praises it.
G.   The author of Passage A explains Lu's study, while the author of Passage B criticizes it.
H.   The author of Passage A analyzes the findings of Lu's study, while the author of Passage B praises it.
J.   Both the author of Passage A and Passage B criticize Lu's study.

Typically, the questions that follow paired passages are arranged in a predictable order: the first questions ask only about the first passage, the next questions ask only about the second passage, and the concluding questions ask you about both passages together.

POWER TIP

Some paired passage items ask you to juxtapose passages, or place them side-by-side to show similarities or differences. This isn't really a different question type. For example, the sample question on the right is a tone question. But it is asking you about two passages instead of one.

Answer:

12. This item asks you to compare the overall tone of the two passages. The author of Passage B finds fault with Lu's study and his findings so both (F) and (H) can be eliminated. The author of Passage B definitely criticizes Lu's study, but the author of Passage A is mainly concerned with analyzing or explaining the study, so the correct answer is (G).

POWER TIP

You will need to keep the two passages straight in answering questions that address both. For example, you don't want to mix up which tone goes with which passage. Jotting down quick notes for each passage can help you organize your thoughts.

SUM IT UP - PAIRED PASSAGES

Paired Passage items ask you to draw conclusions and make inferences based on two sets of passages.

POWER PRACTICE 3

DIRECTIONS: The pair of passages below are followed by a set of items. Read the passages and choose the best answer for each item. You may refer to the passages as often as necessary to answer the items. Answers are on p. 310.

Items #1–10 are based on the following pair of passages.

Prose Fiction: Passage A is a short story called "The Story of an Hour" by Kate Chopin. Passage B is an excerpt from the autobiography *Hell's Guest* by Glenn D. Frazier.

Passage A

Knowing that Mrs. Mallard was afflicted with heart trouble, great care was taken to break to her as gently as possible the news of her husband's death. It was her sister Josephine who told her.
5 Her husband's friend Richards had been in the newspaper office when intelligence of the railroad disaster was received, with Brently Mallard's name leading the list of "killed."

She did not hear the story as many women
10 have heard the same, with a paralyzed inability to accept its significance. She wept at once, with sudden, wild abandonment. When the storm of grief had spent itself she went away to her room alone. There she stood, facing the open window. She was
15 young, with a fair calm face, but now there was a dull stare in her eyes, whose gaze was fixed away off yonder on a patch of blue sky.

When she abandoned herself a little whispered word escaped her slightly parted lips: "free!" She
20 knew that she would weep again when she saw the kind, tender hands folded in death; the face that had never looked save with love upon her, fixed and gray and dead. But she saw beyond that bitter moment a long procession of years to come that would belong
25 to her absolutely. And she opened and spread her arms out to welcome them. She would live for herself. There would be no powerful will bending hers in that blind persistence with which men and women believe they have a right to impose a private
30 will upon a fellow-creature. A kind intention or a cruel intention made the act no less a crime. And yet she had loved him—sometimes.

She descended the stairs. Someone was opening the front door with a latchkey. It was
35 Brently Mallard who entered, a little travel-stained. He had been far from the scene of the accident and did not even know there had been one. He stood amazed at his wife's piercing cry. When the doctors came, they were too late. They said she had died of
40 heart disease—of joy that kills.

Passage B

In the summer of 1941, sixteen-year-old Glenn Frazier, distraught because the girl he loved confessed her devotion to someone else, ran away from his home in Alabama. He lied to Army
45 recruiters about his age and signed up to serve in the Philippines, thinking he would be safe from the war raging in Europe. After the December 7 attack on Pearl Harbor, Frazier became one of thirty-one thousand men under the command of
50 General Douglas MacArthur. The Americans were soon overwhelmed by the more than fifty thousand Japanese troops converging on Manila. MacArthur ordered a retreat to the Bataan Peninsula, a mountainous, malarial place. Short on supplies,
55 the Americans fought off one Japanese attack after another, waiting for the reinforcements MacArthur said were on the way.

The help never came. After four months, Frazier and the other surviving Americans were
60 taken prisoner. They endured brutal treatment at the hands of their captors, beginning with a forced march through the jungle that came to be known as the Bataan Death March. Frazier survived the march but spent the remainder of the war in slave labor
65 camps in Japan. One day, before being relocated to Japan and while on burial detail above a mass grave, he threw his dog tags into the pit. He was certain he would die shortly. Confident that the tags would be found after the war, he wanted to relieve his family
70 of uncertainty about his fate. When the Allies retook the Philippines, they discovered the mass grave with Frazier's dog tags in it. The Army believed that Frazier was dead and notified his family. Frazier's father, however, refused to believe it. He said, "I'm
75 sure if anybody can make it, my son can make it." Miraculously, Frazier survived his internment. When he returned to the United States at the end of the war, he called home. His mother answered the phone

80 and fainted upon hearing the voice of a son she had been told was dead.

1. In Passage A, Mrs. Mallard reacts to the news of her husband's death:

    A. stoically.
    B. indifferently.
    C. with mixed emotions.
    D. without emotion.

2. It can be inferred that Mr. Mallard was:

    F. a calloused individual.
    G. a controlling person.
    H. an abusive husband.
    J. a deceitful man.

3. The key turning in the door in Passage A suggests that the person who will enter is a:

    A. family member.
    B. medical doctor.
    C. coroner.
    D. clergyman.

4. In Passage A, the open window (line 14) suggests:

    F. Mrs. Mallard's devotion to her husband.
    G. Brently Mallard's intense devotion.
    H. Mrs. Mallard's recently acquired freedom.
    J. Josephine's concern for her sister.

5. According to Passage B, Frazier signed up to serve in the Philippines in order to:

    A. fight the Japanese in Manila.
    B. escape the poverty of Alabama.
    C. guard Japanese prisoners of war.
    D. avoid fighting in the war in Europe.

6. According to Passage B, the reinforcements promised by MacArthur to the troops defending Manila:

    F. arrived on December 7.
    G. arrived during the Bataan Death March.
    H. arrived before Frazier discarded his dog tags.
    J. never arrived.

7. According to Passage B, Frazier threw his dog tags into the mass grave so that:

    A. the Army would not be able to find him after the war.
    B. his family would conclude that he had died during the war.
    C. MacArthur would not reassign him to the war in Europe.
    D. he would not be forced to participate in the Bataan Death March.

8. According to Passage B, Frazier's mother fainted upon hearing his voice because:

    F. Frazier had been killed in the Philippines.
    G. she wrongly believed that her son was dead.
    H. Frazier had run away from his home in Alabama.
    J. his father believed Frazier had survived.

9. The emotional reactions of Frazier's mother and Mrs. Mallard can best be described as:

    A. mirror images.
    B. almost identical.
    C. incomprehensible.
    D. predictable.

10. The two stories are both categorized by:

    F. protagonists with character flaws.
    G. unexpected endings.
    H. philosophical digressions.
    J. hidden thoughts not shared with other characters.

CHAPTER 9
Try It Out! Reading Practice

You've learned now about the passages and the item-types, so it's time to put all your new knowledge into practice with the following passages.

DIRECTIONS: Each passage or pair of passages is followed by a set of items. Read the passage and choose the best answer for each item. You may refer to the passage as often as necessary to answer the items. Answers are on p. 310.

Items #1–10 are based on the following pair of passages.

Social Science: The following passages explain two views on judicial review. Judicial review gives the Supreme Court and federal courts authority to interpret the Constitution and make sure all three branches of government follow the Constitution.

Passage A

I think there's a misunderstanding of what the doctrine of judicial review means in practice. Obviously, members of Congress and the president and members of the executive branch are obligated
5 to obey the Constitution, and the doctrine of judicial review doesn't mean they ignore that obligation.

If the majority of members of Congress find something to be desirable but unconstitutional, they ought not to vote for it. If they vote for it and the
10 president decides it's unconstitutional, he ought to veto it. And if two-thirds of Congress overrides the presidential veto, then the Supreme Court ought to throw it out. This is not a case of one branch having supremacy over another; it is a case of a law
15 having to pass everybody's understanding of what is constitutional.

It is being suggested that the Supreme Court should lose its power to declare acts

unconstitutional. This alternative seems very
20 unfortunate to me. While Congress has an obligation to take constitutionality into effect, the question is whether the Supreme Court should lose its power to say "no," an outcome which I find disastrous.

I would add that there is no crisis of judicial
25 activism (judges letting personal beliefs on political or social issues dictate their decisions). Judicial activism is a stick that politicians use to beat things that they don't like.

Various doctrines inherent in the notion of a
30 judiciary restrict judicial activism. One of the most important is judicial restraint: a court should not decide a matter prematurely, should not decide political questions, and should not decide a matter unless there is a genuine case involving controversy.
35 Courts impose on themselves a strict requirement that there be real parties with real interests at stake, that there be a real injury, and that political questions are out of bounds.

Passage B

Courts have an obligation to determine the
40 constitutionality of federal statutes they are asked to apply, and not simply because they are themselves required to obey the Constitution. As Marshall argued, judicial review is an essential element in the constitutional system of checks and balances—
45 designed, as Hamilton said in *The Federalist*, to help keep the legislature within the limits of its authority.

This does not mean that the courts have a monopoly on constitutional interpretation. Members of Congress, like all federal and state officers, are
50 bound by their oaths to support the Constitution. Whenever a bill is introduced, every member of

Congress must inquire whether Congress has the power to enact it. Thus, Congress is continually engaged in interpreting the Constitution. So, of course, is the president. And thus a great deal of constitutional law is made outside the courts, by the legislative and executive branches of government.

The vexing question is therefore not who has power to interpret the Constitution, but whose view prevails in case of conflict. What happens when different branches of government, each acting within its proper sphere of authority, disagree as to what the Constitution means?

There are times when other governmental actors are plainly obliged to accept judicial decisions. Judicial power to decide a case implies authority to render a judgment that binds the parties. Thus, when President Roosevelt contemplated disobeying an anticipated judicial decision requiring the government to pay bondholders in gold, he challenged the very essence of judicial power. Such a course could be defended, if at all, only as an exercise of the natural right of revolution; it was not consistent with the Constitution.

It does not follow that other branches are bound in all cases by judicial interpretations of the Constitution. President Jackson vetoed a new charter for the Bank of the United States after the Supreme Court had upheld congressional power to establish it. President Jefferson pardoned those convicted under the Sedition Act on constitutional grounds that had been rejected by the courts. Both Jackson and Jefferson were well within their rights. Neither of them did anything that interfered with the power of the courts to render binding judgments in particular cases. The pardon power is an express limitation on that principle, and it essentially allows the winning party to waive a judgment in its favor. Nor was either Jefferson's or Jackson's action inconsistent with Marbury's principle that the courts must have power to prevent other branches from exceeding their powers.

On the contrary, Jefferson and Jackson's actions provided an additional check that furnished even greater security for the rights of the states and the people. Indeed, what these two presidents did illustrates the core of our constitutional separation of powers: no measure can be carried out to the detriment of the people or the states unless all three branches agree that it is constitutional.

1. It can be inferred that the author of Passage A believes that claims that judicial activism upsets the proper constitutional balance between the branches of government are:

    A. well-founded.
    B. exaggerated.
    C. misconstrued.
    D. premature.

2. As it is used in line 48, the word "monopoly" means:

    F. a large business.
    G. exclusive control.
    H. unrestricted power.
    J. unlimited authority.

3. It can be inferred that both authors agree that:

    A. only the courts have the power to consider the constitutionality of a law.
    B. only the courts are required to consider the constitutionality of a law.
    C. all three branches of government must assess the constitutionality of a law.
    D. no branch of government is required to assess the constitutionality of a law.

4. It can be inferred that the author of Passage B believes that the Supreme Court's power to judge the constitutionality of a law is:

    F. the exclusive prerogative of the Court and not available to other branches of government.
    G. more extensive than just the obligation of the justices to obey the Constitution.
    H. always binding on the other branches of government when a court interprets the Constitution.
    J. stated explicitly in the provisions of the Constitution itself.

5. In Passage A, what is the author's attitude toward the suggestion that the Supreme Court should be stripped of its power to review the constitutionality of legislation?

A. The author firmly rejects the suggestion.
B. The author is indifferent to the suggestion.
C. The author warmly embraces the suggestion.
D. The author wants clarification of the suggestion.

6. Which of the following, when substituted for the word "vexing" (line 58), would best preserve the intended meaning of the original sentence?

F. Painful
G. Difficult
H. Moot
J. Rhetorical

7. It can be inferred that the author of Passage A believes that the doctrine of judicial restraint:

A. restricts the ability of courts to hear cases that present genuine disputes.
B. is a self-imposed limitation preventing courts from enacting legislation.
C. was enacted by the legislature to prevent courts from abusing their power.
D. is an illegitimate use of the authority of a court to hear a legal case.

8. In the first paragraph of Passage B, the author cites Marshall and Hamilton as authorities for the proposition that:

F. judicial review of the constitutionality of legislation has a broader scope than just a required adherence to the Constitution.
G. courts should conduct a review of legislation pending before Congress to determine its constitutionality.
H. the authority of the legislature to pass laws is limited by the power of the courts.
J. checks and balances is a constitutional provision that increases the authority of the legislature.

9. The author of Passage B believes that Jefferson's pardon of those convicted under the Sedition Act was justified because:

A. the courts had determined that the Sedition Act unfairly restricted free speech.
B. the executive branch, once it had won convictions, was free to give up its victory.
C. the executive branch is in a better position to judge the constitutionality of a law than the courts.
D. the pardon was necessary to prevent the legislature and the courts from exceeding their constitutional authority.

10. Which of the following best characterizes the exchange of views by the two authors?

F. Both authors agree that the doctrine of judicial review, while once important, has outlived its usefulness.
G. Both authors agree that the doctrine of judicial review remains an important element of Constitutional government.
H. The author of Passage A believes that the doctrine of judicial review should only rarely be invoked while the author of Passage B believes the Supreme Court should oversee all aspects of government.
J. The author of Passage A believes that all three branches of government have the power to review the acts of other branches while the author of Passage B believes that only the Supreme Court does.

REVIEW

Questions about paired passages will focus on one of the two passages or ask how the two passages relate. Pay close attention to each question to make sure you are looking to the correct passage for the answer.

Items #11–20 are based on the following passage.

Humanities: This passage explores the authorship of the poem commonly known as "The Night Before Christmas."

"A Visit from St. Nicholas," more commonly known as "The Night Before Christmas," is a poem first published anonymously in New York's *Troy Sentinel* on December 23, 1823, and attributed
5 to Clement Clarke Moore, a professor of Oriental and Greek Literature, in 1837. In that year, Moore claimed authorship and explained that the poem had originally been written for his children and was later sent, without his knowledge, to the
10 newspaper by a housekeeper. The poem was included in an anthology of Moore's work in 1844. It seems indisputable that the poem first appeared on December 23, 1823, in the *Troy Sentinel*, that the manuscript originated in Moore's home, and that the
15 person giving the poem to the newspaper, without Moore's knowledge, believed that it had been written by Moore.

In 1859, however, 26 years after the poem first appeared in print, the children of Major Henry
20 Livingston, Jr., who was born in Poughkeepsie in 1748, claimed to have heard the poem recited by their father as early as 1807—sixteen years before the poem's original publication and 37 years before Moore claimed authorship. The Livingston family
25 also claimed to have found a copy of the poem with edits in Livingston's hand in their father's desk. There is no evidence that Livingston himself ever claimed authorship of the poem. No print record has ever been found with Livingston's name attached
30 to it. The manuscript claimed to have been found by Livingston's family was allegedly destroyed in a house fire. Moore, however, personally made copies of the poem in his own hand as favors for family members and friends.

35 Like Moore, Livingston was an amateur poet with several publishing credits to his name. Unlike Moore, who wrote only one other poem in anapestic form, the meter of "A Visit," Livingston frequently used the anapest. In fact, Livingston
40 was apparently in the habit of writing a holiday poem for his children each Christmas using anapest verse. Many of them borrowed language and form from Christopher Anstey, an English poet who died in 1805, and so resemble "A Visit." But,
45 there is also considerable evidence in the poem to support Moore's authorship: lighthearted, spontaneous-sounding mixed iambs and anapests,

exclamation marks, the rare use of "all" as an adverb, syncopation, and familial affection. In any case,
50 Livingston might have been likelier to employ the anapestic style, but this does not mean that Moore never did so.

Setting aside direct testimony of authorship and the analysis of form, an intriguing bit of
55 evidence is names given in the poem, as originally published, to two of Saint Nicholas' reindeer: *Dunder* and *Blixem*. The names are Dutch for *thunder* and *lightning*. Moore did not speak Dutch; Livingston's mother, however, was Dutch.

60 As intriguing as this point may be, it ignores the then-fashionable Knickerbocker movement which sought to find a Dutch beginning in everything associated with New York. It would have been consistent with the prevailing style for the *Troy*
65 *Sentinel* editor to change the German *Donder* and *Blitzen* to the Dutch equivalents. In fact, later emendations to the poem, in Moore's own hand, changed the names back to the original *Donder* and *Blitzen*.

70 Moore's close friendship with the author Washington Irving, who was closely associated with the Knickerbocker trend, may also help to explain any other Dutch elements that are found in "A Visit." But the Dutch influence proves much
75 more. The Livingston family now claims that the poem was written by Henry Livingston around 1808, but the poem clearly reflects the later influence of Washington Irving, the New York Historical Society, and the Knickerbocker Movement, which date the
80 poem to 1822, consistent with all the other evidence that Moore penned the classic verse.

To be charitable to the Livingston family, perhaps the most likely explanation for the seemingly conflicting evidence is the unreliability
85 of human memory. Assuming that Livingston read to his children a special verse written in anapestic meter each year, it would not be inconceivable that a quarter of a century later, the then-adult children would have a recollection of the meter
90 and Christmas theme. Upon hearing "A Visit," the topical and stylistic similarities would make it easy to conflate "A Visit" and the holiday poems by their father.

11. The author mentions Moore's friendship with Washington Irving in order to show that "A Visit" was probably written around:

    A. 1807
    B. 1822
    C. 1837
    D. 1859

12. The primary purpose of the passage is to:

    F. evaluate the poetic merit of "A Visit."
    G. examine the social setting of the first publication of "A Visit."
    H. assess the evidence for the authorship of "A Visit."
    J. compare the features of "A Visit" to other poems written by Livingston.

13. The fact that Moore's housekeeper submitted "A Visit" to the newspaper without Moore's knowledge helps to explain why:

    A. the poem was written in a meter seldom used by Moore.
    B. Moore did not make a claim of authorship at the time.
    C. "A Visit" has Dutch features even though Moore was not Dutch.
    D. the manuscript supposedly written by Livingston could not be found.

14. The author regards the evidence for Livingston's authorship presented in the third paragraph as:

    F. indisputable.
    G. inconclusive.
    H. irrelevant.
    J. complete.

15. It can be inferred that the author of the passage believes that Dunder and Blixem were names:

    A. used by Moore in his original manuscript.
    B. inserted by Moore into a later version.
    C. chosen by an editor at the *Troy Sentinel*.
    D. selected by Livingston, who knew Dutch.

16. The author's attitude toward the claim of the Livingston heirs to have once been in possession of a copy of "A Visit" handwritten by Livingston can best be described as:

    F. inquisitive.
    G. defensive.
    H. insightful.
    J. skeptical.

17. In context, "conflate" (line 92) means:

    A. confuse.
    B. plagiarize.
    C. approve.
    D. remember.

18. In the final paragraph, the author attempts to:

    F. reconcile the conflicting theories by proposing a third.
    G. show that Moore, rather than Livingston, wrote "A Visit."
    H. correct a longstanding misconception about "A Visit."
    J. excuse the Livingstons' claim as an honest mistake.

19. The use of the words "claimed" (line 30) and "allegedly" (line 31) to describe the loss of the Livingston manuscript suggests that the author is not:

    A. satisfied that Livingston's heir recalled the event accurately.
    B. convinced that the manuscript ever really existed.
    C. aware of any news reports to corroborate the report of the fire.
    D. likely to accept historical facts as proving a theory.

REVIEW

Remember to cross out options that don't work as you find them so that you can eliminate the excess verbiage and think more clearly.

20. Which of the following is regarded by the author as the LEAST firmly established?

F. The poem was first printed in the newspaper on December 23, 1823.

G. Moore had a close friendship with the author Washington Irving.

H. The names Dunder and Blixem appear in the original version published in the newspaper.

J. A housekeeper in the Moore household was responsible for sending the poem to the newspaper.

Items #21–30 are based on the following passage.

Humanities: This passage is adapted from the speech "Is It a Crime for a Citizen of the United States to Vote?" by Susan B. Anthony.

Friends and Fellow Citizens: I stand before you tonight under indictment for the alleged crime of having voted at the last presidential election without having a lawful right to vote. It shall be my work this
5 evening to prove to you that in thus voting, I not only committed no crime, but, instead, simply exercised my citizen's rights, guaranteed to me and all United States citizens by the National Constitution, beyond the power of any State to deny.

10 The preamble of the Federal Constitution begins: "We, the people of the United States, in order to form a more perfect union, establish justice, insure domestic tranquility, provide for the common defense, promote the general welfare,
15 and secure the blessings of liberty to ourselves and our posterity. . . ." It was we, the people, not we, the white male citizens; but we, the whole people, who formed the Union. And we formed it, not to give the blessings of liberty, but to secure them; not to the
20 half of ourselves and the half of our posterity but to the whole people—women as well as men. And it is a downright mockery to talk to women of their enjoyment of the blessings of liberty while they are denied the use of the only means of securing them
25 provided by this government—the ballot.

For any State to make sex a qualification that results in the disfranchisement of one entire half of the people is a violation of the supreme law of the land. By it the blessings of liberty are forever
30 withheld from women and their female posterity. To them this government has no just powers derived from the consent of the governed. To them this government is not a democracy. It is not a republic.

It is a hateful oligarchy of sex. An oligarchy of
35 learning, where the educated govern the ignorant, might be endured; but this oligarchy of sex, which makes father, brothers, husband, sons, the oligarchs or rulers over the mother and sisters, the wife and daughters of every household—which ordains
40 all men sovereigns, all women subjects—carries dissension, discord, and rebellion into every home of the nation.

But, it is urged, the use of the masculine pronouns he, his, and him, in all the constitutions
45 and laws, is proof that only men were meant to be included in their provisions. If you insist on this version of the letter of the law, we shall insist that you be consistent and accept the other horn of the dilemma, which would compel you to exempt
50 women from taxation for the support of the government, and from penalties for the violation of laws.

Though the words *persons, people, inhabitants, electors, citizens,* are all used indiscriminately in the
55 national and state constitutions, there was always a conflict of opinion, prior to the war, as to whether they were synonymous terms, as for instance:

"No person shall be a representative who shall not have been seven years a citizen, and who shall
60 not, when elected, be an inhabitant of that state in which he is chosen. No person shall be a senator who shall not have been a citizen of the United States, and an inhabitant of that state in which he is chosen."

65 But, whatever there was for a doubt, under the old regime, the adoption of the Fourteenth Amendment settled that question forever, in its first sentence: "All persons born or naturalized in the United States and subject to the jurisdiction thereof,
70 are citizens of the United States and of the state wherein they reside."

And the second settles the equal status of all persons—all citizens:

"No states shall make or enforce any law
75 which shall abridge the privileges or immunities of citizens; nor shall any state deprive any person of life, liberty, or property, without due process of law, nor deny to any person within its jurisdiction the equal protection of the laws."

80 The only question left to be settled now is: Are women persons? And I hardly believe any of our opponents will have the hardihood to say we are not. Being persons, then, women are citizens; and no State has a right to make any law, or to enforce
85 any old law, that shall abridge their privileges or immunities. Hence, every discrimination against women in the laws of the States is today null and void.

21. For the purpose of this speech, Anthony assumes the posture of a:

A. defendant on trial in a court.
B. chair of a committee moderating a debate.
C. legislator arguing for a new law.
D. judge making a ruling at a trial.

22. In paragraph four, Anthony infers that if the use of masculine pronouns in the law proves that they apply only to men, then:

F. tax laws and criminal laws do not apply to women.
G. men have the burden of enforcing all the laws.
H. laws, when applied to women, create an unequal burden.
J. the fundamental documents of democracy are null and void.

23. In paragraph six (lines 58–64), Anthony quotes from the US Constitution in order to demonstrate the framers' ambiguous use of the terms:

A. person and citizen.
B. woman and person.
C. woman and man.
D. citizen and man.

24. In the context of Anthony's speech, "regime" (line 66) most nearly means:

F. leadership.
G. command.
H. administration.
J. system.

25. Anthony's argumentative strategy in paragraph four (lines 43–52) is to:

A. challenge her accusers to make their case so that she can answer them.
B. cite authorities to support her interpretation of legal documents.
C. raise a possible objection to her position and offer a rebuttal.
D. demonstrate that the documents she cites are subject to different interpretations.

26. The word "oligarchy" (line 34), as used in this context, refers to a government in which:

F. only men of a certain status may hold positions of power in the government.
G. power is held by a few individuals who share a common characteristic.
H. the wealthy control power and exercise the functions of government.
J. a hereditary monarch has absolute power over the inhabitants of the country.

REVIEW

Remember that vocabulary questions ask about the use of a word in context, not necessarily the most common meaning of a word.

27. Which of the following best explains the dilemma to which Anthony refers in line 49?

A. If women cannot vote because masculine pronouns in the constitutions and laws do not apply to them, then women should not be subject to other laws that use masculine pronouns.

B. When women are denied the right to vote on the basis of gender, then it is equally justifiable to deny men the right to vote on the basis of gender.

C. Once women are granted the right to vote, then it will no longer be legal to deny any individual the right to vote, even if that individual is not able to vote intelligently.

D. If women continue to be excluded from the voting booth, then men and women as groups are necessarily set against each other and a revolution is likely to occur.

28. Which of the following best exhibits the logical structure of Anthony's argument that she has a right to vote?

F. All persons are citizens; all citizens have the right to vote; women are persons; therefore, women have the right to vote.

G. All persons have the right to vote; all persons are citizens; women are citizens; therefore, women have the right to vote.

H. All citizens are persons; all persons have the right to vote; women are persons; therefore, women have the right to vote.

J. All women are persons; all citizens are persons; all citizens have the right to vote; therefore, women have the right to vote.

29. Anthony's main point in paragraph three (lines 26–42) is that:

A. a government by men only creates dissension and instability rather than domestic tranquility.

B. educated persons of both genders should be the only people qualified to vote.

C. men are not uniquely qualified by their gender to make intelligent decisions in the voting booth.

D. the blessings of liberty extend to women even though they are not permitted to vote.

30. Which of the following best describes Anthony's argumentative strategy in the final paragraph?

F. She poses a question, the answer to which she believes is obvious and will be accepted by her opponents.

G. She describes a hypothetical situation that is analogous to her own position and draws conclusions from the comparison.

H. She insists that words are often ambiguous and that important terms like "citizen" can have multiple meanings depending on the context.

J. She points out that her opponents have confused the effect of an event with its cause and offers a different explanation.

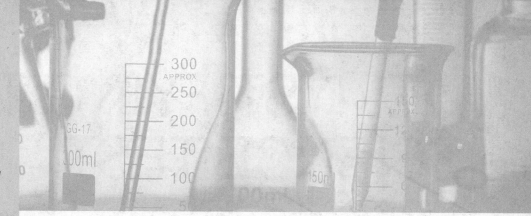

CHAPTER 10

Fast Track to Science Mechanics

DEMYSTIFYING THE SCIENCE TEST

TEST SPECS

Calculators are NOT allowed on the Science Test.

The Science Test consists of 40 multiple-choice questions to be answered in 35 minutes. The questions are divided into six or seven groups. Each group of items is based on a passage. Does this sound like the Reading Test? Well, Science passages are different from Reading passages because Science passages include a lot of diagrams, pictures, tables, and graphs, and they have less text than the Reading passages.

There are three types of Science passages:

- **Data Representations** are reports of data findings
- **Research Summaries** are descriptions of experiments and associated data
- **Conflicting Viewpoints** are debates on different scientific theories

STRATEGY ALERT

The Science Test is "open-book," meaning you can refer to the passage at any time.

Each Science question, or item, has four answer choices. You must select each answer based on what is stated or implied in the passage.

Science passages use content from the following areas:

- **Biology:** botany, cellular biology, ecology, evolution, genetics, microbiology, zoology
- **Chemistry:** biochemistry, organic chemistry, nuclear chemistry, thermochemistry, acids and bases, kinetics and equilibria, properties of matter
- **Earth/Space Sciences:** astronomy, environmental science, geology, meteorology, oceanography
- **Physics:** mechanics, thermodynamics, fluids, solids, electromagnetism, optics

POWER TIP

Science items test reasoning, not content knowledge.

Don't worry if you've taken a biology class and a chemistry class but not a physics class. The Science Test is not a test of science knowledge or science trivia; it's a test of science reasoning. In other words, all of the information necessary to answer the items is included in the context of the accompanying passage, and you can reason the correct answers from the available information. Even if you are not particularly strong in science, you can still do well on the Science Test, as long as you practice your reasoning skills.

ANATOMY OF THE SCIENCE TEST

INSIDE THE DIRECTIONS

The directions below are similar to what appears in the Science Test. There are no surprises here, and on test day, don't waste any time reading them.

SCIENCE DIRECTIONS
Each passage below is followed by several items. After reading a passage, choose the best answer to each item. You may refer to the passages as often as necessary. You are NOT permitted the use of a calculator.

INSIDE THE SCIENCE PASSAGES

As you learned in the last section, there are three types of science passages: Data Representations, Research Summaries, and Conflicting Viewpoints. Some passages include only an introductory sentence and a single figure. Other passages include several paragraphs of text and two or three figures. Passages can be simple or complex depending on their length, the number of figures included, the topic being discussed, and the complexity of the data presented.

Passages may also seem more complex when they discuss unfamiliar topics. There are three ways to approach these passages. The first approach is to read the passage carefully, studying figures and making notes, until you understand the topic and could probably write a research paper about it. The second approach is to panic and stare blankly at your test booklet. The third approach is to calmly preview the passage without trying to memorize any details, gaining a general understanding of the data collection, experiment, or model presented. Which approach is best? Remember, this test measures science reasoning, not science knowledge, so the third approach will get you closest to your goal within the 35-minute time limit.

Let's try a sample passage using this third approach. As you read, underline or star any information about why or how the experiment was conducted. Gloss over words you don't recognize. Remember, you can come back to the passage when you're ready to answer questions.

Example:

A student studied the process by which malodorzane is produced by heating protocrud in a closed system and then releasing it into the surrounding atmosphere.

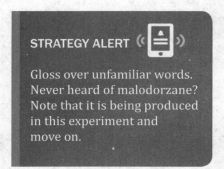

STRATEGY ALERT

Gloss over unfamiliar words. Never heard of malodorzane? Note that it is being produced in this experiment and move on.

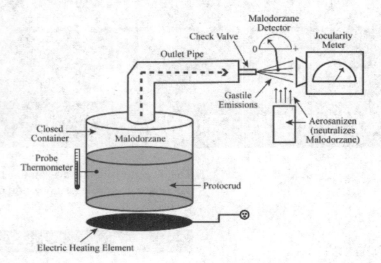

Experiment 1

The concentration of malodorzane produced by the protocrud at various temperatures was measured by determining how much aerosanizen was needed to neutralize the malodorzane (Table 1).

TABLE 1	
Temperature of Protocrud	Aerosanizen (spritz/minute)
20°C	46–198
22.5°C	199–377
25°C	378–612

Experiment 2

The student observed that the release of gastiles, whether or not the malodorzane was counteracted by aerosanizen, produced primary and secondary jocularities. The intensity of the jocularities was measured and recorded for different durations of gastiles (Table 2).

TABLE 2		
	Intensity of Jocularities	
Gastiles (seconds)	Primary Jocularities (decibels)	Secondary Jocularities (decibels)
1.0	30 dB	—*
2.0	35 dB	—*
5.0	40 dB	30 dB
12.0	60 dB	40 dB
19.0	120 dB	60 dB

*Intensity was below measurable levels.

Experiment 3

The student measured and recorded the duration of the jocularities for different durations of gastiles (Table 3).

TABLE 3		
	Duration of Jocularities	
Gastiles (seconds)	Primary Jocularities (seconds)	Secondary Jocularities (seconds)
0.2	3	—*
1.0	7	—*
2.5	13	11
5.0	25	9
12.0	51	4

*Duration was below measurable levels.

See, that wasn't so bad, was it? Actually, that passage is made up of gibberish terms like "malodorzane," "jocularity," and "gastiles" to illustrate that you can do well on the Science Test even without understanding the science content. Could you answer a few questions about the passage, now that you've calmly previewed it? Well, let's see.

INSIDE THE QUESTIONS

Since the Science Test is similar to the Reading Test, it's not surprising that the questions fall into similar categories:

- Some questions ask about the overall purpose of the experiments or the main issue of a debate.
- Some questions require students to locate information. In fact, some Reading questions refer to particular lines in a passage (*In line #, what is...?*), and some Science questions do the same thing (*According to Table #, what...?*).
- Some Reading questions ask students to synthesize information (*If such-and-such were no longer needed, what would the author expect to happen...?*). Science questions can ask the same thing (*Assuming that the temperature doubles, what happens to the so-and-so?*).

Keeping this in mind, try answering the following questions based on the provided passage.

1. Data from the passage indicate that duration was greatest for secondary jocularities produced by gastiles of what duration?

   A. 1.0 seconds
   B. 2.5 seconds
   C. 5.0 seconds
   D. 12.0 seconds

TEST SPECS

ACT answer choices have alternate lettering. The odd-numbered questions have choices lettered A, B, C, and D and the even-numbered questions have choices lettered F, G, H, and J.

2. Gastiles with a duration of 13.0 seconds would probably produce primary jocularities of a duration:

   F. between 3 and 7 seconds.
   G. between 7 and 13 seconds.
   H. between 13 and 25 seconds.
   J. greater than 51 seconds.

3. The data in Table 1 would be most useful in determining whether:

   A. the temperature of aerosanizen affects the chemical's ability to neutralize malodorzane.
   B. the volume of malodorzane varies with the chemical composition of the protocrud.
   C. the closed system produces a greater volume of malodorzane than aerosanizen.
   D. the temperature of the protocrud affects the rate of malodorzane production.

Answers

1. You need to find the table that has the words "jocularities" and "duration": Table 3. The greatest value for "secondary jocularities" is 11, and that corresponds to a "gastile" reading of 2.5 seconds, (B).

2. Again, the answer is in Table 3, but this time there is no entry for 13 seconds in the "gastiles" column. The largest entry is 12.0 seconds. Because primary jocularity duration increases as gastile duration increases, the corresponding entry in the "Primary Jocularities" column, if one existed, would likely be greater than 51 seconds, (J).

3. Table 1 shows the amount of aerosanizen needed to neutralize the quantity of malodorzane at various temperatures: it relates the protocrud temperature to malodorzane output. The data in that table would provide information about how the temperature of the protocrud affects the rate of malodorzane production, (D).

PACING PLAN FOR THE SCIENCE TEST

The passages do not get more difficult as you move through the Science Test, so you should plan on spending approximately the same amount of time on each passage and corresponding question set. For a test with six passages, this is about 6 minutes per passage and question set; for a test with seven passages, it's 5 minutes per passage and question set. The table below illustrates how this approach would work on a test with six passages. As you will learn later, you can customize the order in which you complete the passages, so the passage numbering below refers to the passages as you choose to address them, not necessarily their order on the test.

PACING TIP

Allow yourself one minute to learn about the passage for each set of questions. Learn the main purpose of the data or experiments or the focus of the debate. Then you can easily come back and find the information you need when you answer the questions.

PASSAGE AND CORRESPONDING QUESTIONS	TIME TO SPEND	TOTAL TIME SPENT
I	5 minutes	5 minutes
II	6 minutes	11 minutes
III	6 minutes	17 minutes
IV	6 minutes	23 minutes
V	6 minutes	29 minutes
VI	6 minutes	35 minutes

However, passages can have 5 to 7 items and some have more text or more complex data, so some passages may require less time and others more. This table is helpful as a general guideline.

Within a group of items, the problems do tend to get more difficult with increasing item number. The first item may be just a reading from a table; the second item may be a determination about a maximum or minimum value; the third item may be an interpolation; and the fourth item may be an extrapolation. Finally, the fifth and sixth items might require a higher-level synthesis of the material.

STRATEGY ALERT

Always guess. You have at least a 25% chance of guessing correctly, and your odds improve if you can eliminate one or two choices.

So, if 5 or 6 minutes have passed, and you still haven't gotten to the last item or two in a set, move on. The difficulty meter will reset with the next group of items. You can miss the last question on each passage and still do well on the Science Test.

Ultimately, pacing on the Science Tests requires balancing competing considerations such as the need for speed and desire for accuracy. The best way to find the optimal trade-off is practice.

POWER PRACTICE 1

DIRECTIONS: Give yourself six minutes to work through the following Conflicting Viewpoints passage and accompanying questions. Preview the passage, and then move quickly to the questions to determine where you need focus your attention.

How old is the earth? Two opposing views are presented.

Scientist 1

The earth is approximately five billion years old. We know this to be true because of radioactive dating. Some chemical elements are unstable and will fall apart into smaller pieces over time. This disintegration occurs over a period of time that is very regular for the particular element. In general, we talk about the half-life of the element, which is the time necessary for one-half of the material to disintegrate. This time is constant whether we have an ounce or a ton of the material. So, by measuring the relative amounts of the material left and the disintegration products, we can form an accurate idea of how old the earth is by determining how many half-lives have occurred.

Scientist 2

The argument that supports the hypothesis that the earth is only five billion years old is seriously flawed. What the argument fails to take into account is that the earth is the constant recipient of a shower of cosmic debris in the form of meteorites. These meteorites replenish the stock of radioactive material on the surface of the earth, making it seem as though the earth has gone through fewer half-lives than it really has. Therefore, all estimates of the age of the earth based on radioactive dating are too low.

1. Which of the following is a major assumption of Scientist 1?

   A. The earth has life that recycles carbon-14.
   B. The half-life of all radioactive elements is five billion years.
   C. The radioactive material was formed at the same time as the earth.
   D. There is no longer any radioactivity on the earth.

2. Which of the following is a major assumption of Scientist 2?

   F. The meteorites that land on the earth are radioactive.
   G. Few meteorites have landed on the earth.
   H. The earth is more than five billion years old.
   J. The earth is highly radioactive.

3. Which of the following, if true, would best refute Scientist 2's argument?

   A. Recent meteorites have been found to be radioactive.
   B. The earth has a greater amount of radioactive material on the surface than in the mantle.
   C. The earth's orbit intersects the orbits of a number of meteorites.
   D. Few meteorites have been found to contain radioactive material.

4. Which of the following would be most likely if Scientist 2's hypothesis were correct?

   F. The total amount of radioactive material and its disintegration products on the earth has decreased over time.
   G. The total amount of radioactive material and its disintegration products has increased over time.
   H. The total amount of radioactive material and its disintegration products has stayed essentially the same over time.
   J. The earth will reach a critical mass and explode.

5. Which of the following would be most likely if Scientist 1's hypothesis were correct?

   A. The total amount of radioactive material and its disintegration products has decreased over time.
   B. The total amount of radioactive material and its disintegration products has increased over time.
   C. The total amount of radioactive material and its disintegration products has stayed essentially the same over time.
   D. The earth will reach a critical mass and explode.

ANSWERS

1. **(C)** *Science/Evaluation of Models/Analysis*

   Scientist 1 assumes that the radioactive material was formed at the same time as the earth; otherwise, there is no connection between the radioactive "clock" and the age of the earth.

2. **(F)** *Science/Evaluation of Models/Analysis*

   For the landing of the meteorites to upset the "clock," they would have to contain the radioactive material or its disintegration products. Since Scientist 2 claims that the estimate of the earth's age is too low, the meteorites must contain radioactive material and have landed since the formation of the earth, thus upsetting the "clock."

3. **(D)** *Science/Evaluation of Models/Analysis*

   Since Scientist 2's theory is based on the assumption that the earth is the constant recipient of meteorites that contain radioactive material, finding few meteorites containing radioactive material undermines the theory.

4. **(G)** *Science/Evaluation of Models/Analysis*

   According to Scientist 2, the amount of radioactive material and its disintegration products would increase over time because meteorites would bring more material, while the earth has no way of getting rid of it.

5. **(C)** *Science/Evaluation of Models/Analysis*

   Since there is no additional source for new radioactive material, the amount of radioactive material as it decays through the various disintegration products is constant.

THE CAMBRIDGE GAME PLAN

Okay, so you've learned the basics about the Science Test. Now you need a game plan tailored to your Science needs. Remember, however, that the game plan below includes suggestions, not hard-and-fast rules. Pick what works for you and discard the rest.

BEGIN IN PREVIEW MODE

> **QUICKLY PREVIEW THE TEST, BUT SKIP THE DIRECTIONS**

Check the Science Test before you start to work, especially the number of passages, how many problems are paired with each passage, and which passages are which type.

> **PLAN YOUR ATTACK— EASIEST PASSAGES FIRST**

Before reading any of the Science passages, quickly glance over them and code them according to passage-type: Data Representation (DR), Research Summary (RS), or Conflicting Viewpoints (CV). Coding the passages helps to determine the order in which to attack them. Additionally, the subject matter in a passage may influence the difficulty level you assign to it. Coding the passages should take no more than 20–30 seconds.

Once the coding is done, plan the order of attack—which passages to read first, second, third, etc. Complete the easiest passages first and save the most difficult passages for last. This approach will increase the number of correct answers by ensuring that the easier passages are completed.

One consideration has a higher priority than all the others: save the debate format (Conflicting Viewpoints) passages until last. The need to synthesize information from different viewpoints makes these passages the most challenging for many students. For the other passages, there will be two to four questions requiring nothing more than reading values from a graph or a chart—without any real comprehension required. Complete these passages first!

PACING TIP

Skip the directions. You know what to do—read the passages and answer the accompanying items.

POWER TIP

Contrary to the strategy for the passages on the ACT Reading Test, do NOT preview the Science item stems before reading the corresponding passage. The item stems can be difficult to understand without first having read the information provided in the passage.

PRACTICE BIG PICTURE READING

For the Science Test, "reading the passage" means "reading through" the passage. You can't afford to study the passage, and don't forget that this is an "open-book" test. So, learn generally what is going on and where things are located. Then, let the items tell you where to look more carefully.

READ THE INTRODUCTION

Read any introductory paragraph(s). Not only does this material usually explain why an experiment is being conducted or data are being collected, it often defines a key term that is essential to understanding the connections of the various parts of the passage.

CONSIDER THE FIGURES

Examine any diagrams or schematics. The focus of a passage is often a device that includes beakers, tubing, switches, pulleys, test tubes, and other paraphernalia associated with science. Try to understand what the device is designed to accomplish and how the various parts work together. For example, for a graph, read the title and the labels of the x- and y-axes. For tables, read the column heads and the titles of the rows. However, do not read specific values on a graph or in a table. There are too many and only one or two are likely to be relevant to answering one of the few items based on that passage (compared to all the different questions that the test-writers could have chosen).

STRATEGY ALERT

Try reading the first sentence in each paragraph before reading the entire passage, depending on the difficulty level of the passage.

UNDERLINE KEY WORDS AND PHRASES

When you read the passages, bracket or underline key words and phrases to create quick and easy reference points. For example, in a Research Summary passage, underline the variable that changes in each experiment.

PAY ATTENTION TO DIFFERENCES

Pay attention to the differences in the presented information rather than the similarities. Identify how each table is different from the other tables, how different experimental methods and results are distinct from one another, or how two viewpoints diverge from one another.

WATCH FOR ASSUMPTIONS

Watch for assumptions made in the presented experimental results, arguments, or hypotheses. Identify any assumptions that are not supported by the given information—whether an assumption is in the passage, the item stems, or the answer choices.

LOOK FOR TRENDS

Analyze the tables and graphs, looking for data trends and how those trends vary for each data set. Determine how the investigated factor changes as a function of the controlled parameters. Do the data demonstrate proportional or inverse relationships?

MAKE NOTES TO CLARIFY VIEWPOINTS

Be sure to understand each scientist's viewpoint in Conflicting Viewpoints passages. It may help to take notes in the test booklet, summarizing the viewpoints that are expressed in the passage. Do NOT waste time trying to decide which of the arguments in a Conflicting Viewpoints passage is valid. Items ask for the identification of data trends and assumptions underlying the different arguments, not for judgments of the viewpoints.

POWER PRACTICE 2

DIRECTIONS: The passage below is followed by several items. After reading the passage, choose the best answer to each item. You may refer to the passage as often as necessary. You are NOT permitted the use of a calculator.

To investigate the factors affecting the rate at which starch is broken down to sugar by the digestive enzyme salivary amylase, two experiments were performed. In both experiments, starch (in the form of a cracker) was mixed in a beaker with the enzyme, and samples were removed every 3 minutes. Special sugar indicators were dipped in the sample to determine the presence of starch (indicating that the cracker had not yet been completely digested).

Experiment 1

To test the effects of different pH levels on enzyme activity rate, one cracker and a standard amount of enzyme were placed in three beakers, each containing buffers of different pH. This procedure was repeated using standard amounts of water in place of the enzyme. All tests were carried out at optimal temperature, 37 degrees Celsius. Starch and sugar levels (starch/sugar) from selected samples are shown in Table 1.

TABLE 1					
Contents of Beakers	Approximate pH Levels	Levels of Starch/Sugar			
		After 3 minutes	After 9 minutes	After 15 minutes	After 60 minutes
cracker + enzyme + buffer	5	high/none	high/none	high/low	moderate/moderate
	7	moderate/moderate	low/high	none/high	none/high
	9	high/none	high/none	high/low	moderate/moderate
cracker + water + buffer	5	high/none	high/none	high/none	high/none
	7	high/none	high/none	high/none	high/none
	9	high/none	high/none	high/none	high/none

Experiment 2

To test the effects of temperature on enzyme activity rate, one cracker and a standard amount of enzyme were placed in three beakers, each kept at different temperatures. This was also repeated using standard amounts of water in place of the enzyme. All tests were carried out at optimal pH, 7.40. Starch and sugar levels (starch/sugar) from selected samples are shown in Table 2.

TABLE 2					
Contents of Beakers	Temperatures	Levels of Starch/Sugar			
		After 3 minutes	After 9 minutes	After 15 minutes	After 60 minutes
cracker + enzyme	25°C	high/none	high/none	high/low	moderate/moderate
	37°C	moderate/moderate	low/high	none/high	none/high
	45°C	high/none	high/none	high/low	moderate/moderate
cracker + water	25°C	high/none	high/none	high/none	high/none
	37°C	high/none	high/none	high/none	high/none
	45°C	high/none	high/none	high/none	high/none

1. The ingredient used as a control for both experiments is the:

   A. cracker.
   B. water.
   C. enzyme.
   D. starch/sugar level.

2. Which of the following hypotheses is supported by the results of Experiment 1?

   F. At the appropriate pH level, water can break down starch, but at a slower rate than salivary amylase can.
   G. After any given time interval, no differences in the effects of the three buffers on salivary amylase activity should be detectable.
   H. Salivary amylase can show activity at each of the three pH levels tested.
   J. The duration of time in which starch and enzyme remain in the beakers should have no effect on the amount of sugar produced.

3. Under what conditions does salivary amylase appear to work best?

   A. Any pH level greater than 5 and any temperature greater than 25°C
   B. Any pH level greater than 5 and any temperature less than 45°C
   C. pH level of 9 and temperature equals 37°C
   D. pH level of 7 and temperature equals 37°C

4. Which of the following experimental designs would test the hypothesis that enzyme concentration can affect the rate of starch digestion?

   F. Using the same pH, temperature, and enzyme levels in all beakers, test additional samples at 90 minutes, 120 minutes, and 240 minutes.
   G. Using different pH, temperature, and enzyme levels in all beakers, test additional samples at 90 minutes, 120 minutes, and 240 minutes.
   H. Using the same pH and temperatures in all beakers, test additional samples with the enzyme at one-half the strength, two times the strength, and four times the strength.
   J. Using the same pH, temperature, and enzyme levels in all beakers, test additional samples after stirring for 3 minutes, 9 minutes, 15 minutes, and 60 minutes.

5. On the basis of the results of Experiment 1, what would probably occur if Experiment 2 were carried out at a pH level of 5?

   A. Digestion of starch to sugar would slowly begin in the beakers containing crackers plus water.
   B. Overall, digestion of starch to sugar would probably take place less efficiently.
   C. Overall, digestion of starch to sugar would probably take place more efficiently.
   D. The experimental results would not change.

ANSWERS

1. **(B)** *Science/Scientific Investigation/Analysis*

    The experiments investigate enzyme activity. By comparing experimental groups (enzyme present) with control groups (only water present) under otherwise identical conditions, any differences in the experimental results are attributable to the presence of the enzyme in the experimental groups. Did you note the differences in the experiments in your big picture reading?

2. **(H)** *Science/Interpretation of Data/Analysis*

    Although salivary amylase is most effective when the pH level is 7, the enzyme begins to convert starch to sugar at pH levels of 5 and 9—after 15 minutes, low levels of sugar appear, suggesting the onset of starch digestion; after 60 minutes, moderate levels of starch remain and moderate levels of sugar have accumulated.

3. **(D)** *Science/Interpretation of Data/Analysis*

    Experiment 1 indicates that the digestion of starch is the fastest (after 3 minutes, some starch is gone and sugar is already present) and the most thorough (after 15 minutes, all of the starch has become sugar) at a pH level of 7. Experiment 2 shows similar results when the temperature is 37°C. Did you notice these trends in your big picture reading?

4. **(H)** *Science/Scientific Investigation/Analysis*

    To investigate the effects of enzyme concentration on digestion, all variables must be kept the same for each beaker except for the amount of enzyme.

5. **(B)** *Science/Scientific Investigation/Analysis*

    Originally, Experiment 2 was carried out at an "optimal pH" (probably close to 7). Since a pH level of 5 is less than optimal, as indicated by Experiment 1, the action of salivary amylase in the proposed experiment would probably be less efficient regardless of temperature.

ANSWER THE ITEMS

Locate the relevant information. The first and often last step in answering an item is to locate the information you need. Most item stems use a key word or phrase to tell you where to look. For example, "in Table 2" tells you that the information you need is located in Table 2; "the troposphere" tells you that you need the graph, table, or description that supplies information about the troposphere; and "lowering the temperature" indicates that the answer is in the subpart of the passage that provides information about temperature.

ANSWER THE QUESTION THAT IS BEING ASKED

You must answer the question that is asked (not an implied or assumed question). Pay careful attention to the wording of every item stem. Otherwise, you can easily lose points on items that you are capable of answering correctly.

USE THE ANSWER CHOICES

Study the answer choices for guidance. The answer choices, like an item stem, can direct you to the subpart of the passage that contains the information you need. Consider the following item, in which only the answer choices are visible:

Example:

A. Sodium
B. Potassium
C. Lithium
D. Oxygen

With this array, you know to look at that table, graph, or paragraph that includes that list of terms. The choices will also give you guidance on the degree of precision that is required by the question.

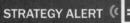

STRATEGY ALERT

Often, the choices are ranges of values, such as $0.015w$ to $0.018w$, rather than specific values, such as simply $0.018w$. Do not look for more precision than the choices allow.

Read the answer choices carefully. The test-writers love to put in wrong answers that look right. For example, if a particular value doubles with a decrease in temperature from 40°C to 20°C, a question might ask, "Assuming the temperature rises from 20°C to 40°C, what happens to the value?" The correct answer is: "The value is reduced by half." You can bet that the wrong answers will include ideas like "doubles," "increases by one-fourth," and "decreases by four"—or some other variation of those ideas.

TRANSCRIBE ANSWERS IN GROUPS

Circle the answers to the ACT Science Test items in the test booklet. For each passage, transcribe the answers to the answer sheet together as a group. Only when the time limit approaches should you transcribe the answers individually to the answer sheet.

ELIMINATE CHOICES, GUESS
(IF NECESSARY), AND MOVE ON

PACING TIP

The ACT test has no penalty for guessing. If you find yourself stuck on a difficult item, eliminate as many choices as possible, guess, and move on!

The items that correspond to a Science passage tend to be arranged from easiest to most difficult. The first item may ask you to find a single number in a table. The second item may ask for a value that is the largest or smallest in a series. And the third item may require you to interpolate a value. Then, the going might get considerably more difficult.

Remember, you get +1 for the hardest item and +1 for the easiest item. Do NOT spend too much time on any one item. When the going gets tough, skip the rest of the questions and go to the next passage where the difficulty resets to the lowest setting.

POWER PRACTICE 3

DIRECTIONS: The passage below is followed by several items. After reading the passage, choose the best answer to each item. You may refer to the passage as often as necessary. You are NOT permitted the use of a calculator.

PASSAGE I

The chart below shows the average blood pressure and relative total surface area associated with the different types of human blood vessels.

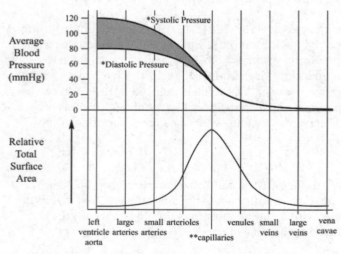

*Pulse pressure is the difference between systolic and diastolic pressure.
**Blood velocity is lowest in the capillaries (averaging 3 cm/sec).

1. According to the diagram, pulse pressure can be detected:

   A. in large arteries only.
   B. in large arteries as well as in large veins.
   C. in blood vessels between the aorta and the capillaries.
   D. primarily in the arterioles, capillaries, and venules.

2. Based on the information in the diagram, average blood pressure:

   F. decreases with increasing blood vessel distance from the left ventricle.
   G. remains approximately constant regardless of blood vessel distance from the left ventricle.
   H. first increases, then decreases with increasing blood vessel distance from the left ventricle.
   J. is highest in blood vessels with the greatest relative total surface area.

3. Which of the following correctly states the relationship between the relative total surface area of blood vessels and the average blood pressure?

   A. As relative total surface area decreases, average blood pressure increases.
   B. As relative total surface area decreases, average blood pressure decreases.
   C. As relative total surface area decreases, average blood pressure may increase or decrease.
   D. Average blood pressure always changes in the opposite direction as the relative total surface area changes.

4. Based on the information in the diagram, which of the following conclusions is correct?

   F. As blood vessel distance from the left ventricle increases, relative total surface area decreases.
   G. As blood vessel distance from the left ventricle increases, pulse pressure increases.
   H. Blood vessels with the greatest relative total surface area have the highest pulse pressure.
   J. Blood vessels closest to and farthest from the left ventricle have the smallest relative total surface area.

5. A physician examining a newly discovered tribe of people deep in the Amazon jungles found that the relative total surface area of their capillaries was greater than that previously reported for any other group of people. If the physician were to predict the average velocity of blood through the capillaries of these people, which of the following values would be most reasonable?

   A. 2 cm/sec
   B. 3 cm/sec
   C. 4 cm/sec
   D. 5 cm/sec

PASSAGE II

What will the end of the universe be like? Two opposing views are presented.

Scientist 1

The universe will die out with a whimper because the energy of the big bang that created the universe will spread itself out over larger and larger regions of space. Since there is only so much energy in the universe, every cubic foot must hold, on the average, less energy as time goes on. In the end everything will get so cold that all motion will stop. That will be the true end of time.

Scientist 2

The idea that the universe will spread itself too thin and freeze is seriously flawed. Such theories do not take into account the gravitational attractions of the bits of matter in the universe for each other. Gravity can act as a cosmic glue to keep the universe from dissolving into nothingness. Theories that state that the universe will eventually re-collapse into a scorching black hole through a reversal of the metric expansion of space are more feasible.

6. Which of the following is a major assumption of Scientist 1?

   F. All matter consists of atoms.
   G. There is a limited amount of energy in the universe.
   H. Gravity does not exist in interstellar space.
   J. The universe is contracting.

7. Which of the following facts, if true, does not help Scientist 2's hypothesis?

   A. It is shown that the galaxies are moving away from each other with a constant speed.
   B. It is shown that the galaxies are moving towards each other with a constant speed.
   C. It is shown that the galaxies are moving towards each other with a constant acceleration.
   D. It is shown that the galaxies are not moving at all relative to each other.

8. It has been calculated that if the universe has a mass greater than or equal to *m*, then the universe will eventually collapse on itself. Scientist 1 would likely say that the mass of the universe:

   F. is equal to *m*.
   G. is less than or equal to *m*.
   H. is greater than *m*.
   J. is less than *m*.

9. If Scientist 2 claims that the universe is contracting, what would he expect the average temperature of the universe to be in 10 billion years?

   A. Higher than now
   B. Lower than now
   C. Same as now
   D. No comparison is possible.

10. What must be true about the energy content of the universe if Scientist 1 is correct?

   F. It is increasing.
   G. It is decreasing.
   H. It is a constant.
   J. It increased at the moment of the big bang and decreased afterwards.

ANSWERS

1. **(C)** *Science/Interpretation of Data/ Comprehension*

   The "*" indicates that the pulse pressure is the difference between systolic and diastolic pressures. According to the diagram, this difference occurs only for blood vessels between the aorta and the capillaries, as indicated by the shaded area in the upper graph.

2. **(F)** *Science/Evaluation of Models/Analysis*

   According to the top graph in the diagram, average blood pressure decreases from left to right across the top graph. This decrease in pressure corresponds to an increase in the distance of vessels from the left ventricle.

3. **(C)** *Science/Interpretation of Data/Analysis*

   In the bottom graph, the relative total surface area peaks in the center (capillaries) and decreases to either side of the peak. In the top graph, vessels to the left of capillaries have higher average blood pressures, while vessels to the right of capillaries have lower average blood pressures. Thus, as surface area decreases, blood pressure may increase or decrease.

4. **(J)** *Science/Evaluation of Models/Analysis*

   In the bottom graph, vessels with the smallest relative total surface area are to the extreme left and extreme right of the center (capillaries), representing the closest to and farthest from the left ventricle of the heart, respectively.

5.   (A) *Science/Scientific Investigation/Application*

Since capillaries have the largest relative total surface area of any vessels (bottom graph), as well as the lowest blood velocity (3 cm/s), it is inferable that an even larger surface area (as in the newly discovered people of the Amazon) should result in slower blood velocity.

6.   (G) *Science/Evaluation of Models/ Comprehension*

The viewpoint of Scientist 1 specifically states that "there is only so much energy in the universe."

7.   (A) *Science/Evaluation of Models/Analysis*

If the galaxies are moving away from each other with a constant speed, then there is no force pulling them back.

8.   (J) *Science/Evaluation of Models/Application*

Scientist 1 argues that the universe will spread out forever, so he would claim that it does not have sufficient mass to collapse. (G) is wrong—if the mass is equal to m, then the universe will collapse.

9.   (A) *Science/Evaluation of Models/Analysis*

Scientist 2 would claim that the average temperature of the universe would be higher in ten billion years than it is now, since the energy will be more concentrated. It is also helpful to note that Scientist 2 states, "The idea that the universe will spread itself too thin and freeze is seriously flawed."

10. (H) *Science/Evaluation of Models/ Comprehension*

Again, Scientist 1 says, "there is only so much energy in the universe."

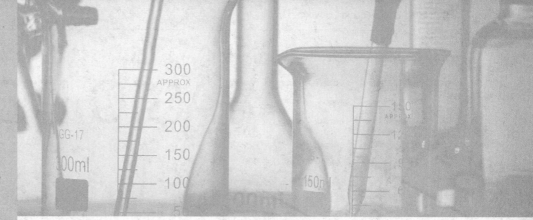

CHAPTER 11

HyperPrep Science

THREE BASIC ITEM TYPES

Science items sort into three general categories: Comprehension, Analysis, and Application. Comprehension items test your ability to recognize and understand basic ideas in text and graphics. Analysis items require you to identify any relationships and trends. Application items ask you to apply the given information to a new situation or to synthesize new information.

COMPREHENSION

Comprehension items frequently require one or more of the following skills:

- Find values on a chart or table
- Perform a calculation using certain values
- Read a graph and understand its labeling
- Identify elements of an experimental design that are explicitly stated
- Identify arguments that are explicitly stated

Examples:

Soil erosion involves the breakdown, detachment, transport, and redistribution of soil particles, most commonly by wind and water. Soil erosion by water occurs most commonly through sheet and rill erosion. Sheet erosion is the planar removal of surface soil by the action of either raindrop splashes or shallow flows of surface water as runoff travels over disturbed ground, picking up and transporting soil particles. The process of sheet erosion is gradual and difficult to detect.

As the shallow flows of water runoff driving sheet erosion combine and increase in velocity, the scouring capacity increases and causes rill erosion. Unlike sheet erosion, which is generally invisible, rill erosion leaves visible scouring of the land in the form of streamlets, or rills. These rills become a further major sediment transport route for soil detached on the sheet erosion areas between rills.

PACING TIP

Comprehension questions tend to be the easiest questions to answer, and they are often the first questions included after each passage. Make sure to attempt all the Comprehension questions on the test.

Soil erosion on cropland, both cultivated and non-cultivated, is of particular interest to farmers as well as land conservationists. In addition to on-site impacts on soil quality and crop productivity, off-site water quantity and quality, air quality, and wildlife habitat are all affected by cropland soil erosion. Figure 1.2 shows cropland soil erosion data collected every five years during a 25-year period.

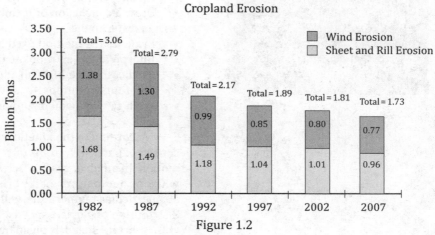

Figure 1.2

Explanations for the example questions are included later in the chapter. Circle your answers now. Later when you reach the explanations at the end of the section, come back and check to make sure you answered the questions correctly.

1. According to the passage, both sheet and rill erosion are:

   A. caused by water.
   B. caused by wind.
   C. easily detected.
   D. independent of soil conditions.

2. According to Figure 1.2, how much land was lost to sheet and rill erosion in 1992?

   F. 0.26 billion tons
   G. 0.95 billion tons
   H. 1.18 billion tons
   J. 2.16 billion tons

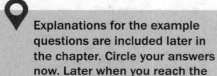

SUM IT UP – COMPREHENSION

Comprehension items ask you to:

- Find values on a chart or table
- Perform a calculation
- Read and understand graphs
- Identify experimental design
- Identify arguments

ANALYSIS

POWER TIP

Pay particular attention to direct (factors change in the same direction) and inverse (factors change in opposite directions) relationships.

Analysis items go a bit deeper than comprehension items. Analysis items frequently require the following skills:

- Identify trends or otherwise explain the data that are presented.
- Draw a conclusion or formulate a hypothesis based on the data of an experiment.
- Evaluate the method used in an experiment.
- Interpolate or extrapolate data from an experiment.
- Predict the results of an additional experimental trial under different conditions.
- Analyze what would support or refute an argument.

Examples:

According to the kinetic molecular theory of gases, all gases consist of particles (atoms or molecules) in continuous, random motion. In an ideal gas, particles move freely without interacting with one another except for brief elastic collisions. Particles of a gas at a particular temperature will have a range of different speeds. The distribution of particle speeds, that is, the number of particles moving with a certain speed, is given by the Maxwell-Boltzmann distribution curves. The most probable speed for the particles is represented by the peak of the curve. For a given distribution, the area under the curve corresponds to the total number of particles of a gas sample.

To illustrate how mass affects molecular speed, Figure 1 gives the Maxwell-Boltzmann distributions for the common gases in Table 1 at a fixed temperature (300 K). To illustrate how temperature affects molecular speed, Figure 2 gives the Maxwell-Boltzmann distributions for nitrogen gas (N_2) at several temperatures.

Table 1: Molar Mass of Common Gases (grams/mole)	
H_2 (hydrogen)	2.02
He (helium)	4.00
N_2 (nitrogen)	28.01
O_2 (oxygen)	32.00
Cl_2 (chlorine)	70.91
Kr (krypton)	83.80

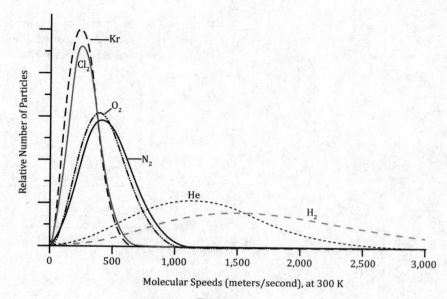

Figure 1

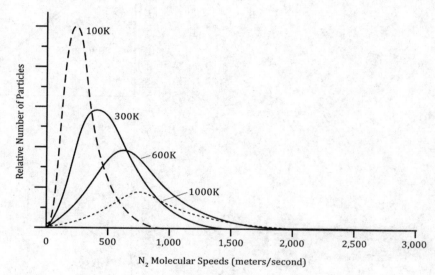

Figure 2

3. A scientist fills one metal cylinder with helium gas and a second metal cylinder with chlorine gas. After the scientist heats both gases to 300 K, which of the following will be true?

A. The molecules in both gases will have the same most probable speed.
B. The helium molecules will have the higher most probable speed.
C. The chlorine molecules will have the higher most probable speed.
D. The chlorine molecules will have a broader range of speeds.

4. Based on the information provided, which of the following graphs best represents the most probable molecular speed for nitrogen as a function of gas temperature?

F.

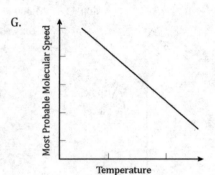

G.

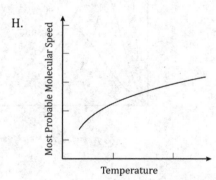

H.

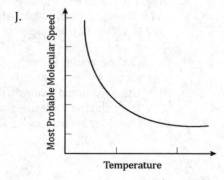

J.

SUM IT UP –
ANALYSIS

Analysis items ask you to:

- Identify trends.
- Draw a conclusion or formulate a hypothesis.
- Evaluate the method used in an experiment.
- Interpolate or extrapolate data.
- Predict the results of an additional experimental trial.
- Analyze what would support or refute an argument.

APPLICATION

Application questions are the most challenging of the three types because they require you to take information from the passage and apply it in some way. Application items frequently require the following:

- Use the results of an experiment to evaluate a new situation.
- Re-evaluate an experiment in light of new information.
- Predict how an author would respond to new information or argumentation.

Examples:

A physics student performed two sets of experiments designed to examine the factors that influence the motion of falling objects.

Experiment 1

A stone was dropped from a steep cliff while a camera, mounted on a tripod on the ground, took photographs at 0.1 second intervals. Back in the laboratory, the same procedure was repeated in the absence (nearly) of air inside a huge vacuum chamber.

Experiment 2

The experiments were repeated (on the cliff and inside the vacuum chamber) using a stone and a cork with identical masses dropped at the same time. At the cliff, the stone hit the ground first. In the vacuum chamber, both objects hit the ground together.

STRATEGY ALERT ((⏏))

Application items are often the last items in a set. If you are having trouble finishing the test, skip the Application items and move on to the next passage, circling back at the end of the test to work on these items. And don't forget to guess if necessary.

5. If part of Experiment 1 were repeated on the moon, where the pull of gravity is one-sixth that of Earth, the stone's downward speed would increase as it falls (i.e., it would accelerate) but the rate of increase in speed would only be one-sixth as great as on Earth. When the photos taken at 0.1-second intervals on the moon are compared to the photos taken on Earth, the series of moon pictures of the stone will be:

A. closer together.
B. farther apart.
C. identical.
D. closer at some times and farther apart at others.

6. In Experiment 1, gravity accelerates the stone as it falls from the cliff, causing it to pick up speed as it drops. Which of the following series of pictures most resembles how the stone appears as it drops?

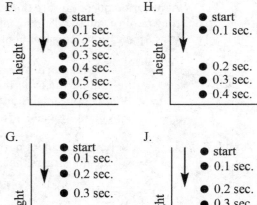

F.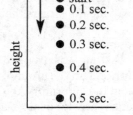

● start
● 0.1 sec.
● 0.2 sec.
● 0.3 sec.
● 0.4 sec.
● 0.5 sec.
● 0.6 sec.

H.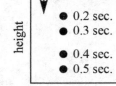

● start
● 0.1 sec.

● 0.2 sec.
● 0.3 sec.
● 0.4 sec.

G.

● start
● 0.1 sec.
● 0.2 sec.

● 0.3 sec.

● 0.4 sec.

● 0.5 sec.

J.

● start
● 0.1 sec.

● 0.2 sec.
● 0.3 sec.

● 0.4 sec.
● 0.5 sec.

Return to the pages below to review each item:
1. p. 197
2. p. 197
3. p. 199
4. p. 200
5. p. 201
6. p. 202

**SUM IT UP –
APPLICATION**

Application items ask you to:

- Use the results of an experiment to evaluate a new situation.
- Reevaluate an experiment in light of new information.
- Predict how an author would respond to new information or argumentation.

Answers:

1. This item tests your ability to find basic information in the text that describes a simple data presentation. Figure 1.2 presents data on soil erosion caused by both wind erosion and sheet and rill erosion. According to the second sentence of the passage, as well as the descriptions given in the first and second paragraphs, both sheet and rill erosion are caused by water, (A).

2. This item tests your ability to extract a piece of information from a simple data presentation. In this case, 1992 corresponds to the third bar of Figure 1.2. Sheet and rill erosion corresponds to the light-gray bottom section of the bar: 1.18 billion tons, (H).

3. Figure 1 gives data for six gases at 300 K, including helium (He) and chlorine (Cl_2). The peaks (most probable molecular speed) are different, so eliminate (A). The range of the speed data is greater for He than for Cl_2, so eliminate (D). Since the peak of He is further to the right at a greater molecular speed than the peak for Cl_2, He molecules have a higher most probable speed at 300 K than the Cl_2 molecules, (B).

4. According to Figure 2, with an increase in temperature (from 100K to 1,000K), the most probable molecular speed also increases (from approximately 300 meters/second to 800 m/s). This is best represented in (H). None of the other graphs show an increase in most probable molecular speed as the temperature increases.

5. Less acceleration means less speed at comparable times, so the lunar photos will show images of the stone that are closer together, (A).

6. Since the stone moves faster as it drops due to acceleration, it will fall farther in each 0.1 second interval, (G).

DATA REPRESENTATION REVIEW AND STRATEGIES

Data Representation passages require you to interpret information presented in graphs, charts, and tables. The ability to read and understand graphs and tables is essential to success on the Data Representation passages, so let's begin our review by focusing on this skill.

UNDERSTANDING FIGURES

A graph or chart consists not just of lines, bars, or other similar devices; it also includes a main title, categories, units, clarifying notes, and other information. These words and numbers are as important for understanding the presented information as the picture itself.

Graphs and charts are always drawn to scale. The function of a graph or chart is to present data in pictorial form, and that function cannot be fulfilled unless the picture is accurately drawn. You can save considerable time by reviewing the graphs and charts visually, without reading the actual numbers. For example, in most cases, a taller column will correspond to a greater amount than a shorter column.

STRAIGHT LINES

CLOSER LOOK

Here are some common Data Representation questions:

1. Select a conclusion that can be supported by Figure 1.
2. Determine what the slope of a given line represents in Figure 2.
3. Predict the results given an assumption or a new situation.
4. Select a statement that is best supported by the data represented in Graph 1.
5. Determine the results based on the difference of time or location.
6. Determine the relationship between the two variables.
7. Determine which conclusion is NOT consistent with the information given in Graph 2.
8. Select an explanation for a given outcome.
9. Identify the LEAST significant assumption made when determining a particular outcome.

A graph with two axes represents the relationship between two variables. There may exist a direct, inverse, or constant relationship. The slope of the line, or the direction of the curve, determines the relationship. A straight line indicates a simple (linear) relationship between two variables.

A direct relationship exists when there is an increase in both variables; in such a case, the slope of the line is positive:

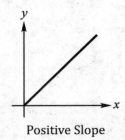

Positive Slope

An inverse relationship exists when there is an increase in one variable and a decrease in the other; in such a case, the slope of the line is negative:

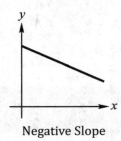

Negative Slope

A constant relationship exists when there is a change in one variable and the other remains constant. For instance, the *y*-value remains unchanged regardless of the increase or decrease in the *x*-value. The result is a horizontal line, which has a slope of zero.

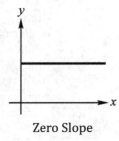

Zero Slope

PARABOLIC CURVES

A parabola is a curve representing an equation in which, in simplest form, one variable is equal to the square of the second variable multiplied by some constant.

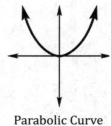

Parabolic Curve

GRAPH READING STRATEGY

STRATEGY ALERT ((▲))

Preview graphs, noting headings, labels, and units. Use this preview method for all graph types, including pie charts.

The strategy for correctly reading graphs and charts is very much like the strategy for reading passages on the Reading Test. Start with the basic parts: look for the main point of the graph, which is sometimes summarized by the main heading or title above the graph.

Next, glance over the general content of the graphs, and look for answers to questions such as: "What do the various categories mean?" and "What units are used?"

Do NOT try to memorize the presented data—rather, take note of the locations of the represented items. Bracket any material of which the significance may not be initially clear. Remember that the accompanying items will indicate the necessary relevant information.

Examples:

The kinetic energy of an object with mass *m* (measured in grams) after a fall from a height *h* (measured in centimeters) was recorded for different heights. A graph was made representing the kinetic energy versus height.

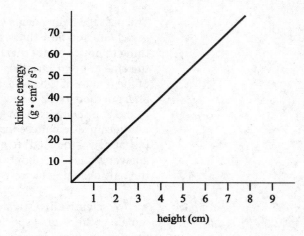

Explanations for the example questions are included later in the chapter. Circle your answers now. Later when you reach the explanations at the end of the section, come back and check to make sure you answered the questions correctly.

1. What would be the approximate kinetic energy (in $g \cdot cm^2 / s^2$) of an object of mass *m* if it were dropped from a height of 4.5 cm?

    A. 4.5
    B. 9.0
    C. 45
    D. 90

2. It is discovered that if the experiment is repeated for an object with twice the mass, the kinetic energy obtained for every height is doubled. The slope of the new set of experiments can be obtained by doing what to the old slope?

    F. Multiplying by 2
    G. Dividing by 2
    H. Squaring
    J. Taking the square root

Items corresponding to Data Representation passages typically address three areas of concern: understanding the nature of the data, recognizing trends, and drawing conclusions.

UNDERSTANDING THE NATURE OF DATA

Understanding a Data Representation passage (and some Research Summary passages) requires understanding the nature of the experiment, how it should be set up or studied, or how the data are arranged. Before any further analysis can be performed, it is necessary to understand what is presented in tables or graphs. In a table, for example, to understand the data, simply read the column headings—these will be the variables in the experiments. Then, check the rows to see what variables were changed in each trial.

The passage below deals with the nature of the animal species *taedi periculum* and how the results of a related study are arranged. The first thing to notice about this Data Representation passage is that it describes the effect of two variables (temperature and food) on the sexual maturity of the female of the species. If you need to answer a question about the effect of food, refer to the "age" column and compare Experiments 1, 2, and 3, or compare Experiments 4, 5, and 6. In each of those groups, temperature remains constant so that a change in age can only be related (as far as is indicated) to a change in amount of food intake. If you need to answer a question about the effect of temperature, compare rows in which the only changing factor is temperature.

Examples: A scientist investigated the variables that affect the age at which a female of the animal species *Taedi periculum* first gives birth. Some of the results of this study are summarized in the table below.

EXPERIMENT	TEMPERATURE (°C)	AVERAGE FOOD INTAKE (grams)	AGE WHEN FIRST GAVE BIRTH (months)
1	25	15	7
2	25	30	6
3	25	45	4
4	35	15	5
5	35	30	3
6	35	45	3

3. Which of the pairs of experiments listed below would be useful for studying the effect of temperature on the age of first birth?

A.   1 and 2
B.   1 and 5
C.   1 and 4
D.   2 and 6

4. Which of the following would be good animals to use for the experiment?

   F. Adult females
   G. Newborn females
   H. Newborn males
   J. Adult males

ANALYZING TRENDS

The second step in understanding a Data Representation passage (and some Research Summary passages) requires the identification of the data trends. To recognize a trend, read each column, noting the trend as the row variable changes. Typical items ask for predictions of what will happen if particular variables are changed in the experiment or for comparisons of the results of two or more trials.

The following two items test the ability to recognize the trends from the previous passage; specifically, the effects of increasing food and increasing temperature on the age of sexual maturity.

5. Which of the following experiments was a control for Experiment 5 when the variable being tested was food intake?

   A. Experiment 1
   B. Experiment 2
   C. Experiment 3
   D. Experiment 6

6. If all other variables are kept constant, which of the following will result in an increase in the age at which the animals give birth?

   F. Decrease in food from 30 grams to 15 grams
   G. Increase in temperature from 25°C to 35°C
   H. Increase in food from 15 grams to 45 grams
   J. Increase in temperature from 25°C to 30°C

MAKING CONCLUSIONS

Finally, take a moment to imagine how the experiments might have been performed. The third step in understanding a Data Representation passage requires going beyond what is specifically stated; it involves evaluating conclusions drawn from the data presented. Avoid conclusions that are not supported by the data.

7. Which of the following conclusions is consistent with the data presented in the table?

A. The weight of the firstborn is proportional to the food intake.
B. The weight of the firstborn is related to the temperature.
C. The age of the mother at time of first offspring's birth increases with decreasing food intake.
D. The age of the mother at time of first offspring's birth decreases with decreasing food intake.

Answers:

Return to the pages below to review each item:
1. p. 205
2. p. 205
3. p. 206
4. p. 207
5. p. 207
6. p. 207
7. p. 208

1. The passage states that the plotted measurements are for an object of mass m, and the y-variable is in units of $g \cdot cm^2/s^2$. Therefore, the kinetic energy of an object of mass m dropped from 4.5 cm is found directly from the graph. (If the item asked about an object of mass $2m$, it would be necessary to double the y-values). Locate 4.5 on the x-axis and the corresponding value on the y-axis. The y-value of this coordinate pair is the kinetic energy for the object of mass m dropped from 4.5 cm: 45 $g \cdot cm^2/s^2$, (C).

2. If the heights ("run") used in the new set of experiments are the same as those used in the original experiment, but the kinetic energy values ("rise") are double the original values, then the denominator of the new slope ("run") is unchanged, while the numerator of the new slope ("rise") is multiplied by two. Therefore, the new slope is equal to twice the original slope, (F).

3. To study the effect of temperature on sexual maturity, experiments in which only temperature is varied must be compared. Of the answer choices, only Experiments 1 and 4, (C), have the same food intake (15 grams) at two different temperatures (25°C and 35°C).

4. A male at any age, (H) and (J), cannot be used to determine the age at which a female gives birth. Furthermore, if the experiment is begun with adults, (F), then there is no way of knowing how big a role the current control of the animals' environment has compared to their past (unknown) environment. Therefore, newborn females, (G), are the best test subjects for the experiment.

5. A controlled experiment for Experiment 5 would have to be identical except for the variable of interest (in this case, temperature). Of the listed choices, only Experiment 6 is identical to Experiment 5 except for the average food intake, (D).

6. Both an increase in temperature, (G) and (J), and an increase in food, (H), cause a decrease in the birthing age. Rather, the item asks for the factor that will cause an increase in the birthing age. If all other variables are kept constant, either a decrease in food, (F), or temperature will result in an increase in the age at which the animals first give birth.

7. In the presented set of experiments, only the effects of temperature and food intake on the mother are known; nothing is known about the offspring at all. Even though it might be reasonable to suppose that some of the extra food goes to the infant, there is no information provided that would back that idea. Therefore, neither (A) nor (B) is correct. In order to decide between (C) and (D), look for a data trend in the table that relates the mother's birthing age to food intake: the age of the mother increases with decreasing food intake, (C).

POWER PRACTICE 1

DIRECTIONS: The passage below is followed by several items. After reading the passage, choose the best answer to each item. You may refer to the passage as often as necessary. You are NOT permitted the use of a calculator. Answers are on page 311.

An object in periodic motion, such as a mass on a spring or a pendulum, vibrates about a fixed position in a regular and repeating fashion. There are two measurable quantities of periodic motion: amplitude and period. The amplitude is the maximum displacement of the object, in either direction, from its resting position. The period is the time it takes the object to complete one cycle of motion: from resting position through the maximum

displacement on both sides of the resting position and then back to the resting position. Note that the period does not depend on how far the spring is initially stretched. This independence is a key feature of all systems that undergo periodic motion.

A student investigates the relationships between position, velocity, and acceleration of a vibrating mass-spring system undergoing periodic motion. A motion sensor placed directly below a mass hung from a spring is used to record the vertical position of the mass for 1 second after the spring is stretched (beyond its resting point) and allowed to "spring back." A computer program is used to analyze the data and plot displacement, velocity, and acceleration of the mass-spring system as a function of time (Figure 1).

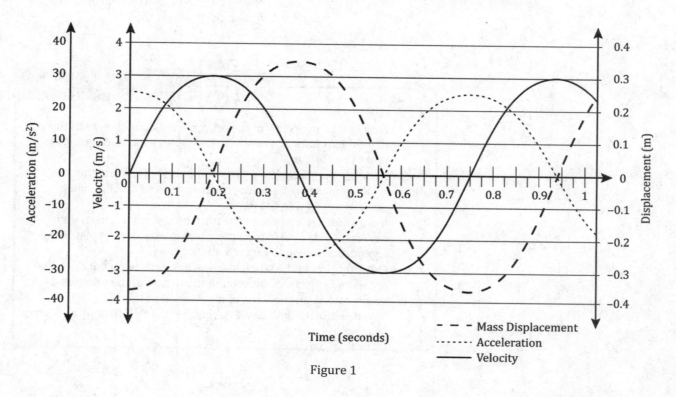

Time (seconds)

- – – Mass Displacement
- .... Acceleration
- ——— Velocity

Figure 1

1. In Figure 1, a positive slope for acceleration data indicates that the mass-spring system is:

   A. moving downward.
   B. moving upward.
   C. slowing down.
   D. speeding up.

2. The period of the mass-spring system is approximately:

   F. 0.375 second.
   G. 0.75 second.
   H. 1 second.
   J. Cannot be determined from the given information

3. Negative values of both displacement and velocity indicate that the mass-spring system is:

   A. below the resting position and moving upward.
   B. moving downward, but speeding up.
   C. below the resting position and moving downward.
   D. approaching the resting position and moving upward.

4. Which of the following statements about the relationship between displacement and velocity for a mass-spring system in periodic motion is best supported by the experimental results?

   F. The velocity magnitude of a mass-spring system decreases as the system moves from maximum positive displacement to its resting position.
   G. The velocity magnitude of a mass-spring system is least as the system passes through its resting position.
   H. The velocity magnitude of a mass-spring system remains constant as the system moves from maximum negative displacement to its resting position.
   J. The velocity magnitude of a mass-spring system is greatest as the system passes through its resting position.

5. The mass-spring system is released from 0.7 meters below its resting position and the experiment repeated. Which of the following results is most likely to occur?

   A. The period of the mass-spring system remains unchanged.
   B. The period of the mass-spring system doubles.
   C. The amplitude of the mass-spring system remains unchanged.
   D. The maximum velocity of the mass-spring system decreases by half.

SUM IT UP –
DECODE THE DATA

1. First, get an overview of the represented data, then read the item(s) carefully and return to the tables, charts, or graphs to find the necessary information.
2. Underline or circle key words and points of information. This strategy makes referencing them easier and quicker when actually answering the items.
3. If data are represented in the form of a graph or chart, then pay particular attention to the scale, the units of measure, the legend, and any noted information.
4. Pay attention to the labeled axes when reviewing data presented in graphs. Determine the nature of the presented information and the units of measurement used.
5. Pay attention to data trends; identify the relationships as direct or inverse.

RESEARCH SUMMARY REVIEW AND STRATEGIES

CLOSER LOOK

Here are some common Research Summary questions:

1. Identify the difference in the experimental design of the two experiments.
2. Predict an outcome based on the results of Experiment 2.
3. Predict the outcome of Experiment 1 when one of the variables is altered.
4. Identify an assumption of Experiment 2 based on the results.
5. Identify a conclusion supported by the results of Experiment 1.
6. Select an experiment that should be conducted in order to test another hypothesis.
7. Identify a hypothesis that was investigated in Experiment 1.

Research Summary passages typically summarize between one and four related experimental studies. This type of passage includes the design, methods, and results of the experiments. A brief introduction may be included to provide additional background information. The experimental results are often illustrated using tables and graphs.

Often, experiments are carried out using a model. Models provide simplified pictures of the processes occurring in real life. The actual values of model measurements are meaningless; however, if the model is valid, then the general trends indicated by the data are useful. For example, a model of an eardrum is made by stretching a thin rubber sheet across a round metal hoop. A set of experiments using this model determines how changes in the frequency or loudness of a sound affect the vibration of the rubber sheet. Even though the actual vibration measurements of the model are irrelevant, the pattern of the measured responses suggests why humans hear shriller noises better than lower pitched ones and why they cannot hear dog whistles.

Research Summary passages describe the methods used for a given set of experiments and the results of those experiments. If any special information is needed, such as the meaning of a particular chemical test result, that information will be detailed in the experiment description. Additionally, before describing any experiments, a Research Summary passage may review the hypothesis that the experiments are intended to test.

Items that correspond to Research Summary passages (and many Data Representation passages) typically address three areas: understanding experimental design, evaluating data, and predicting results.

UNDERSTANDING EXPERIMENTAL DESIGN

Understanding Design of Experiment items ask about what is represented by a particular part of an experiment. These items require an understanding of the information stated in the passage about the design and implementation of the various experiments, as well as any results. In the ear model example, a typical item would ask what the metal hoop represents (the supporting bone for the eardrum). Another item might focus on the controlled variables in the experiment (the rubber sheet and the metal hoop).

Examples:

To test the hypothesis that all antibiotics are equally effective in preventing bacterial growth, the following three experiments were carried out using clear plastic plates filled with nutrient agar (a mixture of ingredients that supports the growth of bacteria). When bacteria reproduce successfully, colonies form on the agar, giving it a cloudy appearance.

Experiment 1

Three plates (A, B, and C) of agar were set up, each with an equal amount of bacterial culture (Bacterium X) spread over the agar surface and with a paper disk placed in the center. Plate A's disk was soaked in Antibiotic I; Plate B's disk was soaked in Antibiotic II; Plate C's disk was soaked in plain water. After incubation overnight at 37°C (body temperature), Plates A and B had a clear area, 2" in diameter surrounding the paper disk, but beyond this 2" region, the plates were cloudy. Plate C was entirely cloudy, including the area adjacent to the paper disk.

Experiment 2

Identical procedures were followed except that Plates A, B, and C were incubated overnight at 22°C (room temperature). After incubation, Plate A had a clear area, 2" in diameter, surrounding the paper disk. Plates B and C were entirely cloudy.

Experiment 3

Identical procedures were followed except that the concentrations of Antibiotic I (Plate A) and Antibiotic II (Plate B) were made twice as strong. After incubation overnight at 22°C, Plates A and B both had clear, 2" areas around the paper disk, while Plate C remained entirely cloudy.

1. After incubation, a clear area around a previously soaked paper disk represents a region where:

    A. agar had washed away.
    B. decomposition had occurred due to high incubation temperatures.
    C. bacterial growth did not occur.
    D. bacteria grew best.

Explanations for the example questions are included later in the chapter. Circle your answers now. Later when you reach the explanations at the end of the section, come back and check to make sure you answered the questions correctly.

2. Which of the following results would indicate that the antibiotics being tested have nothing to do with the control of bacterial growth?

   F.   A clear, 2" region was always observed around the disks soaked in water.

   G. All results remained the same at the two experimental temperatures and at the two antibiotic concentration levels.

   H. Plates A and B always remained clear.

   J.   The disks soaked in water were not used in the experiments at all.

EVALUATING DATA

Evaluating Data items involve relating the experimental results to proposed hypotheses. These items might ask how the experiments can be altered to test a new hypothesis or for the identification of the hypothesis that is best supported by a particular experiment.

If redesigning an experiment to test a new hypothesis, identify which variable is to be investigated and which ones should be held constant. For the correct description of the new experimental methods, only the investigated factor will vary in value. If identifying which hypothesis is best supported by an experiment's data, compare each choice to determine the hypothesis most specifically described by the actual experimental methods and reported data trends.

A hypothesis for the ear model example that says something about flexible membranes on round frames would be better than one that discusses flexible membranes on frames in general. Since the experiment is specific to round frames, the first hypothesis more closely describes the actual experiment and is therefore the better choice.

Examples: **3.** Which hypothesis best explains the observation that the agar plates never appear clear beyond a 2" area surrounding the soaked paper disks?

   A. The bacteria cannot grow well within 2" of any moist paper disks.

   B. The antibiotics cannot seep through the agar beyond a distance of 2".

   C. At the experimental incubation temperatures used, the two antibiotics interfere with each other's effectiveness.

   D. The paper disks can absorb nutrients out of the agar from the distance of 2".

4. Which of the following conclusions is supported by the results of both Experiment 2 and Experiment 3?

    F. Antibiotics I and II have similar effects on bacterial growth, regardless of concentrations.
    G. Antibiotic II and water have similar effects on bacterial growth, regardless of concentrations.
    H. The effectiveness of Antibiotic II at 22°C depends on its concentration.
    J. The effectiveness of Antibiotic I at 22°C depends on its concentration.

PREDICTING RESULTS

Predicting Results items require you to make inferences or predictions based on the presented experimental results and data trends. These items are similar to Data Representation items that require the identification of data trends, except that the answers to Research Summary items are often qualitative rather than quantitative. Therefore, it is important to understand not only the experiment, but also any special results, such as the significance of a certain color or the forming of a solid.

Example: 5. If either Antibiotic I or II could be prescribed for internal use to prevent the spread of Bacterium X infections, which recommendation, based on the experimental results, is appropriate if the cost due to the amount of antibiotic used per dose is the most critical factor (the antibiotics are equal in cost for equal concentrations)?

    A. Either Antibiotic I or II can be taken at equal cost.
    B. Antibiotic I would be less expensive.
    C. Antibiotic II would be less expensive.
    D. Neither Antibiotic I nor II would be effective in preventing the spread of Bacterium X.

Answers: 1. The last sentence of the introduction states that when bacteria reproduce successfully, colonies form on the agar, giving it a cloudy appearance. Therefore, it is inferable that if bacterial reproduction or growth does not occur, the agar will remain clear, (C).

Return to the pages below to review each item:
1. p. 212
2. p. 213
3. p. 213
4. p. 214
5. p. 214

2. The plates with water-soaked paper disks are the experimental controls. A clear 2" area around the water-soaked disks similar to that found around the antibiotic-soaked disks would indicate that the inhibition of bacteria growth was not due to the presence of the antibiotic, (F).

3. Both (A) and (D) are incorrect because neither statement is true with respect to the paper disks soaked in water. (C) is incorrect because the antibiotics cannot interfere with each other if they are not on the same plate of agar. So, by the process of elimination, (B) must be correct. Indeed, since the clear area never extends beyond 2" from the antibiotics, the degree to which substances can diffuse through a thick medium such as agar is limited.

4. In Experiment 2, the normal concentration of Antibiotic II (Plate B) had no effect on bacterial growth; therefore, both Plate B (Antibiotic II) and Plate C (water) were completely cloudy with bacterial growth. In Experiment 3, the concentration of Antibiotic II was doubled and Plate B then had a clear 2" area around the antibiotic-soaked disk, indicating the inhibition of bacterial growth. Therefore, the effectiveness of Antibiotic II at 22°C depends on its concentration, (H).

5. This question underscores the importance of looking at details, such as temperature. Failure to do this would make you draw the faulty conclusion of using all three experiments, when only Experiment 1 is appropriate. Since the antibiotics would be prescribed for internal use, their effects at body temperature (37°C) are most important to consider. Experiment 1 showed that both Antibiotics I and II work equally well in the same concentrations at 37°C (body temperature). Thus, the result is the same, regardless of which one is used. The correct answer is (A).

POWER PRACTICE 2

DIRECTIONS: The passage below is followed by several items. After reading the passage, choose the best answer to each item. You may refer to the passage as often as necessary. You are NOT permitted the use of a calculator. Answers are on page 311.

A useful property of lenses is their ability to form images of objects due to the refraction of light as it passes from one medium to another. If the object and image sizes are h and h', respectively, the magnification of the lens is the ratio of the image size to object size, or:

$$M = \frac{h'}{h} = -\frac{i}{o}$$ (Equation 1)

where o represents the distance between the center of the lens and the object and i represents the distance between the center of the lens and the image. The magnification is represented as a negative number to indicate that an inverted image has a negative height and an upright image has a positive height.

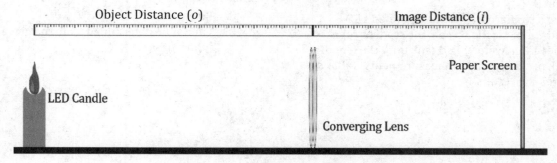

Figure 1

Experiment 1

A student places an LED candle 100 centimeters from a thin converging lens. A paper screen on the other side of the lens is moved until a sharply focused image of the candle light appears on the screen (Figure 1). The image distance and height are measured. The candle is moved 20 centimeters closer to the lens and the experiment repeated until an object distance of 20 centimeters is reached. For each data set, the magnification is calculated (Table 1).

Table 1			
Object Distance, o (cm)	Image Distance, i (cm)	Image Height, h' (cm)	Magnification
100.0	11.1	−0.55	−0.11
80.0	11.4	−0.71	−0.14
60.0	12.0	−1.00	−0.20
40.0	13.3	−1.66	−0.33
20.0	20.0	−5.00	−1.00

Experiment 2

The student repeats Experiment 1 after replacing the single lens with two identical lenses side-by-side and in contact with each other. Table 2 summarizes the results.

Table 2			
Object Distance, o (cm)	Image Distance, i (cm)	Image Height, h' (cm)	Magnification
100.0	5.3	−0.27	−0.05
80.0	5.3	−0.33	−0.07
60.0	5.5	−0.46	−0.09
40.0	5.7	−0.71	−0.14
20.0	6.7	−1.68	−0.34

Experiment 3

Using a similarly sized waterproofed LED candle and white plastic screen, the student repeats Experiment 1 in a water-filled tank until the length of the tank prevents further measurements. Table 3 summarizes the results.

Table 3			
Object Distance, o (cm)	Image Distance, i (cm)	Image Height, h' (cm)	Magnification
100.0	63.9	−3.20	−0.64
80.0	76.1	−4.76	−0.95
60.0	88.1	−7.34	−1.47

1. According to the experimental results, the magnification for the paired converging lenses in air is:

    A. less than that of a single converging lens in air.
    B. greater than that of a single converging lens in air.
    C. equal to that of a single converging lens in air.
    D. greater than that of a single converging lens in water.

2. Which of the following best describes the purpose of Experiment 3?

    F. To study how image formation is affected by changing the object used to form the images
    G. To study how image formation is affected by combining converging lenses
    H. To study how image formation is affected by changing the medium surrounding a converging lens
    J. To study how image formation is affected by changing the position of an object relative to a converging lens

3. Based on the information provided, approximately how tall are the LED candles used in these experiments?

    A. 5 cm
    B. 10 cm
    C. 20 cm
    D. Cannot be determined from the given information

4. Which of the following graphs best represents the relationship between object distance and image distance for a thin converging lens in air?

F.

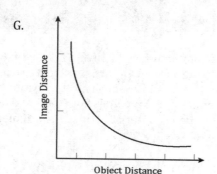

G.

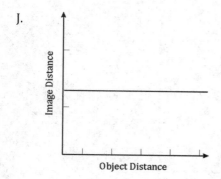

H.

J.

5. Focal length is the distance between the center of a lens and the point at which a clear image of a very distant object is formed. For a thin converging lens in air, the lens formula relates focal length, f, to object distance, o, and image distance, i:

$$\frac{1}{f} = \frac{1}{i} + \frac{1}{o}$$

Using this information, what is the focal length of the lens used in Experiment 1?

A. 33.3 cm
B. 40 cm
C. 10 cm
D. 5 cm

STRATEGY ALERT

Deploy the following Research Summary strategies:

1. Identify the controls and the variables. For a given experiment, the controls are constant—only the investigated factor for that particular experiment is varied.
2. Anticipate how to alter experimental variables to support alternative hypotheses and predict the results of these new experiments.
3. For depicted data trends, determine any proportional or inverse relationships between the investigated factor and the experimental results.
4. If an assumption is faulty because it is not supported by the given information, the experiment may fail to prove the hypothesis, and conclusions based on the assumption may therefore be invalid. Question the validity of any assumptions.

CONFLICTING VIEWPOINT REVIEW AND STRATEGIES

CLOSER LOOK

Here are some examples of Conflicting Viewpoints questions:

1. Predict results based on Scientist 1's argument.
2. Select a generalization that is most accurate given that Scientist 1's argument is correct.
3. Select the findings upon which Scientist 1 and Scientist 2 would NOT agree.
4. Predict which observations support Scientist 1's argument.
5. Select the weakest link in one of the arguments.
6. Select the findings that support the interpretations of both scientists.
7. Select a criticism that Scientist 2 would make about Scientist 1's conclusion.

The third type of Science passage is Conflicting Viewpoints. This passage type presents the hypotheses, arguments, or viewpoints of at least two individuals (e.g., Scientist 1 and Scientist 2) addressing a given question or topic. Scientist 1 may present an argument that includes both facts and an interpretation of the facts; Scientist 2 then counters Scientist 1's argument with an alternative explanation.

Items that correspond to Conflicting Viewpoints passages typically address three areas: predicting results, spotting the assumptions, and picking the best argument.

PREDICTING RESULTS

Predicting Results items ask for a prediction of results based on one of the presented viewpoints. These items are no different from Data Representation and Research Summary items that require using the demonstrated trends to predict additional results. In fact, for the Conflicting Viewpoints passages, the arguments for each presented hypothesis are made using the data trends; therefore, part of the work necessary for these items is already done.

Examples:

Theory 1

Early in the twentieth century, many chemists believed that the stability of the molecule methane, CH_4, could be explained by the "octet" rule, which states that stability occurs when the central atom, in this case carbon, is surrounded by eight "valence," or outer, electrons. Four of these originally came from the outer electrons of the carbon itself, and four came from the four surrounding hydrogen atoms (the hydrogen atom was considered an exception to the rule since it was known to favor a closed shell of two electrons as helium has). According to the octet rule, neither CH_3 nor CH_5 should exist as stable compounds, and this prediction has been borne out by experiment.

Theory 2

While the octet rule predicted many compounds accurately, it also had shortcomings. Ten electrons, for example, surround the compound PCl_5. The greatest shock to the octet rule concerned noble gases such as krypton and xenon, which have eight electrons surrounding them in their atomic states, and therefore should not form compounds since no more electrons would be needed to make an octet. The discovery in 1960 that xenon could form compounds such as XeF_4 forced consideration of a new theory, which held that (a) compounds formed when electrons were completely paired, either in bonds or in non-bonded pairs; (b) the total number of shared electrons around a central atom varied, and could be as high as twelve; (c) the shapes of compounds were such as to keep the pairs of electrons as far from each other as possible.

For example, since six electrons in the atomic state surround sulfur, in the compound SF_6 it acquired six additional shared electrons from the surrounding fluorines for a total of twelve electrons. The shape of the compound is "octahedral," as shown in Figure 1, since this conformation minimizes the overlap of bonding pairs of electrons.

Figure 1

Explanations for the example questions are included later in the chapter. Circle your answers now. Later when you reach the explanations at the end of the section, come back and check to make sure you answered the questions correctly.

1. According to Theory 1, the compound XeF_4:

   A. exists with an octet structure around the xenon.
   B. should not exist since more than eight electrons surround the xenon.
   C. will have similar chemical properties to CH_4.
   D. exists with the xenon surrounded by twelve electrons.

2. The atom boron has three outer electrons, and in bonding to boron, a fluorine atom has a single, unpaired electron to bond with a boron atom. The BF_3 molecule is known to exist. Which of the following is true?

   F. BF_3 obeys Theory 1.
   G. The existence of BF_3 contradicts Theory 2.
   H. According to Theory 2, the structure of BF_3 is a pyramid:

   J. According to Theory 2, the structure of BF_3 is triangular and planar:

SPOTTING ASSUMPTIONS

Spotting the Assumptions items ask you to identify any assumptions regarding the data that were used to support either viewpoint. These assumptions may or may not be justified—the key point is that they were not proven true. Sometimes an assumption is easy to spot because it includes a weak phrase such as "may be," "it is likely that," or "this could indicate."

Examples:

Scientist 1

   The atmosphere of Earth was at one time almost totally lacking in oxygen. One piece of evidence supporting this assertion is the very fact that life got started at all. The first chemical reactions that are necessary for the origin of life, the formation of amino acids, require ultraviolet light. Most of the ultraviolet light coming from the Sun is now absorbed by oxygen in the atmosphere. If there were as much oxygen in the atmosphere then as there is now, there would have been too little ultraviolet light available to enable life to begin. In addition, the oldest bacteria, the ones that have the shortest DNA, are almost all anaerobes—either they do not need oxygen or they die if exposed to oxygen. Most of the oxygen that exists now entered the atmosphere later from volcanic fumes.

Scientist 2

The prevailing opinion is that the atmosphere, though thicker now than it was in the past, is not essentially different in composition. The argument that Earth must originally have been deficient in oxygen is flawed. First, the presence of iron and other oxides in the rocks from this time indicates that there was oxygen available. Second, the requirement for a great deal of ultraviolet light holds only if there is a low concentration of the starting materials in the water. If the water in some prehistoric lake began to freeze, the starting materials would be concentrated in a small volume of unfrozen water. The high concentration of the starting materials would offset the so-called deficiency of ultraviolet light, and life could begin.

3. Underlying Scientist 1's suggestion that the evolutionary record supports the idea of an oxygen deficiency on early Earth is the assumption that the oldest living things:

   A. have the shortest DNA.
   B. have the most fragmented DNA.
   C. have changed radically.
   D. must have died out.

4. Underlying the argument of Scientist 2 is the assumption that the oxygen in the oxides in the rocks was:

   F. always tied up in the rocks.
   G. involved in biological reactions.
   H. completely gaseous during the early days of the atmosphere.
   J. related to the oxygen in the atmosphere at the time.

PICKING THE BEST ARGUMENT

Picking the Best Argument items ask for the argument that best supports or undermines the hypothesis. Concentrate on the central point of the hypothesis and any assumptions that were made regarding the data. Since an assumption is the weakest part of a hypothesis, it will have the greatest impact on the hypothesis whether the argument supports or undermines it.

Examples: 5. To refute Scientist 1's hypothesis, Scientist 2 might best show that:

   A. the amount of oxide in rocks has changed little over the past four billion years.
   B. there are ways of making the biologically important molecules without ultraviolet light.
   C. there are complex anaerobic bacteria.
   D. the atmospheric pressure has not changed over Earth's history.

6. Which of the following is the strongest argument Scientist 1 could use to counter Scientist 2's suggested mechanism for the origin of life?

    F. There was not enough ultraviolet light available.
    G. Chemical reactions occurred differently then.
    H. The temperature at the surface of Earth at that time was always above 35°C because of geothermal heat release.
    J. Most lakes would not have covered large enough areas to guarantee that all the essential building blocks were present.

Answers:

Return to the pages below to review each item:
1. p. 220
2. p. 220
3. p. 221
4. p. 221
5. p. 221
6. p. 222

1. Theory 1 is based on the octet rule: stable compounds form when the central atom is surrounded by eight valence electrons. However, as stated in Theory 2, xenon has eight electrons in its atomic state, so "that xenon could form compounds such as XeF_4 forced consideration of a new theory." This implies that according to Theory 1 and the octet rule, XeF_4 should not exist as a stable compound since it would have more than eight shared electrons, (B): eight electrons from the central xenon atom and four more electrons from the surrounding fluorine atoms.

2. Since the BF_3 molecule has six electrons, it violates Theory 1— eliminate (F) and (G). According to Theory 2, "the shapes of compounds were such as to keep the pairs of electrons as far from each other as possible." The compound's structure in (J) has the fluorine atoms, and thus the shared electrons, farther apart than the arrangement in (H). So, (J) must be correct.

3. Scientist 1 holds that the behavior of the anaerobic bacteria is based on the environment in which they developed, which lacked oxygen. This is significant for early Earth only if the anaerobes were among the oldest living things. Scientist 1 assumes that since the anaerobes have short DNA, they indeed must be among the oldest, (A).

4. It is inferable that Scientist 2 assumes a link between the oxygen in the rock and the oxygen in the air; otherwise, there is no point in bringing up the oxides at all; eliminate (F). Scientist 2's argument is based on the idea that there was once oxygen in the atmosphere, though it does not require that all the oxygen in the rock be free, or that the reactions use the rock oxygen, (H) and (G). The oxygen in the rocks was related to that in the atmosphere, so (J) is correct.

5. The key point of Scientist 1's argument is that life could begin only if ultraviolet light filtered through the atmosphere. This argument is destroyed by eliminating the biological molecules' need for ultraviolet light, (B). (A) could be used as an argument for either side—Scientist 1 could claim that the fact that the amount of oxide does not change demonstrates that it is not relevant to what is going on in the atmosphere; Scientist 2 could claim that it indicates that the atmosphere has also held a constant amount of oxygen. (C) is a weak retort to Scientist 1's second point—Scientist 1 could respond that the complex anaerobe evolved later under special circumstances. (D) says nothing about composition since the pressure can remain unchanged while the relative amounts of the gases change.

6. (F) has an assumption as its argument, which is circular reasoning and incorrect. (G) is an argument without support in the passage. (J) is a weak argument since it is based on probability—a simple "it only had to happen once" refutes the argument. (H) is the strongest argument for countering Scientist 2 because if it were true, there might be no freezing lake at all.

POWER PRACTICE 3 ⚡

DIRECTIONS: The passage below is followed by several items. After reading the passage, choose the best answer to each item. You may refer to the passage as often as necessary. You are NOT permitted the use of a calculator. Answers are on page 311.

How did life originate on planet Earth? Two opposing views are presented.

Scientist 1

The idea that Earth could have given rise to life independently is mistaken. Life on this planet must have come from elsewhere for several reasons. First, complex life appears very suddenly in the geological record. Secondly, all life on Earth has a very similar biochemistry. If life originated on Earth, one would expect regional variations in biochemistry, similar to the variations in species spread over large areas. Finally, the time when life first appeared in the geological record was also a time when large numbers of meteorites struck Earth. The meteorites must have caused life to appear on Earth. The simplest hypothesis is that the meteorites brought life with them.

Scientist 2

Life need not have been imported from outer space. The chemicals required for life existed on the surface of Earth at the time life first appeared. The fact that all life has a similar biochemistry can be explained by considering that any group of chemicals that won the race to life would probably have used the "almost-living" as food. Since we can offer explanations for what happened without relying on a meteorite of unknown composition that might have fallen to Earth, we should stick to hypotheses that have fewer unknowns.

1. Which of the following, if true, most strengthens Scientist 2's argument?

   A. Only five percent more meteors than normal fell on Earth during the time life began.
   B. Only five percent of the meteorites studied contained organic molecules.
   C. A simulation of early Earth chemistry showed the spontaneous formation of complex biomolecules.
   D. Meteorites containing amoebas have been found.

2. Which of the following is an assumption of Scientist 1?

   F. Complex life forms can develop quickly.
   G. Meteorites burn up as soon as they hit Earth's atmosphere.
   H. There is a cause-and-effect relationship between meteors falling and the origin of life.
   J. The changes on Earth's surface due to the presence of life attracted meteor showers.

3. With which explanation of the similar biochemistry of all life on Earth would Scientist 1 most likely agree?

   A. A single chemical pathway to life exists.
   B. Life on Earth arose from a single source.
   C. Life on Earth is not varied.
   D. Meteors are simple.

4. Which of the following, if true, most strengthens Scientist 1's argument?

    F.   Meteorites containing amino acids have been found.

    G.   Only five percent more meteors than normal fell on Earth during the time life began.

    H.   Only five percent of the meteorites studied contained organic molecules.

    J.   A simulation of early Earth chemistry showed the spontaneous formation of complex biomolecules.

5. Which scientist would be likely to disagree with the idea that life on planets other than Earth could have different biochemistries?

    A.   Scientist 1

    B.   Scientist 2

    C.   Neither scientist

    D.   Both scientists

STRATEGY ALERT

Deploy the following strategies when answering Conflicting Viewpoints questions:

1. Be prepared to predict results based on each of the presented viewpoints.
2. Watch for assumptions in each viewpoint—they may or may NOT be justified.
3. Be prepared to identify which argument best addresses the issue. Pay attention to any stated assumptions since they may be the weakest part of the argument.
4. Identify the viewpoints' main point(s) and logical value; identify the differences.
5. Read the viewpoints, but do NOT dwell on the details—the test is "open-book."
6. Read the answer choices carefully. Preparing choices that are workable distractors is more difficult for test-writers than writing the correct response—no more than two or three out of four choices will have any real merit. Distractors, while related to the general topic of the initial statement, ignore the logical structure of the argument.

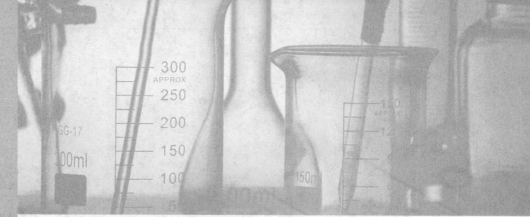

CHAPTER 12
Try It Out! Science Practice

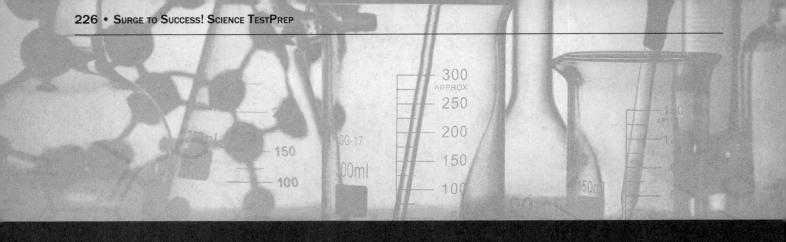

DIRECTIONS: The item numbers in this drill represent the likely position of each problem in a series of 30 multiple-choice questions. Use the "divide and conquer" principle to help solve each problem. Circle your answers. Answers are on page 311.

PASSAGE I

Charles's law states that the volume, *V*, of a gas at constant pressure is proportional to its absolute temperature *T* (temperature in kelvins, K):

$$V \propto T \qquad \text{(Equation 1)}$$

Boyle's law states that the volume of a gas at constant temperature is inversely proportional to its pressure *P* (pressure in pascals, Pa):

$$V \propto 1/P \qquad \text{(Equation 2)}$$

Experiment 1

Students inserted a 100-mL syringe and a thermometer through holes in a rubber stopper and inserted the stopper into a flask that had been cooled in an ice bath to 273 K (Figure 1). The flask was then removed from the ice bath and placed on a hot plate. The gas in the flask expanded as it warmed, slowly pushing the piston up the syringe. Students recorded the temperature and corresponding syringe volume readings as the gas expanded at constant atmospheric pressure (100kPa). To obtain the total volume of the gas in the system, they added the volume of the syringe to the volume of the flask. The students then created a graph of the experimental data (Figure 2).

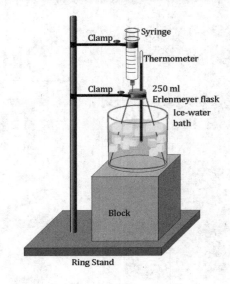

Figure 1

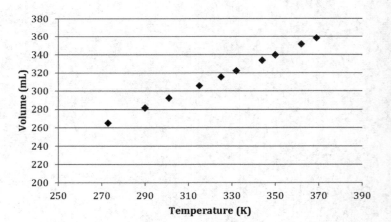

Figure 2

Experiment 2

The students investigated the change in the volume of a gas at room temperature (294 K) at different pressures using the apparatus shown in Figure 3. A glass tube contained a pure nitrogen gas sample (a), and its volume (in mL) was read from the scale. A column of oil (c) transmitted pressure from the reservoir (b), and the pressure value was read on the gauge (d). Table 1 summarizes the data.

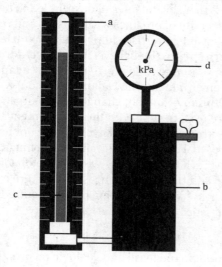

Figure 3

Table 1	
Pressure, P (kPa)	Gas Volume, V (mL)
40	160
50	128
60	107
70	91
80	80
100	64
120	53
140	46
160	40
180	35
200	32

1. Which of the following correctly describes Experiments 1 and 2?

   A. Experiment 1 is designed to study Boyle's law, and gas temperature is the controlled variable; Experiment 2 is designed to study Charles's law, and gas pressure is the controlled variable.

   B. Experiment 1 is designed to study Boyle's law, and gas pressure is the controlled variable; Experiment 2 is designed to study Charles's law, and gas temperature is the controlled variable.

   C. Experiment 1 is designed to study Charles's law, and gas volume is the controlled variable; Experiment 2 is designed to study Boyle's law, and gas pressure is the controlled variable.

   D. Experiment 1 is designed to study Charles's law, and gas pressure is the controlled variable; Experiment 2 is designed to study Boyle's law, and gas temperature is the controlled variable.

2. In the experiment demonstrating Boyle's law, the volume of gas at atmospheric pressure was:

   F. 32 mL.
   G. 64 mL.
   H. 100 mL.
   J. Cannot be determined from the given information

3. In Experiment 2, the function of the column of oil in the experimental apparatus is to:

   A. measure the pressure of the air in the glass tube as it expands or contracts.
   B. measure the temperature of air in the glass tube as it expands or contracts.
   C. transmit pressure from the reservoir to the gas in the glass tube.
   D. transmit air to the gas in the glass tube.

4. Does the graph from Experiment 1 support Charles's law?

F. No; the graph supports Boyle's law because the data demonstrates that volume and temperature are directly proportional.
G. No; the graph does not support Charles's law because the data demonstrates that volume and pressure are inversely proportional.
H. Yes; the graph supports Charles's law because the data demonstrates that volume and temperature are directly proportional.
J. Yes; the graph supports Charles's law because the data demonstrates that volume and temperature are equal.

5. To test the validity of Boyle's law, the students should graph gas volume as a function of:

A. temperature using the data from Experiment 1.
B. temperature using the data from Experiment 2.
C. pressure using the data from Experiment 1.
D. pressure using the data from Experiment 2.

6. Based on the information provided, which of the following is true for the pressure, P, temperature, T, and/or volume, V, of a sample of gas?

F. PV is constant for the same temperature.
G. VT is constant for the same pressure.

H. $\frac{V}{P}$ is constant for the same temperature.

J. PVT is constant for all pressures, volumes, and temperatures.

PASSAGE II

Jean Baptiste Lamarck hypothesized the process of biological evolution before Charles Darwin was born. Some aspects of Lamarck's ideas and Darwin's ideas are presented below.

Lamarckism

Observations of the fossil record led Lamarck to believe that several lines of descent led to nature's broad diversity of organisms. Old fossils and recent fossils showed patterns leading to the characteristics of modern species. He believed that newer forms were more complex and more "perfectly" adapted to their environment. New adaptations could arise as the environment changed. Body organs that were used to cope with the environment became stronger and larger, while those not used deteriorated. For example, giraffes stretching their necks to reach higher leaves would develop longer necks. In addition, such changes in structure could then be passed on to offspring (these acquired characteristics could be inherited).

Darwinism

Based on the fossil and geologic record, Darwin also came to believe that various modern species were related through descent from common ancestors. He also noted that the great diversity of organisms that he observed during his travels were all very well adapted to their environments. The adaptations, however, did not come about through "coping" or usage. Instead, individuals from a population can each show slight genetic or "heritable" differences (variability) in a trait. If such differences, by chance alone, give the individual some reproductive advantage (he or she can successfully produce more offspring than other members of the population), then more individuals with that trait will make up the next generation. Through this "natural selection" of individuals with characteristics that give them a slight advantage in their particular environment, species appear to become very well suited to their natural world. However, "perfection" is not a useful term since the environment is constantly changing. The adaptations that are advantageous "today" may not be advantageous "tomorrow" under different conditions.

7. A major difference between Lamarck and Darwin relates to their views on:

   A. the diversity of organisms in the natural world.
   B. the significance of fossils.
   C. the importance of adaptations to the environment.
   D. the way adaptations come about.

8. Which viewpoint supports the idea that present-day species are descended from earlier forms?

   F. Lamarckism
   G. Darwinism
   H. Both viewpoints
   J. Neither viewpoint

9. Which statement might be used by a Darwinist to explain the extinction of a species?

   A. The environment changed, and not enough individuals had traits or adaptations well suited to the new conditions.
   B. The environment changed, and body parts could not be manipulated enough to adapt to new conditions.
   C. As the environment changed, the individuals present were not "perfect" enough.
   D. As the environment changed, there was no "natural selection."

10. Darwin might dispute the Lamarckian idea of inheriting acquired characteristics by pointing out that:

   F. giraffes with short necks may do just as well as those with long necks.
   G. giraffes that break a leg and walk around on three legs all their lives still do not produce three-legged offspring.
   H. giraffes had shorter necks millions of years ago.
   J. giraffes that break a leg would not be able to reach the highest leaves.

11. Many species of moles live underground in the dark. These species often have small, almost dysfunctional eyes. Which of the following statement(s) would a Lamarckian use to explain this phenomenon?

   I. Moles without eyesight are better adapted for survival underground and therefore produce more offspring.
   II. Disuse of eyes in the dark led to their deterioration in mole species.
   III. Eye deterioration can be passed on to the next generation.

   A. I only
   B. II only
   C. II and III only
   D. I, II, and III

12. Which factor is vital to Darwin's ideas, but not to those of Lamarck?

   F. The fossil record
   G. An examination of modern species
   H. The inheritance of adaptations
   J. Chance

13. A few individuals in a population have an adaptation that enables them to tolerate extremely cold temperatures. In their lifetimes, the environment never reaches such extremes. If all other traits are the same among individuals, what would a Darwinist predict about the number of offspring left in the next generation by these individuals, compared to the number left by other members of the population?

   A. These individuals will leave approximately the same number of offspring.
   B. These individuals will leave more offspring.
   C. These individuals will leave fewer offspring.
   D. These individuals will probably not leave any offspring.

PASSAGE III

The chart below shows the flavor preferences of mice that were offered various fluids to drink at different ages.

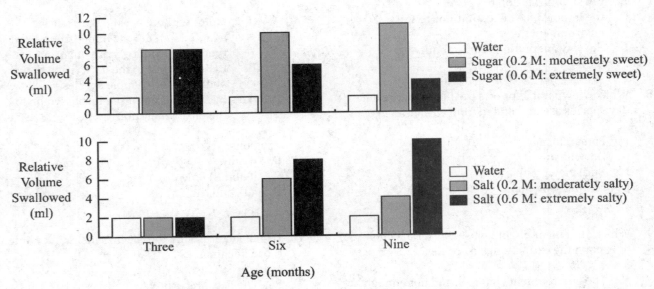

Age (months)

14. Which category on the chart shows no preference between water and the experimental flavor?

    F.   Three months of age/sugar
    G.   Six months of age/salt
    H.   Three months of age/salt
    J.   Nine months of age/sugar

15. Which statement about mice is supported by the information in the chart?

    A.   As age increases, the preference for all tested sugars increases.
    B.   As age increases, the preference for all tested salts increases.
    C.   As age increases, differences between sugars cannot be detected, and differences between salts cannot be detected.
    D.   As age increases, differences between sugars can be detected, and differences between salts can be detected.

16. The flavor preference that fluctuates most irregularly with age is:

    F.   moderately salty.
    G.   moderately sweet.
    H.   extremely salty.
    J.   extremely sweet.

17. Based on the trends shown in the chart, which of the following predictions is most reasonable for one-year-old mice?

    A.   Moderately sweet and moderately salty will be most preferred.
    B.   Extremely sweet and extremely salty will be most preferred.
    C.   Moderately sweet and extremely salty will be most preferred.
    D.   Extremely sweet and moderately salty will be most preferred.

18. Which of the following conclusions about water is NOT consistent with the data in the chart?

    F.   Water is never preferred over any tested flavors.
    G.   Before the age of six months, mice cannot taste the difference between water and sugar or between water and salt.
    H.   At the age of three months, both salty fluids are equal to the water swallowed.
    J.   As age increases, the volume of water swallowed remains the same.

PASSAGE IV

Using electrical circuits, three experiments were performed to investigate the relationship between voltage (volts), resistance (ohms) (total resistance of resistors in series equals the sum of individual resistances), and current (amperes). Each experiment was set up with the following circuit design:

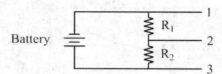

Experiment 1

Using a 6 volt battery and two 1,000 ohm resistors (R_1 and R_2), the measured voltages between points 1 and 2 and between points 2 and 3 were 3 volts each.

Experiment 2

When the battery voltage was increased to 12 volts, and the resistors were kept the same (1,000 ohms each), the measured voltages between points 1 and 2 and between points 2 and 3 were 6 volts each.

Experiment 3

Using the original 6 volt battery, R_1 was replaced with a 2,000 ohm resistor. The voltages measured between points 1 and 2 and between points 2 and 3 were 4 volts and 2 volts, respectively.

19. Judging from the results in Experiment 1 and Experiment 2, if the battery voltage were changed to 1.5 volts and both resistors were 1,000 ohms, what voltage would be expected between point 1 and point 2?

   A.   0.75 volts
   B.   1.5 volts
   C.   3.0 volts
   D.   6.0 volts

20. After studying the measurement made in the previous question, as well as those made earlier in Experiments 1, 2, and 3, the experimenter could reasonably hypothesize that:

   F.   voltage measured across a resistor is inversely proportional to the value of that resistor.
   G.   voltage measured across a resistor is directly proportional to the value of that resistor.
   H.   voltage measured across a resistor is not related to the value of that resistor.
   J.   voltage measured across a resistor equals the battery voltage.

21. When the experimenter recorded the current in the circuit of Experiment 1, it measured 0.003 amperes. In Experiment 3, however, the current measured 0.002 amperes. These results show that current and total resistances are:

   A.   directly proportional.
   B.   inversely proportional.
   C.   equal.
   D.   unrelated.

22. Which of the following formulas for the current in the circuit best summarizes the above results? (The battery voltage is given by V_b and the total resistance is given by R.)

   F. $V_b R$
   G. $\dfrac{R}{V_b}$
   H. $\dfrac{V_b}{R}$
   J. $V_b + R$

23. A new circuit is set up, similar in design to those in the experiments. The battery voltage and the size of the resistors are unknown, but the current measures 0.001 amperes. If the battery voltage is doubled and one of the two resistors is replaced with one having a smaller value, which answer most accurately describes the new current?

   A.   It will be smaller than 0.001 amperes.
   B.   It will be unchanged.
   C.   It will be greater than 0.001 amperes.
   D.   Cannot be determined from the given information

24. Which of the following single changes to Experiment 2 would produce a current of 0.004 amperes?

    F. Decrease the voltage to 4 volts.
    G. Decrease the voltage to 8 volts.
    H. Increase the resistance to 4,000 ohms.
    J. Increase the resistance to 2,000 ohms.

PASSAGE V

Phase diagrams illustrate the relationship between temperature, pressure, and the phases of matter. Each of the three phases—solid, liquid, and gas—is represented by a section of the phase diagram. The curves represent states of equilibrium between two phases—the substance is present in two phases at once as it passes from one phase to the next. All three phases are present at the triple point. For temperatures and pressures both below the triple point, matter passes directly between the solid and gas phases without passing through the liquid phase.

For pressures and temperatures beyond the critical point, the liquid and gas phases converge and become indistinguishable in what is known as a supercritical fluid. Supercritical fluids can dissolve materials like a liquid and effuse through solids like a gas. Beyond the critical point, no amount of pressure will restore a supercritical fluid to its liquid or solid phase without decreasing the temperature.

Figure 1 shows the phase diagram for water, a liquid at room temperature (21°C) and atmospheric pressure (1 atm). Figure 2 shows the phase diagram for carbon dioxide, a gas at room temperature and atmospheric pressure.

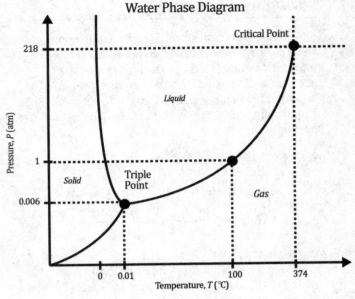

Figure 1

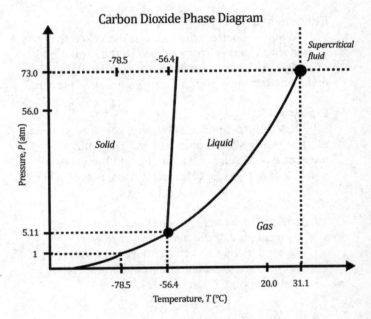

Figure 2

25. According to the information provided and Figure 1, water becomes a supercritical fluid when the temperature and pressure exceed:

   A. 0.006°C and 0.01 atm.
   B. 0.01°C and 0.006 atm.
   C. 218°C and 374 atm.
   D. 374°C and 218 atm.

26. At 100°C, as pressure is decreased from 1.5 atm to 0.006 atm, which of the following is true?

   F. Carbon dioxide changes from a gas to a liquid.
   G. Carbon dioxide changes from a liquid to a gas.
   H. Water changes from a liquid to a gas.
   J. Water changes from a gas to a liquid.

27. Based on the information provided and the phase diagram for water, it can be inferred that the triple point of carbon dioxide occurs at:

   A. −78.5°C and 1 atm.
   B. −56.4°C and 5.11 atm.
   C. 0.01°C and 0.006 atm.
   D. 31.1°C and 73 atm.

28. According to the information provided, both water and carbon dioxide exist solely as liquids at which of the following combinations of pressure and temperature?

   F. 10°C and 56 atm
   G. 0°C and 1 atm
   H. 30°C and 10 atm
   J. There is no point at which both water and carbon dioxide exist solely as liquids.

29. In Figure 1, the line indicating equilibrium between solid water (ice) and liquid water has a negative slope. This indicates that to maintain equilibrium between the two states:

   A. As the temperature is decreased, the pressure must be decreased.
   B. as the temperature is increased, the pressure must be decreased.
   C. as the temperature is increased, the pressure must remain constant.
   D. as the temperature is increased, the pressure must be increased, then decreased.

30. Sublimation occurs when a solid changes to a gas without going through a liquid phase. Under which of the following conditions can sublimation occur?

   F. Water at 0°C and 0.80 atm
   G. Water at 80°C and 0.006 atm
   H. Carbon dioxide at −78.5°C and 1 atm
   J. Carbon dioxide at 0°C and 5.11 atm

CHAPTER 13

Fast Track to Writing Mechanics

DEMYSTIFYING THE WRITING TEST

TEST SPECS

The essay is read by two readers, who give you a score from 2 to 12 in each of the four categories (Ideas and Analysis, Development and Support, Organization, and Language Use and Conventions). The two readers' scores are averaged to give you your final score in each category, and if the essay scores from each grader are not within one point of each other, a third grader will be called on to resolve the conflict. The total score for the essay ranges from 2 to 12 and is based on the category scores.

You write essays for your teachers, so the ACT Writing Test should be no big deal, right? Well, not quite. The essay you are asked to write on the ACT test is different from the essays your teachers assign. But with a little preparation you can ace the ACT Writing Test. There are four things you need to know:

1. **The Writing Test is optional.** Do your homework and find out if any of the schools you're applying to require (or prefer) applicants to submit essay scores.

2. **Your Writing Test score isn't part of your composite test score**. The essay is scored in four categories—Ideas and Analysis, Development and Support, Organization, and Language Use and Conventions—with a score from 2 to 12 in each category.

3. **The directions are always the same.** You can walk into the test knowing exactly what to expect, with a foolproof game plan for the Writing Test.

4. **They tell you what to write (kind of).** The directions tell you to develop your perspective on a provided issue. The directions even give you a list of tasks you should complete in writing your essay.

ANATOMY

CLOSER LOOK

Notice that the prompt does not test a specific body of knowledge. For example, it does not ask, "What were the causes of World War II?" or "What is the best recipe for chocolate cake?" Also, notice that the prompt is constructed so you can provide a very successful response based simply on the perspectives listed and your own personal experience.

DIRECTIONS: You have 40 minutes to plan and write an essay. Read the prompt carefully and make sure you understand the instructions.

The Electoral College

Our indirect method of selecting our president through the Electoral College (all Electoral College votes are declared to the winning candidate in each of the 50 states) has come into question. Direct popular election is the method most often presented as the fairest way to choose a president. Adoption of this process would mean, simply, that the candidate who received the most votes would become president. Some argue that the Electoral College could be kept and votes in the states could be designated to a candidate in a proportional method, so a person who received 60% of a state's votes would receive 60% of its electoral votes. Those who favor this method argue this is the fairest way to choose who will lead the country. However, would changing the constitution be an extreme and unwise change? No matter which side you may choose, this conversation is an important one for our nation's future.

Perspective 1	Perspective 2	Perspective 3
Direct election of the president by popular vote is the fairest way to choose our chief executive. Such a change in our process of selecting the president would reinforce our view that America is a government of the people, by the people, and for the people.	The Electoral College has served the United States for over 250 years. Radical change is not always the best course. A tweaking of the selection process would provide candidates a percentage of the votes earned in each state.	Changing the constitution is never to be done lightly. The founding fathers thought long and hard about this step. We should think long and hard about such a change to our constitution and the possible consequences of such a decision.

CLOSER LOOK

The prompt points you in the right direction. It asks you to evaluate the given perspectives and lists a few specific things you must include in your response.

Essay Task

Write a unified, coherent essay in which you evaluate multiple perspectives on the impact of direct popular election of the President of the United States. In your essay be sure to:
- Analyze and evaluate the perspectives given
- State and develop your own perspective
- Explain the relationship between your perspective and those given

Your perspective may be in full agreement with any of the others, in partial agreement, or wholly different. Whatever the case, support your ideas with logical reasoning and detailed, persuasive examples.

SAMPLE ESSAY OUTLINE

I. **Paragraph 1:** Introduction
    A. Thesis statement: (Agrees with Perspective 1) The Electoral College should be abolished, or at least redesigned, and the president should be elected by a process that gives more power to the popular vote.

II. **Paragraph 2:** The Electoral College undermines the popular vote, and therefore, the outcome of the presidential elections does not necessarily reflect the opinion of the majority of the people.
    A. In a few cases, such as the 2000 election, the outcome went against the popular vote.
    B. If the results of the election are consistent with the popular vote, one could argue that the Electoral College is redundant and serves no real purpose.

III. **Paragraph 3:** The Electoral College forces presidential candidates to focus on winning in key states, rather than winning the votes of the majority of the people.
    A. Campaigning is state-focused; the battleground is in more moderate swing states that may elect either a Democrat or Republican (such as Ohio or Florida), and other states do not receive as much attention.
    B. If you don't live in a swing state, you may feel like your vote doesn't matter and you might be less likely to vote.
    C. Since states contain a mix of Republicans and Democrats, they should not allocate all their Electoral College votes to one candidate; however, this is what usually happens.

IV. **Paragraph 4:** Although it would be a radical change to the Constitution, an amendment would require bipartisan support.
    A. Address Perspectives 2 and 3; abolishing or even modifying the Electoral College would be a radical change, and it is true that it should not be taken lightly.
    B. However, the Constitution has been amended before, and it was designed to be amended. Adding a constitutional amendment is a lengthy legislative process that would require bipartisan support and the approval of three-fourths of the states.
    C. The Constitution has been amended in the past to make voting a more democratic process. For example, amendments were necessary to give racial minorities and women the vote.

V. **Paragraph 5:** Conclusion
    A. Restatement of thesis: Although abolishing the Electoral College would be a radical change to the Constitution, it would make presidential elections a more democratic process by giving greater power to the popular vote.

BEAT THE CLOCK

PACING TIP

The directions are always the same, so read them carefully before the test and understand what is expected before test day. Then, don't waste time reading the directions on test day.

On the ACT test, you will respond to one essay prompt within a 40-minute time limit. During the 40 minutes, you'll need to read the prompt, read the perspectives, analyze the issue and perspectives, outline your response, write your essay, and proofread your essay. This may seem like a lot to accomplish in 40 minutes, but if you break your time down as suggested in the table below, you shouldn't have trouble finishing.

TASK	TIME TO SPEND ON IT	TOTAL TIME SPENT
Read the prompt.	1 minute	1 minute
Evaluate the given perspectives.	2 minutes	3 minutes
Formulate your perspective.	2 minutes	5 minutes
Outline your essay.	2 minutes	7 minutes
Write the introduction.	4 minutes	11 minutes
Write the first paragraph.	7–8 minutes	18–19 minutes
Write the second paragraph.	7–8 minutes	25–27 minutes
Write the third paragraph.	7–8 minutes	32–35 minutes
Write the conclusion.	3 minutes	35–38 minutes
Proofread your essay.	2–5 minutes	40 minutes

If you follow this schedule, you will likely receive at least an average score. After all, your essay will include all the main parts of a successful essay (an introduction that states your position, three supporting paragraphs of text analysis, and a brief conclusion). If your essay is also expressed in clear, precise language and does not include any major grammatical or spelling errors, you will likely receive an even higher score.

GAME PLAN

STEP 1: BEGIN WITH THE PROMPT

To answer the prompt correctly, you have to read and understand the description of the issue and the given perspectives. Do not rush through this first step. Your score is based both on your ability to write clearly and organize ideas and also on your ability to think critically and develop and support an argument. Consider some of the questions that are used by readers to determine your score:

- Does the student understand the prompt?
- Does the student think critically about the presented issue?
- Does the student think critically about the given perspectives?

You need to demonstrate understanding and critical thinking, so make sure you take time before you write to process the prompt.

STEP 2: CHOOSE A POSITION

After you understand the issue and given perspectives, turn to assessing them and decide which perspective you will argue for. Your writing score does NOT depend on which position you choose, so it doesn't matter which perspective you decide to support. In order to choose your own perspective, ask yourself a few questions:

- Do I already have a perspective on this issue?
- Is there a perspective that makes more sense to me than the other perspectives?
- What supporting reasoning and examples will I use in my essay? Which perspective can I best support?

Remember, you can choose any perspective and write a successful essay. So pick one, but be strategic about it. If you already support a perspective, write from that perspective. If you're not sure which perspective to support, think about the evidence you will use and choose the perspective you think you will be able to easily defend.

STEP 3: CREATE AN OUTLINE

Lay out your essay before you begin writing. You know your essay should include an introduction and conclusion. You should also plan to include at least three body paragraphs where you make your main points. Organize your main points from strongest to weakest. Follow this sample outline or create your own outline:

Paragraph 1, Introduction: Concerning [the issue], I use three supporting arguments to argue that [perspective being advanced].
- Overview of support for thesis
- Thesis statement

Paragraph 2, First Argument
- Sub-point 1
- Sub-point 2

Paragraph 3, Second Argument
- Sub-point 1
- Sub-point 2

Paragraph 4, Third Argument
- Sub-point 1
- Sub-point 2

Paragraph 5, Conclusion: I argue that [perspective] on the basis that [first argument], [second argument], and [third argument].
- Restatement of thesis

Once you have created an outline, you should be prepared to successfully write your essay.

STEP 4: WRITE

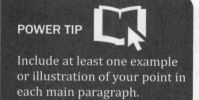

POWER TIP

Include at least one example or illustration of your point in each main paragraph.

Following the outline you created, write your essay. Remember, this prompt is asking you to analyze different perspectives on an issue and then to advance your own. Although your essay should address the complexity of the issue in some detail, it's more important to focus on making a case for why the position you take is the strongest one even given the credibility of other perspectives. Use specific evidence and examples to support your analysis. Whenever you are addressing the relationship between your argument and the perspectives given, describe the strengths and weaknesses of the others and then reiterate why yours is stronger and better supported.

STEP 5: PROOFREAD

POWER TIP

Here are a few extra tips to make your essay successful:

- Use a pencil (not a pen). Using a pencil will let you easily correct anything you might want to change while writing.

- Write clearly and legibly. Readers cannot grade something they cannot read. Taking a little extra time to write clearly will pay off.

- Don't skip lines. Doing so makes it seem like you're trying to pad your essay to make it look longer.

After you've written your essay, take a deep breath. Now all that's left to do is look over your essay. You'll want to spend a few minutes checking for any spelling, grammar, or punctuation errors. Remember that one category on which your essay will be scored is language use and conventions. You won't have time to do a major overhaul of your whole essay, but getting rid of small errors will help increase your score. Use the following good grammar principles to check your essay:

1. Each sentence must have a conjugated (main) verb that agrees with its subject.
2. Each pronoun must have a referent (antecedent) with which it agrees.
3. Similar elements in a sentence must appear in parallel form.
4. Modifiers must agree with what they modify. They must also make sense.
5. Each sentence should use clear and concise language.

POWER PRACTICE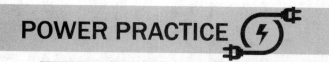

DIRECTIONS: Write an outline for your essay. Then write an introductory paragraph.

Planned Obsolescence

Many technology manufacturers follow a policy of planned obsolescence. Obsolescence describes the condition of no longer being used or useful. Planned obsolescence means that manufacturers make products that are designed to wear out and be replaced quickly. New smartphone applications only function on the latest version of a phone. High repair costs encourage consumers to buy a new laptop instead of fixing a broken one. Spare parts for a computer are no longer available after a few years. Planned obsolescence cuts costs for the manufacturer and the consumer, but what are the risks for both parties when the consumer must frequently replace a product? With the prevalent role of technological devices in our society, planned obsolescence has a strong financial impact on our lives.

Perspective 1	Perspective 2	Perspective 3
Planned obsolescence can be unfair to consumers, forcing them to spend more money than necessary on products that do not offer significant improvements to the older ones. Manufacturers should deliver high quality, long-lasting products. From the manufacturer's perspective, flimsy products could also encourage consumers to buy from a company with a more durable product.	Some industries, such as the automotive industry, are focusing on creating new products that are more environmentally friendly than what is currently available. Planned obsolescence could encourage consumers to buy these newer products and ultimately have a positive impact on the environment.	Planned obsolescence cuts manufacturing costs and encourages companies to design better products in a shorter period of time. This allows for greater innovation in products and ultimately gives the consumer a superior product.

Essay Task

Write a unified, coherent essay in which you evaluate multiple perspectives on the impact of planned obsolescence. In your essay be sure to:
- Analyze and evaluate perspectives given
- State and develop your own perspective
- Explain the relationship between your perspective and those given

Your perspective may be in full agreement with any of the others, in partial agreement or wholly different. Whatever the case, support your ideas with logical reasoning and detailed, persuasive examples.

ANSWERS

SAMPLE OUTLINE

Introduction (Thesis)

- Thesis statement (Agrees with Perspective 1): Planned obsolescence wastes consumers' money by forcing them to buy products that are not designed to last.
- Supporting arguments: Many of the products affected by planned obsolescence are expensive to begin with, and it is misleading for a company to advertise premium products that must be replaced in a few years. A company's reputation will suffer if consumers are not happy with its products. Companies could still create new products and encourage costumers to buy them by using effective advertising rather than creating products that will soon be obsolete.

Paragraph 2 (Subtopic: Many of the products affected by planned obsolescence are expensive to begin with, and it is misleading to the consumer for a company to advertise premium products that, in reality, must be replaced in a few years.)

- Laptops, for example, can cost anywhere from a few hundred to a few thousand dollars. If a consumer pays more for a more expensive laptop, it is reasonable to expect it to last longer than a couple years.
- Technology companies sometimes charge more for repairs than necessary. If consumers research other repair options, they will find more competitive pricing.
- When repair parts are no longer available for a product, the consumer receives the message that the company no longer values the expensive product that was sold to them.

Paragraph 3 (Subtopic: A company's reputation will suffer if consumers are not happy with its products.)

- Consumer support is important for a company's reputation. If a consumer is not happy with a product, he or she is less likely to buy from that company in the future.
- With online consumer reviews, it is easy to research which companies have a reputation for long-lasting, high-quality products.

Paragraph 4 (Subtopic: Companies can still innovate and encourage consumers to buy new products without resorting to planned obsolescence.)

- Address Perspectives 2 and 3: It is important for companies to design new products quickly in order to remain competitive. However, they will not remain competitive by alienating the consumer.
- Companies can encourage consumers to buy new products through effective advertising campaigns. This will make consumers enthusiastic about new products, rather than angry with old ones.

Conclusion (Restatement of thesis): Although it is important for companies to innovate quickly and keep up with their competitors, planned obsolescence can damage the relationship between a company and its customers.

POWER UP!

The Exclusive Cambridge Sample Exam

DIRECTIONS

Practice Test 18B includes five subject tests: English, Mathematics, Reading, Science, and Writing. Calculator use is permitted on the Mathematics Test only.

Cambridge offers several services for schools utilizing our practice tests. Ask your teacher whether your school has decided to send your answers to Cambridge for scoring or to score your answers at your school. If Cambridge is scoring your test, you will use a Scantron™ form provided by your teacher, or you will enter your answers online. If your school is scoring your test, you may use a Scantron™ form provided by your teacher, or you may write your answers on paper.

If you are entering your test answers on a Scantron™ form, please be sure to include the following information on the Scantron™:

Book and Edition	AccelePrep for the ACT Test, 2nd Edition
Practice Test Number	**Practice Test 18B**

If you are only completing a single section of this practice test, make sure to also include the following information:

Subject	English, Mathematics, Reading or Science
Section Number	**Section 1, 2, 3 or 4**

The items in each multiple-choice test are numbered and the answer choices are lettered. The Scantron™ form has numbered rows that correspond to the items on the test. Each row contains lettered ovals to match the answer choices for each item on the test. Each numbered row has a corresponding item on the test.

For each item, first decide on the best answer choice. Then, locate the row number that corresponds to the item. Next, find the oval in that row that matches the letter of the chosen answer. Then, use a soft lead pencil to fill in the oval. DO NOT use a ballpoint pen.

Mark only one answer for each item. If you change your mind about an answer choice, thoroughly erase your first mark before marking your new answer.

Note that only responses marked on your Scantron™ form or written on your paper will be scored. Your score on each test will be based only on the number of items that are correctly answered during the time allowed for that test. You will not be penalized for guessing. Therefore, it is in your best interest to answer every item on the test, even if you must guess.

On the Writing Test, write your response to the prompt using the essay response sheets or loose-leaf paper provided by your teacher. Your teacher might also direct you to enter your essay response online. (Note that the Writing Test is optional.)

You may work on each test only during the time allowed for that test. If you finish a test before time is called, use the time to review your answer choices or work on items about which you are uncertain. You may not return to a test on which time has already been called, and you may not preview another test. You must lay down your pencil immediately when time is called at the end of each test. You may not for any reason fill in or alter ovals for a test after time has expired for that test. Violation of these rules will result in immediate disqualification from the exam.

PRACTICE TEST 18B

1 1 1 1 1 1 1 1 1 1 1 1

SECTION 1: ENGLISH TEST
45 Minutes—75 Items

DIRECTIONS: In the passages below, certain parts of the sentences have been underlined and numbered. In the right-hand column, you will find different ways of writing each underlined part; the original version is indicated by the "NO CHANGE" option. For each item, select the choice that best expresses the intended idea, is most acceptable in standard written English, or is most consistent with the overall tone and style of the passage.

There are also items that ask about a section of the passage or the passage as a whole. These items do not refer to an underlined portion of the passage; these items are preceded by statements that are enclosed in boxes.

Read the passage through once before you begin to answer the accompanying items. Finding the answers to certain items may depend on looking at material that appears several sentences beyond the item. So, be sure that you have read far enough ahead before you select your answer choice. Answers are on page 312.

Answers are on page 312.

PASSAGE I

Basic Principles of Nuclear Weapons

The challenge <u>to start to begin to make</u> timely
                          1
progress toward removing the threat of nuclear war

is the most important challenge in international

relations today. Three general principles guide our

defense and negotiation policies toward such a goal,

principles based on the technical realities of nuclear

war.

First, nuclear weapons are <u>fundamentally</u>
                                              2
<u>different than</u> non-nuclear weapons. These weapons
       2

of mass destruction <u>that could do a lot of harm</u>
                              3

1. A. NO CHANGE
    B. to begin making
    C. to begin the making of
    D. of beginning the making of

2. F. NO CHANGE
    G. different than fundamentally
    H. different from fundamentally
    J. fundamentally different from

3. A. NO CHANGE
    B. (and they could also do a great deal of harm)
    C. (owing to the fact that they could do a lot of harm)
    D. OMIT the underlined portion.

GO ON TO THE NEXT PAGE.

have a long and deadly radioactive <u>memory, the</u>
₄

unknowns of nuclear conflict dwarf the predictable

consequences. The number of deaths resulting <u>from</u>
₅

<u>injuries and the unavailability of medical care</u> and
₅

the economic damage <u>as a result from</u> disruption and
₆

disorganization <u>would be even more devastating than</u>
₇

the direct loss of life and property. 8

    Second, the sole purpose of nuclear weapons

must be to deter nuclear <u>war, it is</u> neither a
₉

substitute for maintaining adequate conventional

military forces to meet vital national security goals

<u>but</u> an effective defense against the almost total
₁₀

mutual annihilation and devastation that results

from a full-scale nuclear war. <u>Third,</u> arms control
₁₁

is an essential part of our national security. Thus

far, we have had no effective controls on offensive

nuclear weaponry, and it is clear that each step

forward in the arms race toward more and improved

---

4. F. NO CHANGE
   G. memory. The
   H. memory the
   J. memory and the

5. A. NO CHANGE
   B. from injuries and also from the unavailability of medical care
   C. from the unavailability of injuries and medical care
   D. both from injuries and also from the unavailability of medical care as well

6. F. NO CHANGE
   G. as a result to
   H. resulting from
   J. with a result of

7. A. NO CHANGE
   B. is even more devastating than
   C. are even more devastating as
   D. might be more devastating even as

8. Which of the following would be an appropriate final sentence for this paragraph?

   F. And so I believe nuclear weapons to be a challenge.
   G. Nuclear war could have no winners.
   H. Nuclear conflict is very dangerous.
   J. Nuclear conflict would be rather wasteful.

9. A. NO CHANGE
   B. war. They are
   C. war they are
   D. war; it is

10. F. NO CHANGE
   G. and
   H. nor
   J. including

11. A. NO CHANGE
   B. Third
   C. (Begin a new paragraph) Third
   D. (Begin a new paragraph) Third,

weapons <u>has made less</u> our security. Before
12

deploying additional weapons, <u>they must develop</u> a
13

coherent arms control strategy.

12. F.   NO CHANGE
    G.   has lessened
    H.   have lessened
    J.   have made less of

13. A.   NO CHANGE
    B.   the development is necessary of
    C.   it is necessary to develop
    D.   it is necessarily to be developed,

> Items #14–15 ask about the preceding passage as a whole.

14. Which of the following best describes the overall structure of the essay?

    F.   A three-part argument
    G.   A two-part narrative
    H.   A three-part comparison
    J.   A four-part argument

15. Which of the following is the thesis of this essay?

    A.   Nuclear weapons are fundamentally different from non-nuclear weapons.
    B.   The sole purpose of nuclear weapons must be to deter nuclear war.
    C.   There are three principles that guide our effort to remove the threat of nuclear war.
    D.   Nuclear war is a frightening possibility.

PASSAGE II

Education for a New Republic

The founders of the Republic <u>viewing their</u>
16

revolution primarily in political terms <u>rather as</u>
17

in economic terms. <u>Therefore,</u> they viewed the
18

kind of education needed for the new Republic

16. F.   NO CHANGE
    G.   having viewed its
    H.   viewed its
    J.   viewed their

17. A.   NO CHANGE
    B.   rather than
    C.   but
    D.   OMIT the underlined portion.

18. F.   NO CHANGE
    G.   Since
    H.   However,
    J.   On the contrary,

GO ON TO THE NEXT PAGE.

largely in political terms instead of <u>as a means to</u>
₁₉
academic excellence or individual self-fulfillment.

<u>Talking about</u> education as a bulwark for liberty,
₂₀
equality, popular consent, and devotion to the public

good, goals that <u>took precedence over</u> the uses of
₂₁
knowledge for self-improvement or occupational

preparation. Over and over again, the Revolutionary

generation, both liberal and conservative in

<u>outlook—assert their</u> faith that the welfare of the
₂₂
Republic rested upon an educated citizenry.

All agreed that the principal ingredients of

a civic education <u>was</u> literacy and inculcation of
₂₃

patriotic and moral <u>virtues some</u> others added the
₂₄
study of history and the study of the principles of the

republican government itself. The founders, as was

the case of almost all their successors, were long on

exhortation and rhetoric regarding the value of civic

<u>education; since</u> they left it to the textbook writers to
₂₅
distill the essence of those values for school children.

Texts in American history and government appeared

as early as the 1790s. The textbook writers <u>turned</u>
₂₆
<u>out being</u> very largely of conservative persuasion,
₂₆
more likely Federalist in outlook than Jeffersonian,

19. A. NO CHANGE
    B. as a means or a way to
    C. to
    D. as

20. F. NO CHANGE
    G. Talking
    H. They talked about
    J. With the talking about

21. A. NO CHANGE
    B. precede
    C. precede over
    D. took precedence on

22. F. NO CHANGE
    G. outlook, asserted its
    H. outlook; asserted its
    J. outlook asserts their

23. A. NO CHANGE
    B. being
    C. were
    D. were like

24. F. NO CHANGE
    G. virtues—some
    H. virtues, some
    J. virtues; some

25. A. NO CHANGE
    B. education. And
    C. education. Since
    D. education, but

26. F. NO CHANGE
    G. turned out to be
    H. turning out to be
    J. having turned out to be

GO ON TO THE NEXT PAGE.

and <u>universally almost agreed</u> that political virtue
₂₇

must rest upon moral and religious precepts. Since

most textbook writers were New Englanders, this

meant that the texts had a decidedly Federalist slant.

In the first half of the Republic, civic education

in the schools emphasized the inculcation of civic

values, put less emphasis on political knowledge,

and <u>no attempt to develop</u> political skills. The
₂₈

development of political skills was left to the local

parties, town meetings, churches, coffeehouses, and

ale houses where men gathered to talk. [29]

27. A. NO CHANGE
    B. almost, agreed universally
    C. almost universally agreed
    D. almost universally, agreed

28. F. NO CHANGE
    G. made no attempt to develop
    H. none at all on the development of
    J. none was put at all on developing

29. Which of the following correctly describes how
    the last paragraph of the essay functions?

    A. It contradicts much of what was said before.
    B. It continues the logical development of the
       essay.
    C. It reiterates what was said in the first para-
       graph.
    D. It is a transitional paragraph to introduce a
       new topic.

Item #30 asks about the preceding passage
as a whole.

---

30. This essay would most likely be published in a:

    F. history textbook.
    G. political science journal.
    H. journal for educators.
    J. biography of Jefferson.

PASSAGE III

Women and World War I

[1]

<u>The contribution of women</u> on the home front
₃₁

during World War I was <u>varied</u>. It included a large
₃₂

31. A. NO CHANGE
    B. Women, their contribution
    C. The contribution of woman
    D. Woman's contribution

32. F. NO CHANGE
    G. diversely varied
    H. diverse and full of variety
    J. full of various diversity

GO ON TO THE NEXT PAGE.

range of activities—from knitting and the operation
                                    33
of drill presses—and engaged a cross section of the
33
female population, from housewives to society girls.

World War I marked the first time in the history of
                    34
the United States that a systematic effort was made,

through organizations like the League for Women's

Service, to utilize the capabilities of women in all
         35
regions of the country.

[2]

While much of this volunteer work falls within
                                        36
the established bounds of women's club work, many

women entered areas of industrial work previously
                                        37
reserved by the male population. Women put on the
37
uniforms of elevator operators, streetcar conductors,

postmen, and industrial workers. However, they
                        38
were employed in aircraft and munitions plants as
38
well as in shipbuilding yards and steel mills.

[3]

Much of the work fell into the traditional

realm of volunteer activity knitting garments for
                        39
the boys overseas, canning for Uncle Sam, planting

victory gardens, etc. Through these activities, every

homemaker could demonstrate their patriotism
                    40
while still fulfilling her role as homemaker. Women

with more time volunteered to hostess at canteens:
                                            41
make bandages, and organize food and clothing
41
drives. The Women's Land Army, dressed in bloomer

uniforms and armed with such slogans as "The

33. A. NO CHANGE
    B. from knitting with the operation of
    C. from knitting and operating
    D. from knitting to operating

34. F. NO CHANGE
    G. has marked the first time
    H. is the first time it is marked
    J. was marked, the first time

35. A. NO CHANGE
    B. being able to utilize
    C. utilizing
    D. and utilize

36. F. NO CHANGE
    G. fell within
    H. having fallen within
    J. fell in

37. A. NO CHANGE
    B. having previously been reserved
    C. previously reserved for
    D. reserved previous to then

38. F. NO CHANGE
    G. workers. They were employed
    H. workers, but they were employed
    J. workers. Since they were employed

39. A. NO CHANGE
    B. activity; knitting
    C. activity: knitting
    D. activity, knitting

40. F. NO CHANGE
    G. be demonstrating
    H. have demonstrated their
    J. demonstrate her

41. A. NO CHANGE
    B. canteens make
    C. canteens, make
    D. canteens; make

GO ON TO THE NEXT PAGE.

Woman with the Hoe Must Defend the Man with

the Musket," was dispatched to assist farmers in
           42

processing crops.

[4]

Women performed ably during the war and laid
                                              43

the foundation for more specialized jobs, increased
    43

wages, better working conditions, and a more

competitive job status in the labor market.

42. F. NO CHANGE
   G. Musket," which was then dispatched
   H. Musket," and it was dispatched
   J. Musket," and it got dispatched

43. A. NO CHANGE
   B. the foundation was laid
   C. the foundation was lain
   D. laying the foundation

Items #44–45 ask about the preceding passage
as a whole.

---

44. Which of the following represents the most
logical order for the paragraphs?

   F. 1, 4, 3, 2
   G. 1, 3, 4, 2
   H. 1, 3, 2, 4
   J. 2, 4, 3, 1

45. Is the use of the sample slogan appropriate to
the essay?

   A. Yes, because it helps the reader to
understand one of the points being made.
   B. Yes, because all general statements should
be illustrated with an example.
   C. No, because it does not help the reader to
understand the point being made.
   D. No, because it is needlessly distracting.

PASSAGE IV

Democracy in Japan

Following the end of World War II, substantial

changes undertaken in Japan to liberate the
        46

individual from authoritarian restraints, including

a general election, women's right to vote, and

suspension of laws that restricted certain political,

religious, and civil liberties. Business and education

were also impacted. Labor unions formed and

monopolies over landholdings were disbanded.

46. F. NO CHANGE
   G. will be undertaken
   H. have been undertaken
   J. were undertaken

GO ON TO THE NEXT PAGE.

Most notably, the new constitution <u>doled</u>
                                    47
<u>out</u> the authority to rule, rather than giving all the
  47
authority to the emperor. The constitution was

modeled after both British and American rule <u>and,</u>
                                              48
<u>while it maintained the position of emperor,</u> the
            48
emperor acted as a symbol rather than the source

of government authority, much like the queen of

England.

The new democratic value system was

<u>acceptable by</u> many teachers, students, intellectuals,
    49

and old <u>liberals, and</u> it was not immediately
              50

embraced by the society as a whole. <u>Japanese</u>
                                      51
<u>traditions were dominated by group values</u>, and
            51
notions of personal freedom and individual rights

<u>being</u> unfamiliar. The support of then-Emperor
  52
Hirohito was instrumental in the acceptance of this

new system. The Emperor publicly rejected the

common belief that the emperor was divine. He also

helped end debates over the proposed constitution

by supporting the model US leaders proposed.

<u>Today, the triumph of</u> democratic processes
        53

47. A. NO CHANGE
    B. divvied up
    C. spread out
    D. distributed

48. Which of the following alternatives to the underlined phrase would NOT be acceptable?

    F. and, although it maintained the position of the emperor,
    G. and—although it maintained the position of the emperor—
    H. and, (while it maintained the position of the emperor)
    J. and (while it maintained the position of the emperor)

49. A. NO CHANGE
    B. excepted to
    C. excepted by
    D. accepted by

50. F. NO CHANGE
    G. liberals, since
    H. liberals, but
    J. liberals; consequently

51. A. NO CHANGE
    B. Dominated by group values were the Japanese traditions
    C. Group values were always dominating the Japanese traditions
    D. Dominating Japanese traditions were group values

52. F. NO CHANGE
    G. were
    H. was
    J. are

53. A. NO CHANGE
    B. (Do NOT begin a new paragraph) Today the triumph, of
    C. Today, the triumph, of
    D. (Do NOT begin a new paragraph) Today, owing to the fact that

GO ON TO THE NEXT PAGE.

is clear evident in the widespread participation of
54

the Japanese in social and political life. Furthermore,
55

there is no universally accepted and stable

value system, values being constantly modified
56

by strong infusions of Western ideas. School

textbooks expound democratic principles, and so
57

emphasizing equality over hierarchy and rationalism
57

over tradition, but in practice, these values are
58

often sometimes misinterpreted and distorted,
58

particularly by the youth that translated the
59

individualistic and humanistic goals of democracy

into egoistic and materialistic ones.

PASSAGE V

Zoological Nature

From the beginning, humankind always has
61

shared some sort of link with the animal world.
61

The earliest and most primitive was surely that of

hunter and prey—with humans possibly playing

the fatal role of victim. Later, of course, humans

reversed the roles as they became more skillful and

more intelligent. The later domestication of certain

54. F. NO CHANGE
G. is
H. is clear and also
J. are clearly

55. A. NO CHANGE
B. Therefore,
C. So,
D. Yet,

56. F. NO CHANGE
G. system with that values are
H. system since that values are
J. system since values are

57. A. NO CHANGE
B. principles, emphasizing
C. principles and the emphasis of
D. principles with the emphasis that

58. F. NO CHANGE
G. had been misinterpreted and distorted often
H. often misinterpreted and distorted
J. are often misinterpreted and distorted

59. A. NO CHANGE
B. that translate
C. who translate
D. translate

60. What type of discussion might logically follow
this last paragraph?

F. A discussion of goals of Japanese youth
G. A discussion of democratic principles
H. A discussion of Western education
J. A discussion of World War II

61. A. NO CHANGE
B. have always shared
C. is always sharing
D. has always shared

animals and also the discovery of agriculture, made
62

for a more settled and stable existence and was

an essential step in the not-so-orderly and very
63

chaotic process of becoming civilized. However, the
63

intellectual distance between regarding an animal

as the source of dinner or of material comfort and

to consider them a worthy subject for study is
64

considerable.

    Not until Aristotle did the animal world

become a subject for serious scientific study.

Although he seemingly writes on every subject,
      65   66

Aristotle's work in zoology—studying animals
66

as animals—is considered his most successful.

He seemed to have had a natural affinity for and

curiosity about all the living creatures of the world,

and he took special interest in marine life.
67

    Aristotle's zoological writings reveal him to be

a remarkably astute observer of the natural world,

wedding his observations to what might be called
68

speculative reason. He was therefore a theorist as

well. His overall theory was simple. In the works
69

of Nature," he said, "purpose and not accident is

predominant." A thing is known then when we know

what it is for. He linked and combined theory and
70

practice by saying that interpretation of an observed

---

62. F. NO CHANGE
    G. animals, also
    H. animals, along with
    J. animals; along with

63. A. NO CHANGE
    B. (and very chaotic)
    C. yet very chaotic
    D. OMIT the underlined portion.

64. F. NO CHANGE
    G. considering it
    H. considering them
    J. then to consider them

65. A. NO CHANGE
    B. he wrote (seemingly) on
    C. writing seemingly on
    D. he wrote on seemingly

66. F. NO CHANGE
    G. subject; Aristotles work
    H. subject Aristotles' work
    J. subject: Aristotle's work

67. A. NO CHANGE
    B. so
    C. but
    D. because

68. F. NO CHANGE
    G. who was wedded to
    H. in that he wedded
    J. with the wedding of

69. A. NO CHANGE
    B. simple—in
    C. simple. "In
    D. simply. "In

70. F. NO CHANGE
    G. combining
    H. to combine
    J. OMIT the underlined portion.

GO ON TO THE NEXT PAGE.

phenomenon must always be made <u>in light of its</u>
                                        71
<u>purpose</u>. His zoological theory was thus a reflection
  71

of the essentially teleological nature of his overall

philosophy. ☐72

71. A.   NO CHANGE
    B.   always keeping its purpose in mind
    C.   without ever forgetting what its purpose is
    D.   given an understanding of what its purpose
         is

72. Is the quote from Aristotle in the last paragraph
    appropriate?

    F.   Yes, because it is important to quote the
         works of people you are talking about.
    G.   Yes, because it is a succinct statement of
         Aristotle's theory.
    H.   No, because the quote is irrelevant to
         what the author is talking about in that
         paragraph.
    J.   No, because it is wrong to quote when you
         can express the idea in your own words.

┌───┐
│ Items #73–75 ask about the preceding passage │
│ as a whole.   │
└───┘

73. The author probably had which of the following
    audiences in mind for this essay?

    A.   Zoologists
    B.   Students who are studying Aristotle
    C.   The average person interested in science
    D.   Teachers of marine biology

74. What is the actual thesis of this essay?

    F.   People have always liked animals.
    G.   Animals and people reversed roles.
    H.   Aristotle was interested in the natural
         world.
    J.   The animal world became a source of
         serious study because of Aristotle.

75. How does the first paragraph of this essay
    function?

    A.   It poses questions to be answered.
    B.   It provides general background for the rest
         of the passage.
    C.   It introduces an argument.
    D.   It provides an anecdote related to the rest of
         the passage.

END OF TEST 1
STOP! DO NOT TURN THE PAGE UNTIL TOLD TO DO SO.

SECTION 2: MATHEMATICS TEST
60 Minutes—60 Items

DIRECTIONS: Solve each item and choose the correct answer choice. Then, fill in the corresponding oval on the bubble sheet.

Allocate time wisely. Try to solve as many items as possible, returning to skipped items if time permits.

Calculator use is permitted on this test; however, some items are best solved without the use of a calculator.

<u>NOTE:</u> All of the following should be assumed, unless otherwise stated.

1. Illustrative figures are NOT necessarily drawn to scale.
2. The word *average* indicates arithmetic mean.
3. The word *line* indicates a straight line.
4. Geometric figures lie in a plane.

Answers are on page 312.

1. If $\dfrac{1}{x} + \dfrac{1}{x} = 8$, then $x = $?

    DO YOUR FIGURING HERE.

    A. $\dfrac{1}{4}$

    B. $\dfrac{1}{2}$

    C. 1
    D. 2
    E. 4

2. If $x = 2$ and $y = -1$, then $3x - 4y = $?

    F. −5
    G. −1
    H. 0
    J. 2
    K. 10

3. In a certain school, there are 600 boys and 400 girls. If 20% of the boys and 30% of the girls are on the honor roll, how many of the students are on the honor roll?

    A. 120
    B. 175
    C. 240
    D. 250
    E. 280

GO ON TO THE NEXT PAGE.

4. If $p, q, r, s,$ and t are whole numbers, the expression $t[r(p+q)+s]$ must be an even number when which of the five numbers is even?

    F. p
    G. q
    H. r
    J. s
    K. t

DO YOUR FIGURING HERE.

5. A student conducting a lab experiment finds that the population of flies in a bottle increases by the same multiple from week to week. If the pattern shown in the table continues, how many flies can the student expect to find in the bottle in Week 5?

Results of Biology Project Conducted by Student X					
Week	1	2	3	4	5
Number of Flies in Bottle	3	12	48	192	?

    A. 195
    B. 240
    C. 384
    D. 564
    E. 768

6. At a school assembly, 3 students are each scheduled to give a short speech. In how many different orders can the speeches be scheduled?

    F. 12
    G. 9
    H. 6
    J. 4
    K. 3

GO ON TO THE NEXT PAGE.

7. If points P and Q lie in the xy-plane and have the coordinates shown below, what is the midpoint of $\overline{PQ}$?

DO YOUR FIGURING HERE.

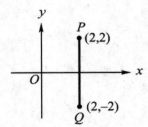

A. (−2,0)
B. (−2,2)
C. (0,2)
D. (2,0)
E. (2,2)

8. If $xy = |xy|$ and $xy \neq 0$, which of the following CANNOT be true?

F. $x > y > 0$
G. $y > x > 0$
H. $x > 0 > y$
J. $0 > x > y$
K. $0 > y > x$

9. In the scale drawing of the floor of a rectangular room shown below, the scale used was 1 cm = 4 m. What is the actual area, in square meters, of the floor of the room?

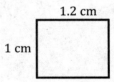

A. 9.6
B. 13.6
C. 15
D. 19.2
E. 38.4

10. If $30,000 \times 20 = 6 \times 10^n$, then $n = ?$

F. 4
G. 5
H. 6
J. 7
K. 8

11. Karen purchased 4 pounds of candy, which was a mix of chocolates and caramels. If chocolates cost $3 per pound and caramels cost $2 per pound, and if Karen spent a total of $10, how many pounds of chocolates did she buy?

A. 1
B. 2
C. 2.5
D. 3
E. 3.5

12. The average of Al's scores on 3 tests was 80. If the average of his scores on the first 2 tests was 77, what was his score on the third test?

F. 86
G. 83
H. 80
J. 77
K. 74

13. A book contains 10 photographs, some in color and some in black-and-white. Which of the following CANNOT be the ratio of color to black-and-white photographs?

A. 9 : 1
B. 4 : 1
C. 5 : 2
D. 3 : 2
E. 1 : 1

14. If $\dfrac{4}{5} = \dfrac{x}{4}$, then $x = ?$

F. 5

G. $\dfrac{16}{5}$

H. $\dfrac{5}{4}$

J. $\dfrac{4}{5}$

K. $\dfrac{5}{16}$

DO YOUR FIGURING HERE.

GO ON TO THE NEXT PAGE.

15. In the figure below, three equilateral triangles have a common vertex. What is the degree measure of $x + y + z$?

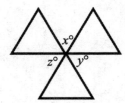

A. 60°
B. 90°
C. 120°
D. 180°
E. 240°

DO YOUR FIGURING HERE.

16. Peter spent $\frac{1}{4}$ of his allowance on Monday and $\frac{1}{3}$ of the remainder on Tuesday. What part of the allowance does Peter still have?

F. $\frac{1}{12}$

G. $\frac{1}{4}$

H. $\frac{1}{2}$

J. $\frac{3}{4}$

K. $\frac{11}{12}$

17. If 100 identical bricks weigh p pounds, then how many pounds do 20 of the identical bricks weigh in terms of p?

A. $\frac{p}{20}$

B. $\frac{p}{5}$

C. $20p$

D. $\frac{5}{p}$

E. $\frac{20}{p}$

18. If the distances between points P, Q, and R are equal, which of the following *could* be true?

DO YOUR FIGURING HERE.

    I. P, Q, and R are points on a circle with center O.

    II. P and Q are points on a circle with center R.

    III. P, Q, and R are vertices of an equilateral triangle.

    F. I only
    G. I and II only
    H. I and III only
    J. II and III only
    K. I, II, and III

19. In the table below, the percentage increase in the price of the item was greatest during which of the following periods?

Year	1980	1985	1990	1995	2000	2005
Price	$2	$4	$7	$12	$20	$50

    A. 1980–1985
    B. 1985–1990
    C. 1990–1995
    D. 1995–2000
    E. 2000–2005

20. Which of the following is a factorization of $x^2 + 4x - 12$?

    F. $(x-2)(x+6)$
    G. $(x-4)(x+3)$
    H. $(x-6)(x+2)$
    J. $(x+2)(x+6)$
    K. $(x+3)(x+4)$

21. Two cartons weigh $3x - 2$ and $2x - 3$ pounds, respectively. If the average weight of the cartons is 10 pounds, the heavier carton weighs how many more pounds than the lighter carton weighs?

    A. 2
    B. 4
    C. 5
    D. 6
    E. 10

22. A group of 15 students took a test that was scored from 0 to 100. If 10 students scored 75 or more on the test, what is the lowest possible value for the average score of all 15 students?

    F.   25
    G.   50
    H.   70
    J.   75
    K.   90

23. For all real numbers x, 16^x is equal to which of the following expressions?

    A. x^{16}
    B. 2^{3x}
    C. 4^{2x}
    D. 8^{2x}
    E. 8^{4x}

24. What is the perimeter of the square in the figure below?

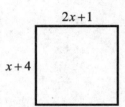

    F.   28
    G.   16
    H.   9
    J.   3
    K.   2

25. If a certain rectangle has a length that is twice its width, what is the ratio of the area of the rectangle to the area of an isosceles right triangle with a hypotenuse equal to the width of the rectangle?

    A. $\dfrac{1}{8}$

    B. $\dfrac{1}{4}$

    C. $\dfrac{1}{2}$

    D. $\dfrac{4}{1}$

    E. $\dfrac{8}{1}$

26. In the coordinate plane, what is the shortest distance between the point with (x,y) coordinates (1,3) and the line with the equation $x = -2$?

    F.   1
    G.   3
    H.   4
    J.   6
    K.   9

DO YOUR FIGURING HERE.

27. If 5 pounds of coffee cost $12, how many pounds of coffee can be purchased for $30?

    A.   7.2
    B.   10
    C.   12.5
    D.   15
    E.   18

28. If the two triangles below are equilateral, what is the ratio of the perimeter of the smaller triangle to that of the larger triangle?

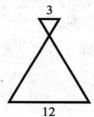

    F. $\dfrac{1}{36}$

    G. $\dfrac{1}{15}$

    H. $\dfrac{1}{9}$

    J. $\dfrac{1}{4}$

    K. $\dfrac{1}{3}$

GO ON TO THE NEXT PAGE.

29. If $f(x) = -3x^3 + 3x^2 - 4x + 8$, then $f(-2) = ?$

DO YOUR FIGURING HERE.

    A. 16
    B. 22
    C. 28
    D. 36
    E. 52

30. A merchant pays $60 wholesale for a dress and then sets the retail price at a 40% markup on the wholesale cost. Two months later, the dress is put on sale at 30% off the retail price. What is the sale price of the dress?

    F. $70.00
    G. $64.70
    H. $58.80
    J. $56.30
    K. $42.00

31. If $\frac{1}{3}$ of a number is 2 more than $\frac{1}{5}$ of the number, then which of the following equations can be used to find the number x?

    A. $\frac{1}{3}x - \frac{1}{5}x = 2$

    B. $\frac{1}{3}x - \frac{1}{5}x = -2$

    C. $\frac{1}{3}x - 2 = -\frac{1}{5}x$

    D. $\frac{1}{3}x + 2 = -\frac{1}{5}x$

    E. $5\left(\frac{1}{3}x + 2\right) = 0$

32. In the figure below, the triangle is equilateral and has a perimeter of 12 centimeters. What is the perimeter, in centimeters, of the square?

    F.   9
    G. 12
    H. 16
    J. 20
    K. 24

GO ON TO THE NEXT PAGE.

33. If one solution of the equation $12x^2 + kx = 6$ is $\frac{2}{3}$, then $k = ?$

   A. 1

   B. $\frac{3}{2}$

   C. 2

   D. 5

   E. 9

DO YOUR FIGURING HERE.

34. If a 6-sided polygon has 2 sides of length $x - 2y$ each and 4 sides of length $2x + y$ each, what is its perimeter?

   F. $6x - 6y$

   G. $6x - y$

   H. $5x$

   J. $6x$

   K. $10x$

35. At the first stop on her route, a driver unloaded $\frac{2}{5}$ of the packages in her van. After she unloaded another 3 packages at her next stop, $\frac{1}{2}$ of the original number of packages in the van remained. How many packages were in the van before the first delivery?

   A. 10

   B. 20

   C. 25

   D. 30

   E. 50

36. For all x and y, $12x^3y^2 - 8x^2y^3 = ?$

   F. $2x^2y^2(4x - y)$

   G. $4x^2y^2(2xy)$

   H. $4x^2y^2(3xy)$

   J. $4x^2y^2(3x - 2y)$

   K. $x^3y^3(12xy - 8xy)$

GO ON TO THE NEXT PAGE.

DO YOUR FIGURING HERE.

37. When $\dfrac{1}{1+\dfrac{1}{x}}$ is defined, it is equivalent to which of the following expressions?

- A. $x+1$
- B. $\dfrac{1}{x+1}$
- C. $\dfrac{x}{x+1}$
- D. $\dfrac{x+1}{x}$
- E. x^2+x

38. If S is 150% of T, what percentage of $S+T$ is T?

- F. $33\dfrac{1}{3}\%$
- G. 40%
- H. 50%
- J. 75%
- K. 80%

39. In $\triangle PQR$, the lengths of $\overline{PQ}$ and $\overline{QR}$ are equal, and the measure of $\angle Q$ is 3 times that of $\angle P$. What is the degree measure of $\angle R$?

- A. 24°
- B. 30°
- C. 36°
- D. 45°
- E. 60°

40. If the cost of b books is d dollars, which of the following equations can be used to find the cost, C, in dollars, of x books at the same rate?

- F. $C=xd$
- G. $C=\dfrac{dx}{b}$
- H. $C=\dfrac{bd}{x}$
- J. $C=bx$
- K. $C=\dfrac{bx}{d}$

GO ON TO THE NEXT PAGE.

41. An article is on sale for 25% off its regular price of $64. If the merchant must also collect a 5% sales tax on this reduced price, what is the total cost of the article including sales tax?

    A. $42.10
    B. $44.20
    C. $49.60
    D. $50.40
    E. $56.70

DO YOUR FIGURING HERE.

42. If $\dfrac{x}{z} = k$ and $\dfrac{y}{z} = k - 1$, then $x = $?

    F. $\dfrac{y}{z}$
    G. $z - y$
    H. $y - 1$
    J. $y + 1$
    K. $y + z$

43. If x is 25% of y, then y is what percentage of x?

    A. 400%
    B. 300%
    C. 250%
    D. 125%
    E.   75%

44. If x is an integer that is a multiple of both 9 and 5, which of the following *must* be true?

    I. x is equal to 45.
    II. x is a multiple of 15.
    III. x is odd.

    F. I only
    G. II only
    H. III only
    J. II and III only
    K. I, II, and III

GO ON TO THE NEXT PAGE.

DO YOUR FIGURING HERE.

45. If each edge of a cube is 2 units long, what is the distance from any vertex (corner of the cube) to the cube's center?

A. $\dfrac{\sqrt{2}}{2}$

B. $\dfrac{3}{2}$

C. $\sqrt{3}$

D. $2\sqrt{2}$

E. $2\sqrt{3}$

46. The figure below shows two circular cylinders, C and C'. If $r = kr'$ and $h = kh'$, what is the ratio of the volume of C' to the volume of C?

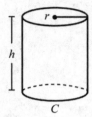 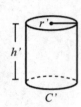

F. $1 : \pi$

G. $\pi : 1$

H. $k\pi : 1$

J. $1 : k^3$

K. $k^3 : 1$

47. In the figure below, if the triangle has an area of 1 square unit, what is the area of the circle, in square units?

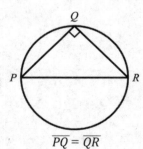

$\overline{PQ} = \overline{QR}$

A. π

B. 2π

C. $2\sqrt{3}\,\pi$

D. 4π

E. $4\sqrt{3}\,\pi$

48. In the figure below, P and Q are the centers of their respective circles and the radius of each circle is 1 inch. What is the perimeter, in inches, of the shaded part of the figure?

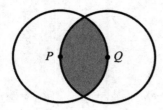

DO YOUR FIGURING HERE.

- F. $\dfrac{4\pi}{3}$
- G. π
- H. $\dfrac{2\pi}{3}$
- J. $\dfrac{\pi}{3}$
- K. $\dfrac{\pi}{6}$

49. A student's final grade in a certain course is the average of his scores on 10 tests graded on a scale of 0 to 100, inclusive. For the first 6 tests, the student's scores averaged 83. If x is the student's final grade for the course, then which of the following must be true?

- A. $8.3 \le x \le 83.0$
- B. $49.8 \le x \le 83.0$
- C. $49.8 \le x \le 89.8$
- D. $54.7 \le x \le 89.8$
- E. $83.0 \le x \le 89.8$

50. What is the multiplicative inverse of the complex number $2 - i$? ($\sqrt{i} = -1$)

- F. $2 + i$
- G. $i - 2$
- H. $\dfrac{2 + i}{3}$
- J. $\dfrac{2 - i}{3}$
- K. $\dfrac{2 + i}{5}$

51. $\log_3 \sqrt{3} = ?$

    A. -1

    B. $\dfrac{1}{3}$

    C. $\dfrac{1}{2}$

    D. $\dfrac{2}{3}$

    E. 2

DO YOUR FIGURING HERE.

52. If $f(x) = (x-1)^2 + 2$, then what value for x creates the minimum value for $f(x)$?

    F. -3

    G. -2

    H. 0

    J. 1

    K. 2

53. If $2^n + 2^n + 2^n + 2^n = x(2^{n+1})$, then $x = ?$

    A. 2

    B. 4

    C. 2^n

    D. 2^{2n}

    E. 2^{n+1}

54. If $f(k) = k^2 + 2k + 1$, then what is the set of all k for which $f(k) = f(-k)$?

    F. $\{0\}$

    G. $\{1\}$

    H. $\{2\}$

    J. $\{1, 2\}$

    K.   All real numbers

55. The limit of a function, $\lim\limits_{x \to a} f(x)$, denotes the value $f(x)$ approaches for values of x approaching a. What is $\lim\limits_{x \to 1} \dfrac{x^2 - 1}{x - 1}$?

    A. -1

    B. 0

    C. 1

    D. 2

    E.   The limit does not exist.

GO ON TO THE NEXT PAGE.

56. If $0 \leq x \leq \pi$ and $\cos x = -1$, then $\cos \dfrac{x}{2} = ?$

DO YOUR FIGURING HERE.

    F. $-\dfrac{\sqrt{3}}{2}$

    G. $-\dfrac{1}{2}$

    H. 0

    J. $\dfrac{1}{2}$

    K. $\dfrac{\sqrt{3}}{2}$

57. Which of the following defines the range of the function $f(x) = \dfrac{1-x}{x}$?

    A.   All real numbers
    B.   All real numbers except –1
    C.   All real numbers except 0
    D.   All real numbers except 1
    E.   All real numbers greater than –1

58. Which of the following graphs represents the equations $x = 3(\sin\theta)$ and $y = 2(\cos\theta)$?

F.

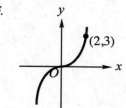

J.

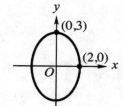

G.

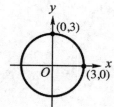

K.

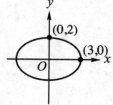

H.

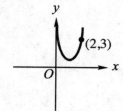

GO ON TO THE NEXT PAGE.

59. For all θ such that $0° < \theta < 90°$, which of the following is equal to $(\sin \theta)(\csc \theta)$?

A. 1
B. $\sqrt{2}$
C. $\tan \theta$
D. $\cot \theta$
E. $\sec \theta$

DO YOUR FIGURING HERE.

60. In the figure below, how many units long is $\overline{BC}$?

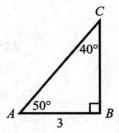

F. 4
G. 5
H. $\sin 10°$
J. $3(\tan 50°)$
K. $3(\tan 40°)$

END OF TEST 2
STOP! DO NOT TURN THE PAGE UNTIL TOLD TO DO SO.
DO NOT RETURN TO THE PREVIOUS TEST.

NO TEST MATERIAL ON THIS PAGE

SECTION 3: READING TEST
35 Minutes—40 Items

DIRECTIONS: Each passage below is followed by a set of items. Read each passage and choose the best answer for each item. Fill in the corresponding oval on your bubble sheet. You may refer to the passage as often as necessary to answer the items. Answers are on page 313.

PASSAGE I

PROSE FICTION: In this passage, a young country man, alone in town for the first time, tries to find a relative, Major Molineux.

It was near nine o'clock of a moonlit evening, when a boat crossed the ferry with a single passenger, who had obtained his conveyance at that unusual hour by the promise of extra fare. When
5 he stood on the landing place, searching in either pocket for the means of fulfilling his agreement, the ferryman lifted a lantern, by the aid of which, and the newly risen moon, he took a very accurate survey of the stranger's figure. He was a youth of
10 barely eighteen years, evidently country-bred, and now upon his first visit to town. He was clad in a coarse gray coat, well worn, but in excellent repair; his under garments were durably constructed of leather, and fitted tight to a pair of serviceable and
15 well-shaped limbs; his stockings of blue yarn were undoubtedly the work of a mother or a sister; and on his head was a three-cornered hat, which in its better days had perhaps sheltered the graver brow of the lad's father. Under his left arm was a heavy
20 cudgel formed of an oak sapling, and retaining a part of the hardened root; and his equipment was completed by a wallet, not so abundantly stocked as to inconvenience the vigorous shoulders on which it hung. Brown, curly hair, well-shaped features, and
25 bright, cheerful eyes were nature's gifts, and worth all that art could have done for his adornment.

The youth, one of whose names was Robin, finally drew from his pocket a little province bill of five shillings, which, in depreciation in that sort
30 of currency, satisfied the ferryman's demand with the addition of a hexagonal piece of parchment, valued at three pence. He then walked forward into the town with as light a step as if his day's journey had not already exceeded thirty miles and with as

35 eager an eye as if he were entering London city, instead of the little metropolis of a New England colony. However, before Robin had proceeded far, it occurred to him that he knew not whither to direct his steps; so he paused and looked up and down
40 the narrow street, scrutinizing the small and mean wooden buildings that were scattered on either side.

"This low hovel cannot be my kinsman's dwelling," thought he, "nor yonder old house, where the moonlight enters at the broken casement; and
45 truly I see none hereabouts that might be worthy of him. It would have been wise to inquire my way of the ferryman, and doubtless, he would have gone with me and earned a shilling from the Major for his pains. But the next man I meet will do as well."

50 He resumed his walk and was glad to perceive that the street now became wide, and the houses were more respectable in their appearance. He soon discerned a figure moving on moderately in advance, and he hastened his steps to overtake it. Robin laid
55 hold of the skirt of the man's old coat, just when the light from the open door and windows of a barber's shop fell upon both their figures.

"Good evening to you, honored sir," said he, making a low bow and still retaining hold of the
60 skirt. "I pray you tell me whereabouts is the dwelling of my kinsman, Major Molineux."

The citizen answered him in a tone of excessive anger and annoyance. "Let go my garment, fellow! I tell you, I know not the man you speak of. What! I
65 have the authority, I have—hem, hem—authority; and if this be the respect you show for your betters, your feet shall be brought acquainted with the stocks by daylight, tomorrow morning!"

Robin released the old man's skirt and
70 hastened away, pursued by an ill-mannered roar

GO ON TO THE NEXT PAGE.

of laughter from the barber's shop. He was at first considerably surprised by the result of his question, but, being a shrewd youth, he soon thought himself able to account for the mystery.

75   "This is some country representative," was his conclusion, "who has never seen the inside of my kinsman's door and lacks the breeding to answer a stranger civilly. The man is old—I might be tempted to turn back and smite him on the nose. Ah, Robin,
80 Robin! Even the barber's boys laugh at you for choosing such a guide! You will be wiser in time, friend Robin."

1. In the final paragraph, the young man is talking to:

    A. the Major.
    B. the man in the coat.
    C. the barbers.
    D. himself.

2. The total cost of the young man's passage on the ferryboat was:

    F. five shillings.
    G. three pence.
    H. five shillings less three pence.
    J. five shillings plus three pence.

3. The young man believes that his relative is a:

    A. barber.
    B. wealthy person.
    C. constable.
    D. builder.

4. The incidents described in the passage take place:

    F. in the late morning.
    G. in the early afternoon.
    H. in the late afternoon.
    J. at night.

5. The passage suggests that thirty miles is:

    A. a long distance to travel in one day.
    B. easily traveled in a single day.
    C. easily traveled in an hour.
    D. a long ferryboat ride.

6. The young man believes that the barbers laughed at him because:

    F. his clothes clearly show that he is from the country.
    G. he asked a question of a stranger who obviously would not know the answer.
    H. he badly needs a haircut and a shave.
    J. the stranger he questioned is actually the man he is looking for.

7. The scenes in the passage are most likely set in which of the following time periods?

    A. Eighteenth century
    B. Nineteenth century
    C. Early twentieth century
    D. Present time

8. The young man approaches the stranger in the coat:

    F. respectfully.
    G. rudely.
    H. coyly.
    J. stealthily.

9. The young man is the only passenger on the ferryboat because:

    A. he paid the ferryman extra for a private charter.
    B. no one else was traveling at that hour.
    C. the Major had sent the boat especially for him.
    D. the ferryman was a good friend of the young man.

10. Just after he gets off the ferry, the young man finds himself in a:

    F. poorer neighborhood.
    G. wealthy neighborhood.
    H. forest.
    J. large city.

GO ON TO THE NEXT PAGE.

PASSAGE II

SOCIAL SCIENCE: These passages discuss Frederick Turner's hypothesis of the American frontier.

Passage A

In 1893, Frederick Jackson Turner presented a paper to a group of historians convening in Chicago during the Columbian Exposition. Entitled "The Significance of the Frontier in American History,"
5 Turner's paper drew little immediate reaction. Yet, no theory of history has had a greater influence on the direction and methodology of inquiry and the issues of debate in American history. Later historians took issue with some of Turner's interpretations;
10 even some of his own students were among those whose research proved some of his views to be wrong. However, these debates merely serve to illustrate the importance of Turner's hypothesis.

Turner's argument was a grand hypothesis
15 about how the settlement of the frontier had shaped the American experience and character. As with all general hypotheses in any field of study, it gave a coherent interpretation to many facts that had been largely ignored by historians up to that time.

20 Turner used statistical evidence from the 1880 census as the basis for a startling conclusion: Prior to 1880 there had been a frontier to be settled. By 1890, Turner pointed out, there was no longer any area of wilderness completely untouched by
25 settlements. The frontier had disappeared. The passing of the frontier, Turner concluded, was a historic moment.

Turner further claimed that the frontier experience had produced a distinctively American
30 character, which was not explainable simply as the predictable behavioral traits molded by English political institutions. Frontier settlers developed inquisitiveness, inventiveness, energy, and a great passion for freedom. These attributes defined a new
35 American character—one evidenced in nationalism, independence, and democracy. This new sense of national identity derived from the fact that people from every section of the country mixed at the Western frontier. Economic independence could
40 be traced to the fact that the settlers no longer depended on England for goods but had become self-sufficient. In addition, the frontier settlers, whose basic social unit was the family, enjoyed freedom from direct governmental interference.
45 Frontier life thus reinforced the fundamental ideals of populist democracy.

In addition, Turner argued that the frontier fostered democracy in the cities of the East. The availability of free land at the frontier provided a
50 "safety-valve" against possible social unrest: those discontented with social inequities and economic injustice could strike out and settle the free land that was available in frontier territories.

Turner's thesis was thus original in both what
55 it said and in the methodology that Turner used in formulating it. Up to the time of Turner's essay, history had been essentially the history of politics. A Midwesterner, Turner challenged this traditional approach of Eastern historians by incorporating
60 techniques of the social sciences, showing how factors of geography, economics, climate, and society influenced the development of the American West. Although now common among historians, at the time this interdisciplinary approach was novel.

Passage B

65 Three years before Turner put forth the frontier thesis, the U.S. Census Bureau had announced the disappearance of a contiguous frontier line. For Turner, the significance of the frontier was its effect on the American character.
70 According to Turner, uniquely American traits were developed by the frontier culture, including a can-do problem-solving attitude, a nervous energy, and rugged individualism.

Turner's essay reached triumphant heights
75 in his belief that the promotion of individualistic democracy was the most important consequence of the frontier. Individuals, forced to rely on their own wits and strength, were necessarily skeptical of hierarchies and fearful of centralized authority.

80 Turner's thesis that the frontier is the key to American history as a whole has rightfully been abandoned. There is too much evidence for the critical influence of factors like slavery and the Civil War, immigration, and the development of industrial
85 capitalism. But even as an account of the West and frontier, Turner's thesis was lacking.

Turner's formulation of "free land" ignored the presence of the numerous Indian peoples whose subjugation was required by the nation's
90 westward march. The many Indian wars started by American expansion belie Turner's argument that the American frontier, in sharp contrast to European borders between nation-states, was "free land."

GO ON TO THE NEXT PAGE.

95 More fundamentally, the very concept of a frontier is dubious, because it applies to too many disparate places and times to be useful. How much do Puritan New England and the California of the transcontinental railroad really have in common? Many such critics have sought to replace the idea

100 of a moving frontier with the idea of the West as a distinctive region, much like the American South.

Additionally, cooperation and communities of various sorts, not isolated individuals, made possible the absorption of the West into the United

105 States. Most migrant wagon trains, for example, were composed of extended kinship networks. Moreover, the role of the federal government and large corporations grew increasingly important. Corporate investors built the railroads; government

110 troops defeated Indian nations; even cowboys, enshrined in popular myth as rugged loners, were generally low-level employees of cattle corporations.

Questions #11–14 ask about Passage A.

11. According to Passage A, Turner's methodology was original in its:

   A. reliance on the history of politics to explain the American experience.

   B. use of an interdisciplinary approach to study a historical question.

   C. reliance on a presentation at a professional conference to announce a theory.

   D. suggestion that key terms like "frontier" have to be more clearly defined.

12. The phrase "even some of his own students" (line 10) implies that students are:

   F. not necessarily familiar with the most recent scholarly work.

   G. ordinarily sympathetic to the views of one of their professors.

   H. not likely to accept a theory until it has been studied for some time.

   J. disposed to propose new theories that have little merit.

13. The attitude of the author of Passage A toward Turner's work can best be described as:

   A. suspicious.

   B. condescending.

   C. undecided.

   D. approving.

14. In this context, "grand" (line 14) means:

   F. incorrect.

   G. comprehensive.

   H. lavish.

   J. tentative.

Questions #15–18 ask about Passage B.

15. The author of Passage B lists the "factors" in lines 83–85 in order to show that:

   A. Turner's thesis did not adequately explain the history of the frontier.

   B. historians prior to Turner had tended to focus on only a single explanatory factor.

   C. the frontier was only one of many important factors in American history.

   D. different regions of America had different experiences of the frontier.

16. The author of Passage B mentions wagon trains (line 105) in order to show that:

   F. frontier land had previously been inhabited by indigenous peoples.

   G. groups were as important in the westward expansion as individuals.

   H. government army troops were needed to secure the safety of settlers.

   J. groups from different regions came into contact at the frontier.

17. It can be inferred that the author of Passage B believes that:

   A. Turner's thesis is still generally valid.

   B. Turner's thesis had very limited usefulness.

   C. Turner was intellectually dishonest.

   D. Turner intentionally ignored evidence.

GO ON TO THE NEXT PAGE.

18. In context, "belie" (line 91) means:

    F. tell an untruth about.
    G. conceal a flaw in.
    H. prove to be false.
    J. retract a point.

Questions #19–20 ask about both passages.

---

19. Both passages mention all of the following as elements of Turner's view regarding the American character EXCEPT:

    A. practical inventiveness.
    B. pro-democracy attitude.
    C. skepticism toward authority.
    D. nationalistic feelings.

20. The evidence in Passage B that frontier land was not free (lines 87–93) most undermines what aspect of Turner's thesis as explained in Passage A?

    F. Safety-valve theory
    G. Census data of 1880
    H. Claim of self-sufficiency
    J. Mixing at the frontier

GO ON TO THE NEXT PAGE.

PASSAGE III

HUMANITIES: In this passage, the author expresses his opinion regarding the role of philosophy.

The service of philosophy, of speculative culture, towards the human spirit is to rouse, to startle it into a life of constant and eager observation. Every moment, some form grows
5　perfect in hand or face; some tone on the hills or the sea is choicer than the rest; some mood of passion or insight or intellectual excitement is irresistibly real and attractive to us—and for that moment only. Not the fruit of experience, but experience itself is
10　the end. Only a counted number of pulses are given to us of a variegated, dramatic life. How may we see in them all that is to be seen in them by the finest senses? How shall we pass most quickly from point to point and be present always at the focus where
15　the greatest number of vital forces unite in their purest energy?

To burn always with this hard, gemlike flame, to maintain this ecstasy, is success in life. In a sense it might even be said that our failure is to form
20　habits: for, after all, habit is relative to a stereotyped world, and in the meantime, it is only the roughness of the eye that makes any two persons, things, or situations seem alike. While all melts under our feet, we may well catch at any exquisite passion, or
25　any knowledge that seems by a lifted horizon to set the spirit free for a moment, or any stirring of the senses, strange dyes, strange colors, curious odors, or work of the artist's hands or the faces of one's friends. Not to discriminate every moment some
30　passionate attitude in those about us, and in the brilliancy of their gifts some tragic dividing of forces of their ways is, on this short day of the frost and sun, to sleep before evening. With this sense of the splendor of our experience and of its awful brevity,
35　gathering all we are into one desperate effort to see and touch, we shall hardly have time to make theories about the things we see and touch.

What we have to do is to be forever curiously testing new opinions and courting new
40　impressions, never acquiescing in a facile orthodoxy. Philosophical theories or ideas, as points of view, instruments of criticism, may help us to gather what might otherwise pass unregarded by us. "Philosophy is the microscope of thought." The theory or idea or
45　system which requires of us the sacrifice of any part of this experience, in consideration of some interest into which we cannot enter, or some abstract theory we have not identified with ourselves, or of what is only conventional, has no real claim upon us.

50　　In one of his most beautiful passages, Rousseau describes the awakening in him of the literary sense. An undefinable taint of death had clung always about him, and now in early manhood he believed himself smitten by mortal disease. He asked himself
55　how he might make as much as possible of the interval that remained; and he was not biased by anything in his previous life when he decided that it must be by intellectual excitement.

We are all under sentence of death but with
60　a sort of indefinite reprieve; we have an interval and then our place knows us no more. Some spend this interval in listlessness, others in high passions, the wisest—at least among the "children of this world"—in art and song. Our one chance
65　lies in expanding this interval—in getting as many pulsations as possible into the given time. Great passions may give us this quickened sense of life, ecstasy and sorrow of love, the various forms of enthusiastic activity, disinterested or otherwise,
70　which comes naturally to many of us. Only be sure it is passion—that it does yield you this fruit of a quickened, multiplied consciousness. Of this wisdom, the poetic passion, the desire of beauty, the love of art for art's sake has most; for art comes
75　to you professing frankly to give nothing but the highest quality to your moments as they pass, and simply for the sake of those moments.

21. Which of the following best describes the overall structure of the passage?

   A.　The author raises a question and then provides an answer.
   B.　The author presents a theory, which he then proves.
   C.　The author studies a widely held belief and then rejects it.
   D.　The author defines a term and then provides examples.

22. In the passage, the author uses the word *pulsations* (line 66) to mean:

   F.　children.
   G.　lives.
   H.　death.
   J.　experiences.

GO ON TO THE NEXT PAGE.

23. According to the author, the function of art is to:

    A. depict reality accurately.
    B. stimulate strong emotions.
    C. encourage social reform.
    D. express the artist's feelings.

24. With which of the following statements would the author most likely agree?

    F. A person's lifetime is merely preparation for what comes after death.
    G. Only an artist can truly enjoy life.
    H. The original experience is more important than the memory of it.
    J. A perceptive person understands that all experience is repetitious.

25. The tone of the passage can best be described as:

    A. impassioned.
    B. scholarly.
    C. informative.
    D. speculative.

26. In the context of this passage, the phrase "short day of the frost and sun" (lines 32–33) refers to:

    F. the transient effect of poetry.
    G. a brief moment of passion.
    H. the life of a person.
    J. stimulation of the senses.

27. The phrase "awful brevity" (line 34) means that:

    A. philosophy is not really useful.
    B. art may not satisfy everyone.
    C. life is short.
    D. passion is the greatest virtue.

28. The "children of this world" (line 63–64) are NOT:

    F. passionate.
    G. wise.
    H. lovers of art and song.
    J. listless.

29. According to the author, the greatest passion is the love of:

    A. beauty.
    B. one's spouse.
    C. wealth.
    D. security.

30. The phrase "then our place knows us no more" (lines 61) means that we:

    F. move to another town.
    G. have children.
    H. die.
    J. divorce.

GO ON TO THE NEXT PAGE.

PASSAGE IV

NATURAL SCIENCE: This passage explains how energy becomes usable through photosynthesis.

Every living cell must acquire energy in a usable form. According to the First Law of Thermodynamics, energy, which is the capacity for doing work, can be converted from one form into [5] another without any net gain or loss. An organism must have an outside source of usable energy. The Second Law of Thermodynamics states that every energy transformation reduces the free (usable) energy of the system. Living cells primarily use [10] chemical energy derived from complex organic compounds.

Photosynthesis is the process by which green plants transform sunlight into a usable energy source. Green plants utilize the energy of light to [15] combine carbon dioxide with water to form organic material (sugar) and oxygen.

$$6CO_2 + 12H_2O + light \xrightarrow{\text{chlorophyll}} 6O_2 + C_6H_{12}O_6 + 6H_2O$$

Photosynthesis is a reduction reaction. Reduction is the addition of one or more electrons [20] to an atom or molecule. Oxidation is the removal of electrons from an atom or molecule. Reduction stores energy, while oxidation releases it. Biological systems rely on the addition or removal of an electron from hydrogen. Photosynthesis is based [25] on two key processes. Light energy is trapped and stored, and hydrogen atoms are transformed from water to carbon dioxide to form carbohydrate.

Photosynthesis takes place within the chloroplasts. The pigments within the chloroplasts [30] are precisely arranged within the membranes of flattened sacs called thylakoids. Thylakoids often lie close together in sacks called grana. The light reactions of photosynthesis take place within the thylakoid membranes, while the dark reactions take [35] place in the colorless matrix (stroma) surrounding the thylakoids.

Different wavelengths of light, especially red and blue light, are trapped by various pigment molecules contained within chloroplasts. When a [40] photon of light strikes a pigment molecule and is absorbed, the energy is transferred to an electron, which is raised to a high-energy state. A specialized form of chlorophyll passes the energized electron to an acceptor molecule, X, which has a high affinity [45] for electrons. X passes the electron to a series of acceptor molecules, each at a slightly lower energy

level. After being passed from molecule to molecule, the electron may return to the chlorophyll from which it started. Some of the energy released as [50] the electron is passed down the energy gradient is used to synthesize the compound ATP from ADP and inorganic phosphate.

ATP is a universal energy packet used by cells to do work. ATP is synthesized from [55] ADP and inorganic phosphate in a process called phosphorylation. Phosphorylation is a very high energy-demanding process. Cyclic photophosphorylation occurs when the energy used for ATP synthesis comes from light-energized [60] electrons as they are returned to the chlorophyll molecules from which they originated.

Another process that occurs in green plants is noncyclic photophosphorylation. In this reaction, some electrons are passed from the chlorophyll to a [65] different type of acceptor molecule called $NAPD_{ox}$, which retains the electron and is therefore reduced to become $NAPD_{re}$.

The ATP and $NAPD_{re}$ produced in the light reaction are used to reduce carbon dioxide to [70] carbohydrate in a series of reactions called the Calvin cycle (dark reaction). Basically, a five-carbon sugar, ribulose diphosphate (RuDP), is combined with CO_2. This process is called carboxylation. The products are then phosphorylated by ATP and [75] reduced by $NAPD_{re}$ to form PGAL, a three-carbon sugar.

Under certain conditions, the very same enzyme that under more agreeable conditions would facilitate its carboxylation oxidizes RuDP. [80] This process, called photorespiration, is seemingly a wasteful process since no ATP is created. Photorespiration predominates over photosynthesis when CO_2 levels are low and O_2 levels are high.

Some tropical angiosperm plants have a [85] unique leaf structure known as Kranz anatomy (C_4 plants). In Kranz plants, the bundle-sheath cells have numerous chloroplasts (other plants usually do not), and the mesophyll cells are clustered in a ring-like arrangement around the bundle sheath. These plants [90] can carry out photosynthesis under conditions of high temperature and concentrated light, when loss of water induces closure of the stomata. When the stomata close, the concentration of CO_2 in the air spaces inside the leaf falls, and the concentration of [95] O_2 rises. Under these conditions most plants (C_3) would experience a net loss of CO_2 because of photorespiration. Kranz plants (C_4) do not because

GO ON TO THE NEXT PAGE.

of their specialized way of initially fixing CO_2. They combine CO_2 with a three-carbon compound in the
100 mesophyll cells to form a four-carbon compound that passes into the bundle-sheath cells, where the CO_2 is regenerated. Therefore, Kranz plants can maintain a CO_2 level in the bundle-sheath cells that allows carboxylation of RuDP in the Calvin cycle to
105 predominate over its oxidation in photorespiration.

31. According to this passage, "the capacity for doing work" (lines 3–4) is the definition of:

    A. photosynthesis.
    B. energy.
    C. oxidation.
    D. thermodynamics.

32. In the equation in line 17, $C_6H_{12}O_6$ apparently names:

    F. oxygen.
    G. carbon dioxide.
    H. a sugar.
    J. photosynthesis.

33. Which of these could be considered the reverse of reduction?

    A. Oxidation
    B. Photosynthesis
    C. Transformation
    D. Phosphorylation

34. Which of the following conclusions is (are) suggested by the third paragraph?

    I. Photosynthesis involves the addition of electrons.
    II. Photosynthesis involves action on hydrogen.
    III. Photosynthesis is a form of energy release.

    F. I only
    G. II only
    H. III only
    J. I and II only

35. The fifth paragraph deals mainly with:

    A. defining terms related to plant growth.
    B. comparing one reduction reaction to another.
    C. explaining the process of photosynthesis.
    D. expressing the author's opinion.

36. Which of the following statements is NOT true about ATP?

    F. It mixes with phosphate to make ADP.
    G. It is created through phosphorylation.
    H. It serves a purpose in the Calvin cycle.
    J. It is used by cells to do work.

37. The Calvin cycle involves:

    A. the combination of carbon dioxide and a five-carbon sugar, with a three-carbon sugar as the result.
    B. the combination of oxygen and a three-carbon sugar, with a five-carbon sugar as the result.
    C. a mix of ATP and sugar to create carbon dioxide.
    D. a reduction of carbohydrate to form carbon dioxide.

38. By "more agreeable conditions" (line 78), the author probably means:

    F. conditions that produce higher levels of oxygen.
    G. conditions that produce higher levels of CO_2.
    H. conditions with higher temperatures.
    J. conditions with longer growing periods.

39. Which of the following statements names a difference between photorespiration and photosynthesis?

    I. Photorespiration involves RuDP.
    II. In photosynthesis, ATP is synthesized.
    III. Photorespiration is a reduction reaction.

    A. I only
    B. I and II only
    C. II and III only
    D. I, II, and III

40. Unlike the preceding paragraphs, the final paragraph discusses:

    F. plants that do not photosynthesize.
    G. living matter other than plants.
    H. plants with an unusual structure.
    J. plants that transform carbon dioxide into carbohydrate.

END OF TEST 3
STOP! DO NOT TURN THE PAGE UNTIL TOLD TO DO SO.
DO NOT RETURN TO THE PREVIOUS TEST.

4 4 4 4 4 4 4 4 4 4 4 4 4

SECTION 4: SCIENCE TEST
35 Minutes—40 Items

DIRECTIONS: Each passage below is followed by several items. After reading a passage, choose the best answer for each item. Fill in the corresponding oval on your bubble sheet. You may refer to the passage as often as necessary. You are NOT permitted the use of a calculator on this test. Answers are on page 313.

PASSAGE I

Alkanes are open-chain organic compounds that have the general chemical formula C_nH_{2n+2}. For example, propane has the following structural formula:

$$CH_3 — CH_2 — CH_3$$

For propane, $n = 3$ (the number of carbon atoms), and $2(3) + 2 = 8$ (the number of hydrogen atoms). The series of linked carbon atoms is called the carbon backbone of the compound, and the number of carbon atoms in the backbone gives the compounds their different names. Alkanes that differ by one carbon atom differ in molecular mass by 14u (one carbon atom of mass 12u and two hydrogen atoms of mass 1u each).

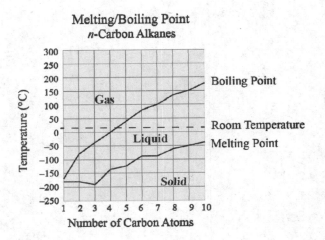

Melting/Boiling Point
n-Carbon Alkanes

Physical Properties of Straight-Chain Alkanes					
Name	# of Carbons	Boiling Point (°C)	Melting Point (°C)	Molecular Mass (atomic mass unit, u)	Flash Point (°C)	Density (g/cm³ at 290°C)
methane	1	−162	−183	16	–	0.466
ethane	2	−89	−183	30	–	0.572
propane	3	−42	−188	44	–	0.585
butane	4	0	−138	58	–	0.601
pentane	5	36	−130	72	−49	0.626
hexane	6	69	−95	86	−??	0.660
heptane	7	98	−91	100	−?	0.684
octane	8	126	−57	114	13	0.703
nonane	9	151	−54	128	31	0.718
decane	10	174	−30	142	46	0.730

GO ON TO THE NEXT PAGE.

1. According to the table, as the number of carbon atoms in the backbone of the alkane molecule increases, the:

   A. molecular mass decreases.
   B. boiling point increases.
   C. melting point decreases.
   D. density at 290°C decreases.

2. Which of the following is the structural formula for butane?

   F. CH_3—CH_3—CH_3—CH_3
   G. CH_2—CH_3—CH_3—CH_2
   H. CH_3—CH_2—CH_2—CH_3
   J. CH_{12}—CH_{10}—CH_{10}—CH_{12}

3. Considering the alkanes listed, if alkane X has a higher boiling point than alkane Y, then alkane X also has:

   A. a lower flash point.
   B. a lower molecular mass.
   C. more carbon atoms.
   D. fewer hydrogen atoms.

4. The alkane undecane has a backbone of 11 carbon atoms. What is the approximate molecular mass of the compound expressed in atomic mass units?

   F. 154
   G. 155
   H. 156
   J. 157

5. The alkane dodecane has a backbone of 12 carbon atoms. The compound has how many hydrogen atoms?

   A. 14
   B. 24
   C. 26
   D. 28

6. Which of the following is not a gas at room temperature?

   F. Methane
   G. Ethane
   H. Butane
   J. Hexane

7. Which of the following graphs most accurately depicts the density of the first ten alkanes as a function of the number of atoms in the carbon backbone in the alkanes?

A.

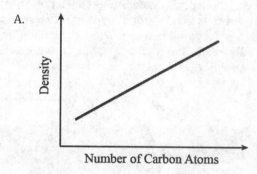

B.

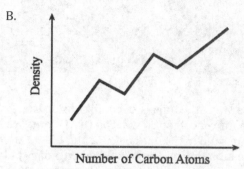

C.

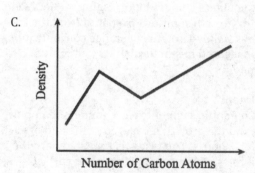

D.

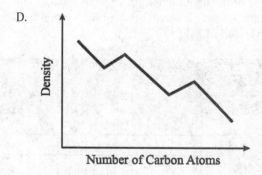

GO ON TO THE NEXT PAGE.

PASSAGE II

The protective sheath that covers the emerging shoot tip of monocotyledons, such as grasses, is called the coleoptile. Coleoptiles consist of specialized cells that do not divide but increase in size as they accumulate water. When the coleoptile pushes above the soil surface, it stops growing as the flag leaves emerge from it and continue to grow.

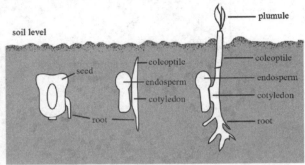

Figure 1

To study the impact of conditions on the growth rate of coleoptiles, *Avena* (oat) plants were grown in sand in the dark at 25°C and 85–90% relative humidity and harvested when 4 days old. Shoot tips 3 to 5 millimeters long were removed from the plants 2 hours before being immersed in water or growth solutions prepared from the fungus *Rhizopus suinus*. Growth substance concentrations were measured in standard units per cubic centimeter.

Experiment 1

Coleoptile segments were immersed in pure water and the growth measured at the end of each hour for 7 hours. The test was repeated with the tops of the segments above the water surface. The growth of each coleoptile segment per hour as a percent of the original length was calculated. The averages across all segments for both tests are summarized in Table 1.

Table 1: Growth of Coleoptile Segments in Water								
Average Growth per Hour as a Percentage of Original Length								
Test	End of Hour *n*							
	1	2	3	4	5	6	7	Total
1 (tops in water)	1.8	1.5	1.2	0.7	0.6	0.4	0.4	6.6
2 (tops in air)	2.5	2.5	4.0	4.3	4.7	3.3	–	21.3

The growth of the coleoptiles entirely immersed in water is attributable to a residuum of growth substance that remained after their removal from the plants. Those whose tops extended into the air produced additional growth substance.

Experiment 2

Coleoptile segments were submerged in growth substance solutions of varying concentrations and the growth was measured after 2, 4, and 24 hours. The cumulative growth of each coleoptile segment as a percentage of the original length was calculated after 2, 4, and 24 hours. The results are summarized in Table 2.

Table 2: Growth of Coleoptile Segments in Growth Substance Solutions			
Cumulative Growth			
Growth Substance Concentration (standard units per cm³)	End of Hour *n*		
	2	4	24
80	3.3	2.1	0.4
40	4.3	8.0	7.2
20	7.4	10.8	15.4
10	11.7	19.9	31.0
1	8.4	15.7	27.0
0.1	6.5	12.1	17.5
0.01	4.5	7.0	15.5
0	3.3	5.6	11.9

Coleoptiles in solutions of high concentrations of growth substance showed a shrinkage after 4 hours and, at the end of 24 hours, lost their turgidity due to a toxic effect of the high concentration of growth substance.

Experiment 3

The researchers theorized that either the action of the growth substance is a simple physical change of the cell wall or it depends on processes of a metabolic nature. If the action of the growth substance were a simple physical change, then it would not be affected by the presence of cyanide. If, however, it depends on metabolic processes, cyanide should inhibit the action of the growth substance. A series of tests were conducted to determine the impact of potassium cyanide (KCN) on the growth of coleoptile segments. Table 3 summarizes the results.

Table 3: Inhibition of Growth of Coleoptile Segments by KCN	
Solution	Total Percent Growth
Growth substance alone	23
Growth substance + 2×10^{-4} M KCN	5
Growth substance + 1×10^{-3} M KCN	2
Growth substance + 2×10^{-3} M KCN	−4
Growth substance + 2×10^{-2} M KCN	−3
Water + 2×10^{-2} M KCN	−4

8. The "flag leaves" referred to in the introductory paragraph of the passage correspond to which of the features shown in Figure 1?

F.   Plumule
G.   Endosperm
H.   Coyledon
J.   Root

9. According to the information provided, the greater growth rate recorded in Test 2 in Experiment 1 is explained by the:

A.   addition of growth substance to the water used to immerse the coleoptiles.
B.   production by the coleoptiles of additional growth substance following clipping.
C.   retention by the coleoptiles of growth substance already present in the plants.
D.   metabolism by the coleoptiles of a growth substance present in the air.

10. Which of the three experiments used water and no growth solution?

F.   Experiment 1 only
G.   Experiment 2 only
H.   Experiments 1 and 2 only
J.   Experiments 2 and 3 only

11. Which of the following graphs most accurately represents the average growth of the coleoptile segments as a percentage of original length for Test 1 in Experiment 1?

A.
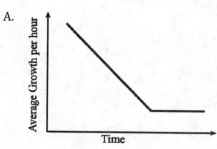

B.
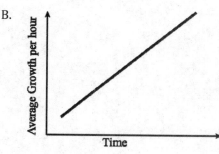

C.
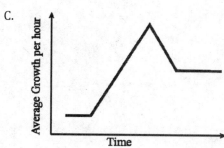

D.
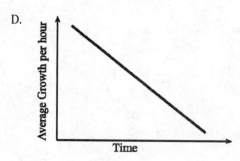

12. According to the data provided, the greatest growth of the coleoptile segments after 24 hours was for which concentration of growth substance in solution (in standard units per cubic centimeter)?

F.   0
G.   1
H.   10
J.   80

GO ON TO THE NEXT PAGE.

13. According to the data provided, the lowest concentration of growth substance in solution (in standard units per cubic centimeter) that showed any period of shrinkage of coleoptile segments was:

A   0
B.   1
C.   40
D.   80

14. The hypothesis that the action of the growth substance depends on metabolic processes is:

F.   disproved by the data in Table 3.
G.   weakened slightly by the data in Table 3.
H.   weakly supported by the data in Table 3.
J.   strongly supported by the data in Table 3.

PASSAGE III

Osmosis is the spontaneous movement of solvent molecules through a semi-permeable membrane into a region of higher solute concentration. The molecules move in the direction that tends to equalize solute concentration on both sides of the membrane.

Figure 1 shows a semi-permeable membrane between two sugar (sucrose) solutions of different concentrations. Osmosis occurs as the water molecules pass through the membrane to the side with higher sugar concentration. The sugar molecules, on the other hand, are too large to pass through the pore spaces in the semi-permeable membrane.

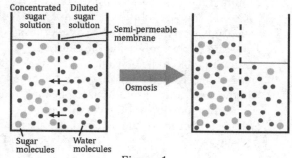

Figure 1

To observe the effect of osmosis, a group of students conducts experiments using plant tissues. In the experiments, the walls of the cells in the plant tissues function as the semi-permeable membrane separating regions of different solution concentrations.

Experiment 1

The students prepare shallow dishes with sugar solutions of varying concentrations. Using tweezers, the students gently pull off small strips of tissue, 3 to 10 millimeters in length and one cell layer thick, from the outer layer of an onion. Each strip is submerged in one of the prepared dishes.

After 45 minutes, the students mount the strips on slides and, using a microscope, examine the tissues for evidence of plasmolysis—the shrinkage of a cell's protoplasm and separation from the cell wall due to water loss from the cell. Forty to sixty-five cells from each onion strip are analyzed and scored as either plasmolyzed or not plasmolyzed. Any cells not clearly plasmolyzed are classified as not plasmolyzed. Table 1 summarizes the experimental results.

Table 1: Plasmolyzed Onion Cell Counts			
Sugar Solution Concentration (mol/kg)*	Number of Cells Analyzed	Number of Plasmolyzed Cells	Percentage of Plasmolyzed Cells
0.55	50	50	100
0.50	50	46	92.0
0.45	64	50	78.1
0.40	64	44	68.8
0.35	50	25	50.0
0.30	62	12	19.4
0.25	48	5	10.4
0.20	55	3	5.5
0.15	57	2	3.5
0.10	41	1	2.4
0.05	40	0	0.0
0.00	50	0	0.0

*moles of sugar per kilogram of water

Experiment 2

The students conduct a second experiment with beets. Beakers are prepared with sugar solutions of the same concentrations as in Experiment 1. Using an 8-millimeter diameter cork borer, cylinders of tissue are extracted from the beets. The tissue cylinders are sliced into disks approximately 3 millimeters thick. Each disk is weighed before being submerged in one of the prepared beakers.

After 75 minutes, the students extract, blot dry, and weigh each of the disks. The percentage of weight change in the disks are calculated. Table 2 summarizes the experimental results.

Table 2: Changes in Beet Tissue Weights			
Sugar Solution Concentration (mol/kg)	Original Weight (g)	Final Weight (g)	Percentage of Weight Change
0.55	2.865	2.460	−14.14
0.50	2.732	2.407	−11.90
0.45	2.807	2.666	−5.02
0.40	2.474	2.422	−2.10
0.35	3.101	3.152	+1.64
0.30	3.060	3.118	+1.90
0.25	2.549	2.642	+3.65
0.20	2.801	2.889	+3.50
0.15	2.357	2.428	+3.01
0.10	2.675	2.754	+2.95
0.05	2.413	2.528	+4.77
0.00	2.880	3.060	+6.25

15. In Experiment 1, osmosis proceeds due to the cell wall permitting:

   A. sugar molecules but not water molecules to pass.
   B. water molecules but not sugar molecules to pass.
   C. neither sugar nor water molecules to pass.
   D. certain water and certain sugar molecules to pass.

16. The purpose of Experiment 1 is to measure the:

   F. solute concentrations of the solutions in which the onion strips are submerged.
   G. quantity of water gained or lost by the onion cells due to osmosis.
   H. number of cells plasmolyzed due to the effect of osmosis.
   J. solute concentration threshold at which osmosis is triggered in onion cells submerged in a sugar solution.

17. Which of the following best explains why the students analyze 40 to 65 cells from each onion strip in Experiment 1?

   A. The number of plasmolyzed cells in an onion strip ranges from 40 to 65 cells.
   B. A sampling adequate to determine the effect of osmosis on onion cells requires 40 to 65 cells.
   C. The average number of cells in an onion strip is 40 to 65 cells.
   D. The unanalyzed cells of the onion strips do not show the effects of osmosis.

18. Which of the following best explains why no plasmolyzed cells are observed for the 0.05 mol/kg sugar solution?

   F. The concentration of sugar inside the cells is greater than 0.05 mol/kg.
   G. The concentration of sugar inside the cells is less than 0.05 mol/kg.
   H. The concentration of sugar inside the cells is greater than 0.55 mol/kg.
   J. The concentration of sugar inside the cells is less than 0.55 mol/kg.

19. The students identify the same number of plasmolyzed cells in both samples from the onion strips submerged in the 0.55 mol/kg and the 0.45 mol/kg sugar solutions yet calculate a value of "Percentage of Plasmolyzed Cells" of 100% for the 0.55 mol/kg solution but only 78.1% for the 0.45 mol/kg solution. This difference in percentage of plasmolyzed cells is due to the fact that:

   A. the cells plasmolyzed by the 0.45 mol/kg solution are less completely depleted than those plasmolyzed by the 0.55 mol/kg solution.
   B. the students analyzed 50 cells from the onion strip submerged in the 0.55 mol/kg solution and 64 cells from the onion strip submerged in the 0.45 mol/kg solution.
   C. the 0.55 mol/kg solution acts more vigorously on the onion cells, accelerating the rate of plasmolysis on the cells submerged in that solution.
   D. all of the cells in the onion strip submerged in the 0.45 mol/kg solution are plasmolyzed but only a portion of those in the onion strip submerged in the 0.55 mol/kg are are plasmolyzed.

20. Which of the following best explains the change in weight of the beet disk before and after submersion in the beaker containing the 0.00 mol/kg sugar solution?

   F. The disk is dehydrated, causing it to absorb water while submerged in the solution.
   G. The disk has a sugar concentration greater than 0.00 mol/kg of water, causing it to absorb water while submerged in the solution due to osmosis.
   H. The disk has a sugar concentration less than 0.00 mol/kg of water and loses water while submerged in the solution due to osmosis.
   J. No sugar molecules are available in the 0.00 mol/kg solution to migrate across the semi-permeable membranes of the cells in the beet disk.

GO ON TO THE NEXT PAGE.

21. Which of the following graphs best represents the percentage of weight change for the beet disks in Experiment 2?

A.

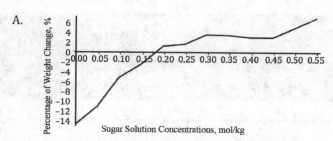

B.

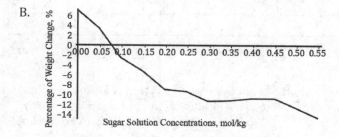

C.

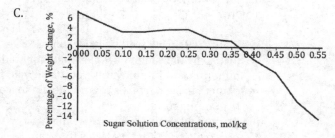

D.

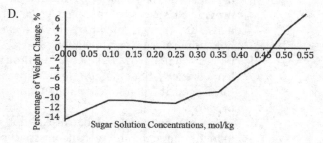

22. It can be inferred from the results of Experiment 2 that the average concentration of sugar per kilogram of water in the sampled beets is:

F. 0.45–0.50 moles.
G. 0.40–0.45 moles.
H. 0.35–0.40 moles.
J. 0.30–0.35 moles.

<u>PASSAGE IV</u>

The chart below shows various physical characteristics of soil components.

Physical Characteristics of Soil Components				
Soil Components	Diameter of Particles, d (μm)	Relative Ability* to Hold Positively Charged Minerals (Ca^{+2}, K^+, Mg^{+2})	Relative Ability* to Maintain Air Spaces	Relative Ability* to Retain Water
Clay	$d < 2$	1	4	1
Silt	$2 \leq d < 20$	2	3	2
Sand	$20 \leq d < 200$	3	2	3
Coarse Sand	$200 \leq d \leq 2{,}000$	4	1	4

*Relative abilities are rated from 1, indicating the most able, to 4, indicating the least able.

23. The soil type that is LEAST able to hold substances such as magnesium (Mg^{+2}) is:

   A. sand.
   B. coarse sand.
   C. silt.
   D. clay.

24. Based on the information in the chart, which of the following statements best describes the relationship between a soil's particle size and its other physical characteristics?

   F. As particle size increases, the ability to hold positively charged minerals increases.
   G. As particle size decreases, the ability to retain water decreases.
   H. As particle size decreases, the ability to maintain air spaces increases.
   J. As particle size increases, the ability to retain water decreases.

25. The size of particles in the soil type that is neither most able nor least able for any of the listed abilities must be:

   A. less than 20 μm.
   B. greater than or equal to 20 μm.
   C. greater than or equal to 2 μm and less than 200 μm.
   D. greater than or equal to 2 μm and less than or equal to 2,000 μm.

26. Loam is a type of soil that is mostly clay, but it also contains some sand and silt particles. Which prediction is most likely to be accurate about the ability of loam to support plant growth?

   F. Plants will grow well because loam primarily has small particles that can hold minerals and retain water, yet it also has enough large particles to provide air spaces containing oxygen.
   G. Plants will grow well because loam primarily has large particles that can provide air spaces containing oxygen, yet it also has enough small particles that can hold minerals and retain water.
   H. Plants will not grow well because although loam is excellent at maintaining air spaces for oxygen, it will not hold enough minerals or water.
   J. Plants will not grow well because although loam has enough minerals and air spaces for oxygen, it cannot retain enough water.

GO ON TO THE NEXT PAGE.

27. Based on the information provided in the chart, which of the following conclusions about soil types is NOT correct?

   A.   Soils most able to retain water are also most able to hold positively charged minerals.
   B.   No two soil types have the exact same combination of relative abilities.
   C.   Clay and coarse sand are the soil types that are most different in every physical characteristic.
   D.   No soil type is best for more than one category of relative ability.

PASSAGE V

Theory 1

The rate of a chemical reaction is defined as the number of moles of a specified product formed per unit of time. Reactants must collide in order for a reaction to occur. Therefore, at higher concentrations, the greater presence of particles increases the likelihood of effective collisions. For example, in the reaction: rate = $k[\text{HCl}]^2$, where k is the rate constant, and the exponents reflect the coefficients in front of the reactants in the reaction. The relationship between numbers of reactant particles and exponents in the rate law is a general one.

Theory 2

Theory 1 is sometimes true, for it expresses the reasonable insight that the greater the concentration of reactants, the greater the rate of a reaction. It has a great shortcoming, however, in its assumption that all reactions proceed in one fell swoop rather than in several skirmishes.

For example, let letters A and B stand for molecules. In the reaction $A + 2B \Rightarrow AB_2$, Theory 1 predicts a rate law as follows: rate = $k[A][B]^2$.

However, if the reaction actually proceeds in two stages, the first one would be $A + B \Rightarrow AB$ (slow) and the second one would be $AB + B \Rightarrow AB_2$ (fast).

Thus, Theory 2 implies that one must understand the details of the reaction, including the relative speeds of the sub-reactions, in order to predict a rate law. For example, if in a three-stage reaction stage 1 and stage 2 are completed in seconds and stage 3 requires several hours to complete, then the reaction rate is primarily determined by the reaction rate of stage 3. Theory 1 is not completely wrong, just incomplete.

28. Theory 1 relates:

F. reaction rate to the concentration of products.
G. reaction rate to the concentration and coefficients of reactants.
H. the relative amounts of products to one another.
J. reaction rate to the individual rates of various stages of the reaction.

29. According to a proponent of Theory 2, Theory 1:

A. can never give a correct prediction for a rate law.
B. will give a correct result if the reactant coefficients are all equal to 1.
C. will give a correct result only for a single-stage reaction.
D. is in error because it claims that collisions are required for reactions to occur.

30. According to Theory 1, the rate of the reaction $3M + 2N \Rightarrow M_3N_2$ will be given by:

F. $k[M][N]$.
G. $k[M]^3[N]^2$.
H. $k[M]^3[N]^2[P]^4$.
J. $k([M]^3 + [N]^2)$.

31. A chemist studies the rate of the reaction $2NO_2 + F_2 \Rightarrow 2NO_2F$. According to Theory 1, the rate of the reaction is proportional to:

A. the first power of $[NO_2]$ and the first power of F_2.
B. the second power of $[NO_2]$ and the second power of $[NO_2F]$.
C. the second power of $[NO_2]$ and the second power of $[F_2]$.
D. the second power of $[NO_2]$ and the first power of $[F_2]$.

32. Supporters of Theory 2 would best be able to defend their positions if:

F. they could show that a chemical reaction occurs in more than one stage.
G. they could show that the rate of reaction speeds up with increasing concentration of products.
H. they sped the reaction up with additional heat.
J. they eliminated all collisions.

33. According to Theory 2, if in a two-stage reaction Stage 1 is much slower than Stage 2, then the overall reaction rate will be:

A. primarily determined by the rate of Stage 1.
B. primarily determined by the rate of Stage 2.
C. undeterminable unless all collisions are counted.
D. undeterminable unless the rate law is measured experimentally.

34. When discussing the rates of reactions that have more than one stage, Theory 2 would not be necessary if:

F. there were exactly two stages.
G. all stages had different rates.
H. the sum of the rates of each stage always equaled the rate of the reaction as a whole.
J. the sum of the rates of each stage was never equal to the rate of the reaction as a whole.

<u>PASSAGE VI</u>

Closely related species of butterflies are often found living in very different environments. A pair of experiments was performed in which butterfly species previously captured in either desert areas or mountain areas were tested in laboratory incubators to determine the conditions at which they could carry out important life functions such as mating, oviposition (egg-laying), and pupation (the stage in which the stationary cocoon undergoes its final development into an adult).

Experiment 1

Under conditions of 100% relative humidity (maximum moisture content of the air), 100 desert butterflies (Species D) and 100 mountain butterflies (Species M) were tested at temperature intervals of 2°C (from 0°C to 40°C) to determine if they could mate, oviposit, and pupate. Each species achieved at least 90% success at the following ranges of temperatures:

Table 1			
	Temperature Ranges (°C)		
	Mating	Oviposition	Pupation
Species D	26–36	28–36	4–38
Species M	24–34	29–33	4–34

Experiment 2

The experiment was repeated at 50% relative humidity. Each species achieved at least 90% success at the following ranges of temperatures:

Table 2			
	Temperature Ranges (°C)		
	Mating	Oviposition	Pupation
Species D	26–36	28–36	4–38
Species M	24–32	29–32	4–28

35. Results of Experiments 1 and 2 indicate that the life function with the narrowest range of temperature at which both species achieve 90% success is:

    A. mating.
    B. oviposition.
    C. pupation.
    D. different in Experiment 1 than it is in Experiment 2.

36. Which condition decreases the success of Species M in mating, oviposition, and pupation?

    F. 100% relative humidity at low temperatures
    G. 100% relative humidity at high temperatures
    H. 50% relative humidity at low temperatures
    J. 50% relative humidity at high temperatures

37. A third experiment was conducted at 100% relative humidity in which the temperature range for caterpillar survival (another life function) was tested in Species D and Species M. Species D achieved 90% success at 12–36 (°C), while Species M achieved 90% success at 8–30 (°C). Which temperature range is a good prediction of caterpillar survival in Species D at 50% relative humidity?

    A. 8°C–30°C
    B. 8°C–24°C
    C. 12°C–36°C
    D. 12°C–30°C

38. If an investigator wanted to set up an experiment to determine the effects of light and dark on mating ability in Species D and Species M at 100% relative humidity, which set of conditions would provide the most complete results?

    F. Test both species at 20°C in the light and 20°C in the dark.
    G. Test both species at 30°C in the light and 30°C in the dark.
    H. Test both species at 34°C in the light and 34°C in the dark.
    J. Test both species at 34°C in the light and 30°C in the dark.

GO ON TO THE NEXT PAGE.

39. Which hypothesis is NOT supported by the results of Experiment 1 and Experiment 2?

A. For all tested life functions, 50% relative humidity only affects Species M at the high end of its temperature ranges.

B. For all tested life functions, 50% relative humidity has no effect on the temperature ranges of the desert species.

C. Species D does better than Species M at high temperatures in all tested life functions.

D. Species M does better than Species D at low temperatures for pupation.

40. Which of the following statements best explains the broad range of temperatures for pupation observed in both butterfly species?

F. Since the cocoon is stationary, it must be able to survive changing temperature conditions until the adult butterfly emerges.

G. Deserts can get very hot and mountains can get very cold.

H. Mountain butterflies would not survive long in the desert, and desert butterflies would not survive long in the mountains.

J. The stationary cocoon must be able to survive under light and dark conditions until the adult butterfly emerges.

PRACTICE TEST 18B

5 5 5 5 5 5 5 5 5 5 5 5 5

SECTION 5: WRITING TEST (OPTIONAL)
40 Minutes—1 Essay Prompt

DIRECTIONS: You have 40 minutes to plan and write an essay. Read the prompt carefully and make sure you understand the instructions. A successful essay will have the following features: it will take a position on the issue presented in the writing prompt; it will maintain a consistent focus on the topic; it will use logical reasoning and provide supporting ideas; it will present ideas in an organized manner; and, finally, it will include clear and effective language in accordance with the conventions of standard written English. Sample essay responses begin on page 313.

Plastic Bag Use

Some countries and states have banned free plastic bags at grocery stores because of the environmental problems they cause. Plastic bags worsen communities' litter problems and can suffocate animals that come into contact with them. Some bags are also non-biodegradable and accumulate in landfills. Because of these environmental risks, some governments have required stores to sell paper or reusable bags to customers, instead of providing plastic bags for free. However, some argue that banning bags is impractical and would inconvenience customers. As more cities and states debate whether to ban free plastic bags, this issue will potentially affect millions of shoppers.

Perspective 1	Perspective 2	Perspective 3
It is impractical to ban free plastic bags in stores, and it will inconvenience shoppers who forget to bring reusable bags with them. Plastic bags can also be reused as trash bags at home.	Free plastic bags should be banned, but stores should have more paper or more durable plastic bags available for sale. Having to pay for bags will encourage shoppers to reuse them, either at home or on their next shopping trip.	Plastic bags should be banned at all stores, and shoppers should either buy recyclable paper bags or bring their own reusable bags. Although this may initially annoy consumers, the environmental risks outweigh the convenience of free plastic bags.

Essay Task

Write a unified, coherent essay in which you evaluate multiple perspectives on the issue of plastic bag use in grocery stores. In your essay be sure to:

- Analyze and evaluate perspectives given
- State and develop your own perspective
- Explain the relationship between your perspective and those given

Your perspective may be in full agreement with any of the others, in partial agreement, or wholly different. Whatever the case, support your ideas with logical reasoning and detailed, persuasive examples.

END OF TEST 5
STOP! DO NOT TURN THE PAGE UNTIL TOLD TO DO SO.
DO NOT RETURN TO THE PREVIOUS TEST.

Take a Test Drive!
Post-Test

TAKE THE POST-TEST

At the end of the course, you will take a post-test. This post-test is an ACT, Inc. ACT practice exam. When you take the post-test, you should bring the following items to the classroom, in addition to anything else your teacher instructs you to bring:

1. Sharpened, soft-lead No. 2 pencils.
2. A calculator that is approved for use on the test. This includes any four-function, scientific, or graphing calculator, except for the following:

   - Devices with built-in computer algebra systems.
   - Pocket organizers or PDAs.
   - Handheld, laptop, or tablet computers.
   - Electronic writing pad or pen-input devices.
   - Calculators built into any electronic communication device, such as a cell phone.
   - Models with a QWERTY (typewriter) keypad. (Calculators with letters on the keys are permitted as long as the keys are not arranged in a QWERTY keypad.)

You may use the following types of calculators if you make appropriate modifications:

   - Calculators that can hold programs or documents: remove all documents and remove all programs that have computer algebra system functionality.
   - Models with paper tape: the paper must be removed.
   - Models that make noise: the sound feature must be turned off.
   - Models that have an infrared data port: the port must be covered with duct tape, electrician's tape, or another heavy, opaque material.
   - Models that have a power cord: the power cord must be removed.

(For more detailed information on calculator usage, go to www.actstudent. org/faq/calculator.html.)

3. A watch (to pace yourself as you work through each test section).

USE THE POST-TEST REPORTS

You will receive the results of your post-test in the form of a Student Summary and Student Item Analysis approximately six days after taking the test. These reports provide details about your performance and will help you to determine where to focus your efforts from now until your test date by targeting those skills, concepts, and strategies that will help you to improve in your areas of weakness. Just as you did with the pre-test, review the details of the sample reports on pages 4–5 of this student text so that you are familiar with their contents.

Once you have received your post-test reports, you can develop a Personal Action Plan. Make connections between the reports and the specific skills, concepts, and strategies that you need to study, then complete the "to do" list on the following page.

SKILL, CONCEPT, OR STRATEGY	START DATE	DATE TO BE COMPLETED	DATE COMPLETED

PLAN FOR FURTHER STUDY

You have received the results of your post-test. You have finished the Cambridge AccelePrep for the ACT® Test program. Now what?

In most cases you will have some spare time before the test day, so planning a study schedule between the post-test and the real test is critical to reinforcing and maintaining the skills, concepts, and strategies that you have learned throughout the course. Below are three steps that will help you make the most of your time.

STEP 1: TAKE THE PRACTICE TEST

Most students understand the concepts tested, but many struggle with time management. If you have not yet done so, take the Practice Test on page 246. The test:

- reinforces skills and strategies;
- simulates the experience of the real test by using time restrictions to emphasize time management; and
- is an excellent guide to targeting your study plan.

STEP 2: CREATE A WRITTEN STUDY PLAN

Use the results of your post-test and practice test to determine a day-by-day schedule that will create a clear and dependable guide for study. Create this plan based on the amount of time you have before the test day.

Several weeks before the test day:

- Plan to review all material equally.
- As the test date approaches, devote your time to any particular areas of weakness.

Remember: picking a few subjects to focus on each week will help you manage your time between now and the test.

A few days before test day:

- Focus on core subjects that are giving you difficulty or areas in which you would like to improve.
- Divide your time proportionally among these subjects based on your assessment of their difficulty.

Determine the topics you will study each day and allot the proper amount of time to study those sections of the book and complete relevant exercises.

STEP 3: STICK TO THE PLAN

Once you have determined your plan for study, stick to it without fail. Such discipline will be rewarded on the day of the test. Follow these helpful hints:

- Ask your teacher for insight. She can help you set goals for each core subject and may be able to suggest further strategies or a re-allotment of your time.
- Do not study too much. An hour or two of studying each day will be more productive than a severe study schedule.
- Practice every day.

Appendix

ENGLISH

CHAPTER 2 | HYPERPREP ENGLISH (p. 29)

Power Practice 1 (p. 39)	Power Practice 2 (p. 43)	Power Practice 3 (p. 49)	Power Practice 4 (p. 55)	Power Practice 5 (p. 60)
1. C	1. D	1. C	1. B	1. B
2. H	2. H	2. F	2. F	2. J
3. B	3. B	3. A	3. A	3. B
4. H	4. J	4. G	4. G	4. G
5. B	5. D	5. B	5. B	5. B

CHAPTER 3 | TRY IT OUT! ENGLISH PRACTICE (p. 61)

1. B	7. C	13. A	19. B	25. C
2. H	8. H	14. H	20. J	26. H
3. B	9. D	15. C	21. C	27. A
4. F	10. J	16. H	22. G	28. F
5. C	11. C	17. C	23. A	29. B
6. F	12. G	18. F	24. F	30. H

MATH

CHAPTER 5 | HYPERPREP MATH (p. 95)

Power Practice 1
(p. 103)
1. C
2. G
3. C
4. F
5. B

Power Practice 2
(p. 111)
1. E
2. J
3. B
4. H
5. D

Power Practice 3
(p. 118)
1. D
2. J
3. B
4. H
5. A

Power Practice 4
(p. 119)
1. A
2. J
3. B
4. K
5. C
6. K

7. B
8. J
9. D
10. H

CHAPTER 6 | TRY IT OUT! MATH PRACTICE (p. 121)

1. E
2. H
3. D
4. J
5. C
6. J
7. E

8. F
9. A
10. G
11. C
12. F
13. B
14. H

15. B
16. J
17. A
18. H
19. A
20. F
21. E

22. K
23. D
24. K
25. C
26. H
27. B
28. F

29. D
30. F

READING

CHAPTER 8 | HYPERPREP READING (p. 147)

Power Practice 1 (p. 155)
1. B
2. F
3. B
4. F
5. A

Power Practice 2 (p. 160)
1. D
2. F
3. C
4. G
5. D

Power Practice 3 (p. 163)
1. C
2. G
3. A
4. H
5. D
6. J
7. B
8. G
9. A
10. G

CHAPTER 9 | TRY IT OUT! READING PRACTICE (p. 165)

1. B
2. G
3. C
4. J
5. A
6. G
7. B
8. F
9. B
10. G
11. B
12. H
13. B
14. G
15. C
16. J
17. A
18. J
19. A
20. J
21. A
22. F
23. A
24. J
25. C
26. G
27. A
28. F
29. A
30. F

SCIENCE

CHAPTER 11 | HYPERPREP SCIENCE (p. 195)

Power Practice 1 (p. 209)
1. A
2. G
3. C
4. J
5. A

Power Practice 2 (p. 215)
1. A
2. H
3. A
4. G
5. C

Power Practice 3 (p. 223)
1. C
2. H
3. B
4. F
5. C

CHAPTER 12 | TRY IT OUT! SCIENCE PRACTICE (p. 225)

1. D
2. G
3. C
4. H
5. D
6. F
7. D
8. H
9. A
10. G
11. C
12. J
13. A
14. H
15. D
16. F
17. C
18. G
19. A
20. G
21. B
22. H
23. C
24. G
25. D
26. H
27. B
28. F
29. B
30. H

PRACTICE TEST

ANSWER KEY

DIRECTIONS: Circle each correct answer. Total the number of circled answers to determine the raw score for that test.

SECTION 1: ENGLISH TEST (p. 247)

1. B	14. F	27. C	40. J	53. A	66. F
2. J	15. C	28. G	41. C	54. G	67. A
3. D	16. J	29. B	42. F	55. D	68. F
4. G	17. B	30. H	43. A	56. J	69. C
5. A	18. F	31. A	44. H	57. B	70. J
6. H	19. A	32. F	45. A	58. J	71. A
7. A	20. H	33. D	46. J	59. C	72. G
8. G	21. A	34. F	47. D	60. F	73. B
9. B	22. G	35. A	48. H	61. D	74. J
10. H	23. C	36. G	49. D	62. H	75. B
11. D	24. J	37. C	50. H	63. D	
12. G	25. D	38. G	51. A	64. G	
13. C	26. G	39. C	52. G	65. D	

SECTION 2: MATH TEST (p. 258)

1. A	11. B	21. D	31. A	41. D	51. C
2. K	12. F	22. G	32. H	42. K	52. J
3. C	13. C	23. C	33. A	43. A	53. A
4. K	14. G	24. F	34. K	44. G	54. F
5. E	15. D	25. E	35. D	45. C	55. D
6. H	16. H	26. G	36. J	46. J	56. H
7. D	17. B	27. C	37. C	47. A	57. B
8. H	18. K	28. J	38. G	48. F	58. K
9. D	19. E	29. E	39. C	49. C	59. A
10. G	20. F	30. H	40. G	50. K	60. J

SECTION 3: READING TEST (p. 276)

1.	D	9.	B	17.	B	25.	A	33.	A
2.	J	10.	F	18.	H	26.	H	34.	J
3.	B	11.	B	19.	D	27.	C	35.	C
4.	J	12.	G	20.	F	28.	J	36.	F
5.	A	13.	D	21.	A	29.	A	37.	A
6.	G	14.	G	22.	J	30.	H	38.	G
7.	A	15.	C	23.	B	31.	B	39.	B
8.	F	16.	G	24.	H	32.	H	40.	H

SECTION 4: SCIENCE TEST (p. 286)

1.	B	9.	B	17.	B	25.	C	33.	A
2.	H	10.	F	18.	F	26.	F	34.	H
3.	C	11.	A	19.	B	27.	D	35.	B
4.	H	12.	H	20.	G	28.	G	36.	J
5.	C	13.	C	21.	C	29.	C	37.	C
6.	J	14.	J	22.	H	30.	G	38.	G
7.	A	15.	B	23.	B	31.	D	39.	D
8.	F	16.	H	24.	J	32.	F	40.	F

SECTION 5: WRITING TEST (OPTIONAL) (p. 300)

Above Average Response

If you walk through a suburban parking lot, on a city street, or even along a beach, you are likely to see grocery bags littering the ground. Because of the environmental risks they pose, free plastic and paper bags should be eliminated and be replaced with cloth bags or purchased bags that are designed for reuse. Non-reusable bags have a harmful impact on the environment, and consumers needlessly accumulate them. Although eliminating free grocery bags would be an unwelcome change for some consumers and manufacturers, it is a long-term change that needs to be made for the good of the environment.

The production and use of both plastic and paper bags have a negative impact on the environment. As litter, plastic bags are more dangerous than paper because often, they are not biodegradable. They accumulate in landfills and can kill animals that attempt to eat them or that become entangled in them and suffocate. Plastic bags can be especially harmful in coastal cities because they can float into bodies of water, where they are difficult to recover and can kill marine life. Paper bags, however, require more energy to manufacture, which produces more greenhouse gases. Unless paper bags are made from recycled material, trees must be cut down to manufacture them. Paper bags are also harder to reuse because some plastic bags are waterproof and more durable. Because both types of cause environmental problems, it is best to shop with reusable, cloth bags.

Grocery bags are also an example of waste because Americans accumulate more bags than necessary. One may argue that some sources of pollution, such as gasoline, cannot be eliminated because there is no widely available substitute. However, paper and plastic bags can easily be replaced with more environmentally-friendly products. It is wasteful to manufacture a product that harms the environment and that is used for about 20 minutes before being thrown out.

Because these bags are so rapidly disposed, they accumulate in shoppers' homes, or worse, outside. Some California cities, for example, have banned plastic bags because of the pollution they cause when they accumulate in natural environments. Stores should cut down on the number of non-reusable bags they distribute by charging for paper and plastic bags and also by having cloth bags available for sale.

Opponents of banning plastic bags claim that a ban would be inconvenient for consumers and would harm manufacturers. For consumers, however, the ban would cease to be an annoyance once they adjusted to bringing their own bags. Shoppers could keep bags in their cars or backpacks for last-minute trips to the store, and initially, stores could reward customers who bring their own bags. For example, some stores enter shoppers with their own bags in a raffle for free groceries. Some consumers argue that they reuse plastic bags for garbage; however, they would still be able to purchase durable plastic bags at a low cost. The biggest challenge to eliminating plastic bags would be the threat to bag manufacturers. In California, a statewide ban was delayed because it would have eliminated manufacturers' jobs. Before implementing a ban, states should devise plans to minimize job loss; for example, factories could transition into making fewer, more durable bags.

Although eliminating free grocery bags would be an adjustment for many Americans, it would be worth the long-term environmental benefits. The large quantities of bags that Americans currently use is wasteful, and their convenience does not justify the threat they pose for the environment.

Ideas and Analysis:

The writer clearly states his or her thesis in the introduction: free, non-reusable shopping bags are a threat to the environment and should be banned. The writer's thesis largely agrees with Perspective 2, but the writer adds that paper bags can also harm the environment. The author addresses Perspective 3's argument by arguing that both paper and plastic bags can be harmful, and the quantity of bags overall should be reduced.

The essay also counters Perspective 1's claim that the convenience of free bags makes them necessary for consumers.

Development and Support:

- The introduction opens with a hook, and the description of litter in different environments illustrates that it is a widespread problem.
- The writer clearly states the thesis in the second sentence of the introduction and previews the three main arguments.
- The body paragraphs begin with topic sentences that state the main point or argument to be made in the paragraph.
- The body paragraphs include concrete examples to support the writer's opinions.
    1. Body paragraph 1: The writer describes specific effects of both paper and plastic bags on the environment.
    2. Body paragraph 2: The writer argues that the accumulation of non-reusable bags is harmful and unnecessary and uses the California ban to illustrate this claim.
    3. Body paragraph 3: The writer acknowledges the opposing viewpoint. Although the writer does not have specific, proven examples of how to prevent job loss when fewer bags are manufactured, he or she provides practical advice on how to make the transition easier for consumers.

Organization:

- The writer introduces each paragraph with a topic sentence.
- The writer uses transitions to connect ideas between and within paragraphs. See, for example, the first sentence of the second body paragraph: "Grocery bags are also an example of waste because Americans accumulate more bags than necessary."
- The main ideas are arranged in a logical progression:

    1. Non-reusable bags are harmful for the environment.
    2. These risks are unnecessary because non-reusable bags can be replaced with products that are more environmentally friendly.

3. Consumers and companies can think of solutions to make the elimination of non-reusable bags easier for customers and manufacturers.

- The second body paragraph becomes slightly repetitive because both the first and second body paragraphs mention the accumulation of paper and plastic bags.
- Language Use and Conventions: The essay contains at least three principal strengths in this area:
- The essay does not have any mechanics/usage errors. As a result, the reader's attention is not distracted from the substance of the essay.
- The essay does not have any informal language.
- Stylistically, the writer varies sentence structures throughout most of the essay.

Summary and Conclusions:

This essay demonstrates writing skills that are well developed and provides arguments, as well as practical suggestions for eliminating non-reusable shopping bags. The writer also addresses all three perspectives throughout the essay. This essay would likely receive a score of 10.

Below Average Response

Eliminating paper and plastic bags might be good for the environment but its just not doable in America. Shopping bags are really convenient for shoppers and can be used around the house. Also, we do other things also have a bad affect on the environment, so I don't see why people have to care so much about plastic bags.

Shopping bags are very convenient, and it would be too much of a burden on customers if they were eliminated. Often, my parents just stop by the store on the way home from work to pick up a few things they need. They would never remember to bring a reusable bag with them to work in case they needed to go shopping afterwards. I think it would be unfair to consumers to have to buy bags every single time they went shopping because the reality is that shoppers aren't used to bringing bags with them, and it would take a long time for them to get used to this. Also, plastic bags can be used around the house. I often use them as trash bags, since they're waterproof, they're very useful for this purpose. Sometimes when it's raining, I also use them to protect my books and my calculator because my backpack isn't completely waterproof.

Also, it is impossible not to harm the environment. So many things that we do harm the environment, like driving, taking long showers, and using gas stoves. However, theres never going to be a law banning these activities, so why should shopping bags be banned?

Although in an ideal world we'd be able to ban non-reusable shopping bags, this wouldn't work in the US. It would be too hard for Americans to adjust to the change.

Ideas and Analysis:

The writer has a clear thesis and three main supporting arguments. However, while the essay defends Perspective 1, it does not take into account the opposing arguments in Perspectives 2 and 3. The writer's analysis of the situation is weak because he or she claims to speak for all "Americans" but only offers arguments and examples from his or her personal life. The essay would be stronger if it analyzed a wider range of viewpoints, instead of relying on generalizations.

Development and Support:

- The writer states his or her thesis in the first sentence of the introduction, and the introduction also previews the three main supporting arguments.
- In the body paragraphs, the writer uses several personal examples, but he or she generalizes from these examples and claims that banning plastic bags would be difficult for everyone.
- The second body paragraph does not develop the writer's argument well. The writer provides two

examples of uses of plastic bags but does not explain that these activities make plastic bags a less wasteful product.

- The third body paragraph, in particular, contains a superficial argument. The writer does not acknowledge that activities like driving and cooking are necessary parts of one's daily life, whereas there is a feasible alternative to using plastic bags.

Organization:

- The organization of the essay is clear and easy to follow. The writer states his or her thesis in the introduction, and each body paragraph has a topic sentence.
- The writer uses transitions, but the transitions sometimes sound repetitive and awkward. For example, both the second and third body paragraphs begin with the transition "also." The writer needs to vary transitions to make the essay flow more smoothly.

Language Use and Conventions:

- The essay contains several weaknesses in this area:
- The essay contains some usage and mechanics errors.

  1. Introduction: In the first sentence, "its" should be changed to "it's." (Explain that "its" is the possessive form, and "it's" means "it is.")
  2. Introduction: In the last sentence, "affect" should be changed to "effect." (Explain that usually, "affect" is a verb and "effect" is a noun.)
  3. Body paragraph 2: The second sentence has a comma splice. (I often use them as trash bags, since they're waterproof, they're very useful for this purpose.) The writer should begin a new sentence after "bags" or replace the comma with a semicolon.
  4. Body paragraph 3: In the final sentence, "theres" should be changed to "there's."

- The essay contains many examples of informal language. For example, in the conclusion, the writer says, "this wouldn't work in the US." Instead, the writer should say, "banning non-reusable bags would not be practical in the US."
- The essay also uses repetitive language. For example, the introduction states that "Shopping bags are really convenient for shoppers." The writer should use a synonym for "shoppers," such as "consumers," to avoid sounding repetitive.

Summary and Conclusions:

The essay has a clear thesis and three main arguments. However, the writer does not use developed reasoning or a variety of examples to support these arguments. Furthermore, the writer does not consider the opposing viewpoints. This essay would likely receive a score of 5.

Cambridge *AccelePrep for the ACT* Test
Error Correction and Suggestion Form

Name/Location: _____

Day Phone: _____

E-mail Address: _____

Part of Materials:
- ☐ Student Text, Specify Subject: _____ Page: _____ Item: _____
- ☐ Teacher's Guide, Specify Subject: _____ Page: _____ Item: _____
- ☐ Test Explanation, Specify Code: _____ Page: _____ Item: _____

Error/Suggestion: _____
_____
_____

Part of Materials:
- ☐ Student Text, Specify Subject: _____ Page: _____ Item: _____
- ☐ Teacher's Guide, Specify Subject: _____ Page: _____ Item: _____
- ☐ Test Explanation, Specify Code: _____ Page: _____ Item: _____

Error/Suggestion: _____
_____
_____

Part of Materials:
- ☐ Student Text, Specify Subject: _____ Page: _____ Item: _____
- ☐ Teacher's Guide, Specify Subject: _____ Page: _____ Item: _____
- ☐ Test Explanation, Specify Code: _____ Page: _____ Item: _____

Error/Suggestion: _____
_____
_____

Part of Materials:
- ☐ Student Text, Specify Subject: _____ Page: _____ Item: _____
- ☐ Teacher's Guide, Specify Subject: _____ Page: _____ Item: _____
- ☐ Test Explanation, Specify Code: _____ Page: _____ Item: _____

Error/Suggestion: _____
_____
_____

Part of Materials:
- ☐ Student Text, Specify Subject: _____ Page: _____ Item: _____
- ☐ Teacher's Guide, Specify Subject: _____ Page: _____ Item: _____
- ☐ Test Explanation, Specify Code: _____ Page: _____ Item: _____

Error/Suggestion: _____
_____
_____

Mail form to Cambridge Educational Services, Inc. or fax form to 1-847-299-2933.
For teacher's assistance, call 1-847-299-2930 or email solutions@CambridgeEd.com.
Visit our website at www.CambridgeEd.com.